Managing Local Government

To my mentor:
JAMES H. SVARA

—KLN

To my mentors:
JOSEPH F. ZIMMERMAN
DAVID B. WALKER

—CWS

Sara Miller McCune founded SAGE Publishing in 1965 to support the dissemination of usable knowledge and educate a global community. SAGE publishes more than 1000 journals and over 800 new books each year, spanning a wide range of subject areas. Our growing selection of library products includes archives, data, case studies and video. SAGE remains majority owned by our founder and after her lifetime will become owned by a charitable trust that secures the company's continued independence.

Los Angeles | London | New Delhi | Singapore | Washington DC | Melbourne

Managing Local Government

An Essential Guide for Municipal and County Managers

Kimberly L. Nelson

Carl W. Stenberg

University of North Carolina at Chapel Hill

FOR INFORMATION:

CQ Press

An imprint of SAGE Publications, Inc.

2455 Teller Road

Thousand Oaks, California 91320

E-mail: order@sagepub.com

SAGE Publications Ltd.

1 Oliver's Yard

55 City Road

London EC1Y 1SP

United Kingdom

SAGE Publications India Pvt. Ltd.

B 1/I 1 Mohan Cooperative Industrial Area

Mathura Road, New Delhi 110 044

India

SAGE Publications Asia-Pacific Pte. Ltd.

3 Church Street

#10-04 Samsung Hub

Singapore 049483

Executive Publisher: Monica Eckman

Editorial Assistant: Duncan Marchbank

Production Editor: Bennie Clark Allen

Copy Editor: Erin Livingston

Typesetter: C&M Digitals (P) Ltd.

Proofreader: Jen Grubba

Indexer: Judy Hunt

Cover Designer: Michael Dubowe

Marketing Manager: Jennifer Jones

Library of Congress Cataloging-in-Publication Data

Names: Nelson, Kimberly L., author. | Stenberg, Carl W., author.

Title: Managing local government : an essential guide for municipal and county managers / Kimberly Nelson, Carl W. Stenberg, University of North Carolina at Chapel Hill.

Description: First edition. | Washington, D.C. : CQ Press, [2018] | Includes index.

Identifiers: LCCN 2017011652 | ISBN 9781506323374

Subjects: LCSH: Local government—United States. | Municipal government—United States. | Municipal services—United States—Management.

Classification: LCC JS331 .N45 2018 | DDC 352.140973—dc23

LC record available at https://lccn.loc.gov/2017011652

17 18 19 20 21 10 9 8 7 6 5 4 3 2 1

BRIEF CONTENTS

DETAILED CONTENTS

PREFACE

This book was written as a response to the admonition "stop complaining and start doing something." For several years, the authors have taught local government management to graduate students at three universities (North Carolina, Northern Illinois, and Virginia), advised and assisted municipal and county managers, and developed leadership training programs for state manager's associations. From these interactions and experiences, we have observed some common, critical concerns.

Practitioners are worried that the pipeline of graduates who aspire to management positions will not be sufficiently full to replace the "silver tsunami" of retiring managers over the next decade. Another concern is that recent graduates who have filled entry-level management positions were not well-exposed to the realities of local government in their classes and internships and were too theory- and public policy bound. A frequent lament at International City/County Management Association (ICMA) and state association conferences is that too few college and university professors participate in these meetings, reflecting a paucity of academic thought leaders in the field who are interested in conducting research on problems and issues relevant to practitioners and capable of communicating the results in practical and applied ways.

At the same time, students have expressed reservations about pursuing careers in local government and instead are turning to nonprofit management or to state and federal agencies for opportunities they believe will be more fulfilling. These students are interested in transforming organizations, helping people, and improving communities, not transacting the business of government. They are also concerned about the insecurity of municipal and county manager positions, the breakdown of civility on governing bodies and tensions between elected officials and professional staff, and the public's growing negativism about and mistrust of government and public service.

Our role as university professors often places us in the middle of these two points of view. We consider ourselves "pracademics," contributing to both scholarship and practice. Over the years, we have sought books, journal articles, and research reports that we could use to encourage students to enter municipal and county management careers and to equip them with the tools to be successful from day one on the job. While scholars and organizations such as ICMA have provided useful material, often, the work has been grounded in either theory or practice. We have found no book that in one place bridges these worlds. And so, our colleagues have urged us to stop complaining and fill this void. That is why we have written this book.

The main audiences for the book are graduate students who are considering pursuing careers in local government management and recently appointed municipal and county managers. We have focused the subject matter on the topics the students and managers we teach and advise have told us would be important in deciding whether to enter the manager profession and in navigating the early days, weeks, and months on the job. These topics fall into three general areas—the changing structure, forms, and functions of local governments (particularly in metropolitan areas); the dynamics of intergovernmental, intersectoral, and interpersonal relationships; and the tools and strategies that contribute to effective local government management and solution of problems that increasingly ignore boundaries, sectors, and disciplines.

We have drawn upon the works of academic and practitioner thought leaders in the field of local government management and have sought in each chapter to connect theory with practice. Some topics have been covered in a general manner—such as budgeting and grants-in-aid or strategic planning and performance measurement— because other literature is available that provides more hands-on information and guidance. This book is intended as a broad introduction for students interested in a career in local government management.

ORGANIZATION OF THE BOOK

This book is both an examination of the history, theory, and terminology that forms the foundation for local government management and an introduction to the career of the local government manager. After the introduction in Chapter 1, we start with the birth of local governments in the United States. Chapter 2 traces the history and legacy of urban and suburban development. Were it not for the corruption and dysfunction in early American cities, the professionalization of local governance may have never come to be.

Chapter 3 provides an overview of the authority and structural arrangements of the U.S. local government system. Local governments, while primarily influenced by their state governments, are not immune to leverage from the federal government. The intergovernmental system in the U.S. is one of the most complicated in the world, with thousands of local governments having varying levels of authority and overlapping responsibilities.

This complicated environment makes working with other governmental entities a necessity but also an enormous challenge for local government leaders. In Chapter 4, we discuss the rationale for working across boundaries and the formal and informal methods and arrangements to do so.

The next section of the book turns to the people in the local government arena. Chapter 5 explores the career of the local government manager—Who are the people serving as managers? Why do they love their jobs? What is the career like? How do managers become leaders? Chapter 6 discusses the political and administrative roles of the municipal and county manager vis-à-vis the elected officials. Perhaps the most challenging part of the manager's career is learning to effectively navigate the political aspects of the job. A critical part of managing relationships with elected officials is helping to improve the effectiveness of the municipal council or county commission. Chapter 7 speaks to the manager's role in this critical function of local governance.

Finishing out the book, the final four chapters introduce the manager's role in service delivery. Citizen engagement has become an integral part of running a local government. Chapter 8 explains how engaging citizens can enhance the policy process and the challenges presented when engaging citizens. Chapter 9 provides an overview of the alternatives to in-house provision of services and building capacity for innovation. The manager's toolbox—strategic planning, performance budgeting, succession planning, and other tools managers can use to improve government performance—are the subject of Chapter 10. Concluding the book is a discussion of the major emerging issues that will be affecting local governments in the future.

ACKNOWLEDGMENTS

We want to express our appreciation to the hundreds of students and managers who have shared their insights and experiences with us over the years and, in doing so, have unknowingly helped shape this book. We have been inspired by the quality and enthusiasm of our graduates who decide to enter the profession and by the dedication and resiliency of new and established managers. As the chapters that follow demonstrate, the challenges and opportunities confronting local governments are greater now than at any time in recent memory. We are confident that the future of local government is in good hands, and we salute those municipal and county managers who are making a difference in improving the daily lives of their citizens. We also want to thank the managers and academic colleagues who reviewed the first draft of this book. Their insights proved invaluable in our revision process.

SAGE also wishes to thank the following reviewers for their kind assistance:

Joshua Ambrosius, *University of Dayton*

Sabawit Bishu, *Florida Atlantic University*

Robert Bruner, *Michigan Municipal Services Authority*

Raymond Cox, *University of Akron*

Joan Gibran, *Tennessee State University*

James Gilsinan, *St. Louis University*

Steve Harding, *Northwestern University*

Paula Holoviak, *Kutztown University*

Nick Kachiroubas, *DePaul University*

Dennis Lambries, *University of South Carolina*

Mark Levin, *Indiana University, Bloomington*

Lindsey Lupo, *Point Loma Nazarene University*

Marcus Mauldin, *The University of Tennessee at Chattanooga*

John Mero, *Campbell University*

Shane Nordyke, *University of South Dakota*

Christine Kelleher Palus, *Villanova University*

Gregory Streib, *Georgia State University*

James Svara, *University of North Carolina at Chapel Hill*

ABOUT THE AUTHORS

Kimberly L. Nelson is associate professor of public administration and government at the School of Government at the University of North Carolina at Chapel Hill. Her research and teaching interests focus on local government management, local government form and structure, and innovation in local government. Her research on the effects of form of government on municipal performance and innovation have been published in leading journals, including *Public Administration Review, The American Review of Public Administration, Urban Affairs Review,* and *State and Local Government Review.*

Dr. Nelson uses her research experience to inform her work with local government managers and elected officials in strategic planning and improving local government–administrative relations as well as to train local government leaders in leadership and promoting innovative practices. She serves on the editorial boards of *Public Administration Review* and *The American Review of Public Administration.* She received her BA from Virginia Tech and her PhD in public administration from North Carolina State University.

Carl W. Stenberg is the James E. Holshouser, Jr. Distinguished Professor of Public Administration and Government at the School of Government at the University of North Carolina (UNC) at Chapel Hill.

Prior to joining UNC, he was dean of the Yale Gordon College of Liberal Arts at the University of Baltimore, director of the Weldon Cooper Center for Public Service at the University of Virginia, executive director of the Council of State Governments, and assistant director of the U.S. Advisory Commission on Intergovernmental Relations.

He is a Fellow and former chair of the board of directors of the National Academy of Public Administration, past president of the American Society for Public Administration, and a recipient of the International City/County Management Association's Academic Award in memory of Stephen B. Sweeney for "outstanding contribution to the formal education of students pursuing careers in local government."

He received his BA from Allegheny College and his MPA and PhD from the State University of New York at Albany.

MANAGING LOCAL GOVERNMENTS IN A DYNAMIC WORLD

All good government begins at home.

—H. W. Haweis (Wood, 1893, p. 9)

There are more than 30,000 county, municipal, and township governments in the United States (U.S. Census Bureau, 2012). While most land area in the country is still designated as rural, more than 80% of Americans live in one of the 381 metropolitan areas in the United States. Metropolitan regions are comprised of an urban core area with a population of at least 50,000 and surrounding communities that are socially and economically integrated with that core. The high degree of integration between communities in a metropolis necessitates that community leaders at all levels build relationships with one another. The success of an individual community is, to a large degree, dependent on the success of the metropolitan system in which it exists. For this reason, local government managers must understand the functioning of their local governments within the context of this larger system and must recognize the importance of skills for forging successful relationships with their neighbors.

This book is designed to help future local government managers lead their communities effectively while successfully navigating the complex metropolitan environment in which most local governments operate. While big cities may come to mind for many people when they think about local governments, the reality is that most local governments in the United States have populations under 50,000. Most professional local government managers will serve throughout their careers in small to medium jurisdictions. This book focuses on concerns that are experienced in municipalities and counties of all sizes, not only large urban areas.

PURPOSE AND ORGANIZATION OF THE BOOK

The purpose of this book is to provide local government managers with the knowledge necessary to successfully navigate their organizations through this increasingly complex environment. As an introductory text in managing local government, it is intended to provide a broad introduction to concepts local government managers must be familiar with. This book is not intended to teach the nuts and bolts of day-to-day operations. It is written to offer readers a historical, theoretical, and practical foundation for managing municipalities and counties.

Written principally for future municipal and county managers, issues discussed in the book will be examined from the manager's perspective. The manager's roles as an organizational leader, especially relating to the tools needed to build high-performing organizations, and a community leader, including strategies for working across sectoral boundaries and engaging citizens, have received limited attention in earlier books. Given the increasing political polarization in government generally, another major theme throughout the book is the manager's sensitivity to the relationships between his or her governing unit's professional staff and elected officials.

The book begins with an exploration of the history behind the development of cities and suburbs to provide the reader with a foundational understanding of how and why professional management developed at the local level. Chapters 2 through 4 explore the complex structural and political nature of the United States' intergovernmental system. Chapter 5 describes the career of the municipal or county manager, which includes potential career paths and patterns, how managers balance the demands of career and personal life, and the differences in the duties of a manager in a council–manager government with those of a chief administrative officer in a mayor–council government. The next section of the book, Chapters 6 and 7, turns to local elected officials. These chapters address the roles elected officials play in local government and how best to create productive working relationships between elected officials and staff. Finishing out the book are three chapters that deal with maximizing organizational performance—engaging citizens, innovating in service delivery, and developing a manager's toolbox.

Modern Metropolitan Complexity

Life in metropolitan America can be complicated. This does not derive solely from the abovementioned interconnected and codependent nature of the metropolis. Rather, a key contributor to the increased complexity is the growing number of jurisdictions in most areas. While the number of local governments has declined by close to 23% since 1952 (U.S. Census Bureau, 2012), the number of special districts (government units providing only limited sets of services) has gone up by nearly 48% in this same time period. Special districts can increase the fragmentation in a region, and they often share the tax base with general-purpose local governments, limiting the fiscal discretion of the general-purpose and special-purpose governments. The rising number of special districts, coupled with a lack of authoritative regional governance structures in most metropolitan areas, leads to even greater fragmentation and a tendency to resist efforts to consolidate authority or service provision.

The fragmented nature of modern U.S. local governance, in turn, can lead to economic and racial segregation, transportation and public works infrastructures that are under stress and inadequately maintained, and competition for scarce natural resources, all of which will further test the capacity of local governments in the future.

Even in the states that have retained a centralized system of local governance (meaning that the state retains a considerable amount of structural and functional authority), local government leaders are finding that their well-being is affected by that of neighboring jurisdictions. In the past, the relationships between neighboring jurisdictions were more competitive than collaborative. However, modern economic stressors are forcing local jurisdictions to work together. The municipal and county managers of the region are often tasked with the responsibility for developing productive relationships with these neighboring entities.

Management Challenges

The issue of how municipalities and counties can best adapt to the challenges inherent in the new economy and information age, as well as to the changing political and intergovernmental landscape, has been a key topic of conversation among government reformers, public officials, civic groups, and students of local government. Increasingly, boundaries between local governments have become blurred, responsibilities for service delivery have become shared, and partnerships and collaborative approaches across jurisdictions and sectors have become commonplace. Local governments are expected to be entrepreneurial and equitable, to engage their citizens, and to be efficient and effective. And their professional managers are being looked to as community leaders and change agents.

It was not always this way. Historically, municipalities and counties were responsible for the basic services needed to support their communities, such as public safety, libraries, public utilities, public works, and cemeteries. Counties acted as the arms of the state government in unincorporated areas, and townships served citizens in rural areas in twenty states. Public education was provided by school districts that were usually separate from general-purpose local governments. In most cases, functions such as the ones listed above were predominantly or exclusively local in the sense that their performance entailed little or no collaboration with other local jurisdictions or units, no receipt of external funds, and no regulation by state and federal authorities.

During the twentieth century, a new set of services was added to local governments' responsibilities as our nation's population grew and became more urbanized. These included land use planning, zoning and subdivision control, urban renewal, housing, parks and recreation, and public health and welfare. The past eighty years witnessed a continuation of local service expansion and diversification. Joining the mix of municipal and county responsibilities were animal control, job training, juvenile and senior centers, Meals on Wheels programs, community and economic development, emergency preparedness, leisure services, and environmental protection.

This changing world has led some reformers to criticize what they see as an irrational pattern of local governmental units, an excessive number of small jurisdictions performing a limited range of duties, costly duplication of functions, parochial orientations on the part of local leaders, and a lack of coordination between special districts, school districts, and general-purpose local units. Reformers also express concerns about the time and expertise limitations of part-time elected officials and governing bodies and the antiquated budgetary, personnel, and procurement rules under which many local governments operate. These factors give rise to the perspective that many communities are not prepared to tackle complex and costly problems that spill across local boundary lines and are unable to take timely collective and authoritative remedial actions. These constraints make it difficult to provide the quality of life needed to attract and retain businesses and taxpayers in the competitive global economy of the twenty-first century.

On the other hand, supporters of the jurisdictional status quo argue the virtues of having government units that are close to citizens, citing accessibility and affordability, the need for local autonomy and control, and the cost-effectiveness of voluntary leadership. This is the case that is often made when communities vote to incorporate into a municipal government. They contend that democratic values such as responsiveness and fairness, the part and parcel of accessible local governments, are more important than the technocratic values of efficiency and effectiveness that are endemic in different governing systems. Moreover, they point out that while local government structure and operations may not be perfect, in most places, they satisfactorily deliver services demanded by the public at prices (i.e., taxes and fees) citizens are willing to pay. Part-time elected officials, rather than professional politicians served by professional managers and their staff, are the appropriate leaders of grassroots community governments because they are close to both the problems and the citizens.

Other challenges in the local government landscape involve the increasing popularity of contracted services. Today, these contracts go far beyond the provision of specific services, such as solid waste collection. There are more than a half dozen communities that are contract-only municipalities in which few, if any, staff are employees of the municipality. Examples include Sandy Springs, Georgia, and Centennial, Colorado.

As is often the case in such debates, the truth likely lies somewhere between the extremes. But the question remains: How can local governments continue to provide the level of services expected by their citizens in a rapidly changing world? Often, the answer is through professional local government management.

THE CONTEMPORARY CONTEXT: CONTINUITY AND CHANGE

Contemporary local government service delivery and management have been shaped by powerful ideological and political forces and trends that have generated discussion and debate over the role of government in American society, the size and scope of governmental activities, and the cost of government. These developments have had profound impacts in at least four areas: the role of citizens, the values and views of elected officials, the manager's roles and responsibilities, and the ways in which local governments conduct their business (Stenberg, 2007). These areas will receive in-depth attention in the chapters that follow.

The Citizen as Customer

Public opinion polls conducted since the early 1970s show a consistent pattern of citizen preference for local governments. When asked, most citizens responded that their local governments were more trustworthy and efficient than their state governments or the national government. They also indicated a desire for local governments to be more empowered to enable them to identify citizen needs, set priorities, and find the most suitable ways to address problems.

Citizens also have been consistent in their desire for the provision of quality services at the local level. At the same time, however, the public often resists tax increases to pay for improvements or new services. This "more for less" environment poses significant challenges in resource reallocation and cutback management.

These enduring attitudes have changed the rules of the game for public managers. Beginning with the Reinventing Government movement of the early 1990s, managers viewed citizens in new ways. Citizens have always been seen as the owners of government in that they elect, give legitimacy to, and hold accountable councils and boards (and, through these governing bodies, professional managers and staff, too). Citizens also have traditionally been considered clients of local agencies, such as health and human services departments. Reinventing Government called upon public managers to treat citizens as customers and coproducers.

The "citizen as customer" concept builds on the view that the local government system is a marketplace, offering choices among multiple jurisdictions for citizens who will "vote with their feet" in search of services they desire at tax and fee rates they are willing to pay. The customer service orientation also applies within individual local governments, calling upon managers to abandon one-size-fits-all approaches and to customize or tailor services such as police patrol or solid waste collection to the preferences of various neighborhoods. Local personnel are expected to have a strong customer service orientation and attitudes comparable to companies recognized nationally for excellence in this area.

Another dimension of the citizen's role is that of *coproducer*, wherein the public is engaged with managers in the provision of a local service. A wide range of possibilities exist for this role—from neighborhood watch police programs to volunteer fire departments, citizen advisory boards, planning departments, or faith-based organizations in human services—but the common factor is professional managers working alongside amateur citizens. Just as the *customer* expectation creates performance pressures on managers to deliver a given service at competitive levels of quality and cost satisfaction, the *coproducer* role requires managers to put aside "we know best" and "we/they" attitudes. Both dimensions of the citizen's role potentially expand the manager's accountability beyond the governing body to include the larger community.

Finally, citizens care more about the quality and cost of services than about which unit provides them. The wide range of special- and general-purpose local units that exists across the country is neither understood nor appreciated by most citizens. They look to the professional manager and governing body of the community to ensure that their expectations are met, even though service provision might be done jointly with other localities or contracted out to the private sector and despite the fact that responsibility for performance might be beyond the control of these officials.

Elected Officials' Values and Views

A second major area where the rules of the game for local government service delivery and management have changed involves the expectations of those who run for and serve on governing bodies. The basic roles of these bodies have not changed dramatically over time—representing citizens and constituents, making policy, overseeing administration, and attending to politics. But the ways in which these roles are carried out, as well as the orientations of the officials who serve in them, have changed in important respects.

Representative democracy, not to mention electoral success, requires that elected officials listen to constituents and seek to address their needs and meet their expectations in ways that are consistent with the community's core values. As local governments replace nonpartisan electoral systems with partisan ones and as more and more municipal council and county board members are elected from districts rather than from a jurisdiction at large, it has become increasingly challenging for local governments to find a general will or guiding public interest to serve as the foundation of policy. It also has become more difficult to reconcile conflicting public values, leading to political and economic polarization between communities, neighborhoods, and citizens.

Consequently, the policy-making process has changed. The growth of single-issue and antigovernment candidates has made it harder for elected officials to build coalitions on the governing body, find common ground, and reach consensus. These conditions make it less likely that managers will receive clear or consistent direction on implementation priorities. Managers prefer to take a less visible role in the policy process, but when incumbents who seek long-term careers in municipal or county elective office are reluctant to take on leadership roles or make unpopular or controversial decisions that could jeopardize their political futures, managers may be expected to take the lead.

These trends reinforce a short-term orientation on the part of elected officials and encourage incremental approaches to policy making by governing bodies that do not consider the larger context of a vision for the community, strategic goals and objectives, or action plans and priorities for decisions on programs and budgets. These trends also contribute to growing gaps between professional managers, governing bodies, and citizens arising from their differing backgrounds, expectations, and competencies. All of this makes it difficult for governing bodies to set clear and realistic expectations for managers—or to set them for themselves as councils or boards—and to effectively oversee and fairly evaluate administration.

In these respects, the world of local governing bodies has become more political and more partisan in trying to balance complex and competing interests, positions, personalities, and values both within the organization as well as outside of it. And the world of local managers has changed as well.

The Manager's Changing Roles and Responsibilities

Over time, managers have become part of the policy-making process and are now asked to do more than provide accurate information and impartial advice. Today's managers are called upon to identify and assess options and to make recommendations for the governing body to consider. The dichotomy between politics and administration first raised by Woodrow Wilson no longer exists (if it ever did). To varying degrees, managers and governing bodies share responsibility in the spheres of mission, policy, administration, and management.

Contributors to the third edition of the International City/County Management Association's book, *The Effective Local Government Manager* (2004), noted other developments and trends that have changed the manager's job and, at times, created tension in his or her relationships with elected officials and community leaders. These include (1) the perpetuation of antigovernment feelings among the public, leading to distrust of elected and appointed officials and to support for local candidates running against the government; (2) unrealistic citizen "more for less" expectations relative to services and taxes; (3) a shift from trustee to delegate or activist roles of local elected officials and a corresponding emphasis on constituent service instead of common problem solving; (4) increasing visibility, powers, and political ambitions of mayors; (5) a growing tendency on the part of local elected officials to become more focused on implementation and to micromanage administration; (6) a demand from governing bodies that managers place more emphasis on privatization as a preferred management tool; and (7) the access that the technology revolution has given citizens and interest groups to information about local operations, enabling them to easily register complaints, monitor performance, and put administration under the spotlight (Svara, 2004).

These trends have changed the manager's formal authority and created voids that must be addressed to effectively provide quality services. As a result, managers must devote more attention to policy, leadership, and constituent relations in their dealings with governing bodies. This partnership rests on the recognition that while the parties are mutually dependent and share responsibility for most aspects of local government, they still need to divide up some responsibility to efficiently, effectively, and equitably fulfill the expectations of citizens.

How Local Governments Conduct Business

A fourth dimension of the changing rules of the game for managers involves a shift from *government* to *governance*. Structural constraints placed on the capacity of local governments to respond to contemporary challenges and to operate in the businesslike, entrepreneurial manner are a key factor behind this pivot.

In most parts of the United States, the typical local government is by nature fragmented and separated, small in terms of both territory and population, and limited with respect to its powers and range of responsibilities. The number of units within a local government and the relationship between general- and special-purpose units can be very important if efficiency, effectiveness, equity, and economies of scale are defined as core values in service delivery. On the other hand, these values may collide with what are considered other important virtues of the local government system—closeness, responsiveness, smallness, and customization. Reconciling these competing and conflicting values is the job of both elected officials and professional managers, and this balancing act sometimes exacerbates the gaps between elected officials' priorities for building the community and representing citizens and professional administrators' needs to modernize the governmental organization and manage local services.

Recognition of the fact that successfully addressing most important public problems requires working across jurisdictional and sector boundaries—with other communities, agencies, nonprofit organizations, businesses, citizen groups, and volunteers—has only added to the complexity of local government operations. Since the 1990s, the term *governance* has been used to describe the reality that the government is only one of multiple players in local service delivery, albeit a critical one.

The need to manage within and to work with a diverse array of horizontal and vertical networks of governmental partners, public–private organizations, and regional and community groups has altered the traditional authority of both managers and governing bodies. Increasingly, managers have taken on the roles of facilitator, broker, and networkers while operating less and less in a hierarchical command-and-control model. While their respective responsibilities have grown, their authority has become more shared and more collective.

In summary, the trends outlined above have had a profound impact on the work of county and municipal managers. Among their other roles, managers are more frequently being called on to serve as a bridge over troubled waters. Gaps continue to widen in many communities—between the education and experience of professional full-time managers and amateur part-time governing bodies; between the basic roles of elected officials to represent and make policy for the community and those of managers to build organizational capacity to effectively carry out policy; between citizen "more for less," "we want it our way," "just in time," and "quicker, better, cheaper" expectations for service delivery and the need for representation of community interests and deliberative decision making; and between the community place-based orientation of elected officials and other local leaders and the boundary-spanning nature of contemporary problem solving and service delivery.

THE INTERGOVERNMENTAL LANDSCAPE: WHO'S IN CHARGE?

Over the past half century, the roles and relationships among local, state, and national governments in the United States have undergone dramatic changes. The interactions between these governments and private profit-making and not-for-profit organizations have also experienced marked shifts. Attention has been focused on the fiscal aspects of these changes, especially on grants-in-aid and tax policy. Equally significant, however, are the regulatory and administrative facets of these developments. Growing intergovernmental and public–private collaboration has raised questions about who, precisely, is in charge: Who is responsible for the delivery of services, the payment for services, and the performance of services? The following section reviews recent trends in intergovernmental relations as they relate to local management.

The number and structure of local government units vary widely across the country. The general pattern is, as discussed above, a fragmented structure of many small (with populations under 2,500) units having overlapping responsibilities and limited boundaries. These overlapping responsibilities, combined with the cross-boundary nature of many social, political, and economic problems, means that it has become difficult to identify purely local problems—those over which individual counties, municipalities, or other general-purpose units exercise control without significant policy, financial, or regulatory involvement of neighboring jurisdictions or state or federal authorities. So-called wicked problems involving environmental quality, economic development, health care, and infrastructure ignore these boundaries altogether and defy single jurisdictional remedial actions. Even traditional local functions such as police and fire protection, libraries, and streets are intergovernmental. Others, such as schools, while remaining legally separate from municipalities and counties in most places, have received state and federal grants accompanied by standards and requirements as conditions of aid.

In addition to structural limitations, the powers of local governments are constrained by state constitutions and statutes. Many states operate under a legal interpretation that local governments are creations of the states, which allows states to have authority over the local units' form of government, functional responsibilities, personnel, and finances. Studies have found wide variation among states as to the extent to which constitutions and statutes grant home rule or discretionary authority to various types of general-purpose local governments. In general, states have been more willing to give local governments greater authority over their form of government, functional responsibilities, and personnel policies than over their finances. Legislatures have been less willing to grant home rule to counties than to municipalities, due mainly to the traditional role of county governments as administrative arms of their state. Even in states where local governments have been granted broad home-rule powers, judges, attorneys general, bond counsels, and legislators have imposed sometimes formidable constraints on the exercise of those powers.

In response to legal constraints, local governments have taken to using a variety of collaborative mechanisms. Foremost among them have been formal and informal interlocal contracts and agreements for joint provision of services as well as mutual assistance pacts between police, fire, and emergency medical services departments. In nearly all cases, these arrangements have involved two units and a single service. A second local government response has been privatization of services, a phenomenon that grew in popularity during the 1990s through contracting with for-profit and nonprofit organizations for the performance of local functions. Lastly, a variety of fiscal instruments has been adopted by local officials—such as tax increment financing, revenue bonds, and leasing—in the search for ways to circumvent state restrictions on taxing and spending.

In addition to procedural and fiscal responses, since the 1960s, there have been three major institutional responses to boundary-crossing problems: the reorganized or urban county, special districts and public authorities, and regional planning and coordinating bodies. These strategies have been implemented with varying degrees of success and have usually occurred in tandem with traditional legal and procedural mechanisms that states have granted to municipalities and counties to enable them to address interlocal matters. Besides contracts and agreements, these include extraterritorial powers, annexation, and interlocal functional transfers. Opposition from citizens and public employees, however, has limited the use of these tools.

Another dimension of the changing intergovernmental landscape involves the federal government's role in local government. Beginning in the 1960s, the federal government's domestic role and responsibilities steadily expanded. This growth was a reaction to a number of political and ideological factors, including a regulatory green light given to Congress and federal agencies by the U.S. Supreme Court in its broad interpretations of the Commerce Clause, the Necessary and Proper Clause, the Supremacy Clause, and other implied powers provisions of the U.S. Constitution; public opinion supportive of a strong national role in such areas as civil rights, environmental quality, public health protection, poverty reduction, occupational safety, and community development; and growth in public interest and special interest lobbying groups that advocated for national involvement in local government. The heightened federal role was also a response to concerns about the limited capacity and uneven commitment of localities and states to adequately fund, effectively plan, and equitably administer programs to tackle problems such as poverty, illiteracy, crime, disease, pollution, and infrastructure deterioration.

These factors continue to be relevant, despite concerns about centralization of authority in Washington, D.C. More recently, the demands and pressures of globalization and the new economy have called for the United States to speak with one national voice, not 50 state voices or 39,044 municipal, township, and county voices, furthering trends toward centralization. The vehicles for this expansion of the federal government's domestic role have been grants-in-aid, regulations, and preemptions.

The contemporary federal fiscal picture is dark, as the 4 Ds—deficits, debt, demographics, and defense—could significantly reduce the discretionary portion of the federal budget, putting localities and states on a possible fiscal collision course. Some are predicting that a period of "fend for yourself" localism lies ahead because of decreased federal discretionary spending, domestic spending cuts, and elimination of deductions for certain local taxes. At the same time, there are no indications that the rate of increase in intergovernmental regulations, mandates, and preemption activities will diminish as the national government's financial role declines; in fact, they are likely to continue to increase, while hopes for turning more authority over to states and localities fade.

MANAGING CHALLENGES: CRITICAL COMPETENCIES FOR CLOSING THE GAP

The trends described in this chapter will impact various types and sizes of local governments in different ways, but one thing is certain: All municipalities and counties will be affected. Managers will need to recognize and relate to a web of other jurisdictions, agencies, and organizations involved in governance. What key knowledge, skills, and abilities are needed for twenty-first century municipal and county managers to succeed in this dynamic world of local government (Stenberg, 2007)?

From the inception of the council–manager form of government, governing bodies have expected their chief executive officer to ensure that municipal or county operations run smoothly, that services are provided efficiently and effectively, and that prudent fiscal practices are followed. This heritage continues. Within their organizations, managers will need to be managerial capacity builders, applying contemporary business management practices to local government, including workforce and succession planning, job enlargement and work sharing, team building, mentoring, and coaching. The manager must demonstrate a commitment to diversity in both hiring and service delivery decisions, loyalty to those in the organization, and dedication to the highest ethical standards, as specified in the code of ethics of the International City/County Management Association (ICMA) and in local policies. Managers will need to have a strong moral compass for moving the community forward.

The manager must be a process leader and a problem solver, applying his or her expertise, discretionary authority, and creativity to building a high-performing organization to facilitate technical and systemic change. He or she must also be a skillful communicator of needs, expectations, and accomplishments both within and outside of the organization. Adept use of management tools such as strategic planning, performance measurement, benchmarking, and program evaluation as well as technologies such as e-government will be essential. Adoption of practices used in the private sector to achieve greater efficiency by eliminating unnecessary steps that add both time and personnel to the delivery of services will also prove useful.

Professionalism and lifelong learning are important aspects of these tasks. It is now common for position vacancy announcements for managers, assistant managers, and department heads to require applicants to hold a master's degree. As of 2016, 1,465 managers successfully completed ICMA's Voluntary Credentialing Program and committed to an additional 40 hours of professional development each year to retain their credentials (http://www.icma.org).

The twenty-first century manager will need to be a gap closer, filling in the void between the experience and knowledge found in the offices of the manager and department heads and possessed by elected officials. As an educator, the manager will need to orient newly elected governing body members on local operations so that they can hit the ground running, and he or she must also find ways to present complicated information and updates on matters of interest to busy elected officials in clear and concise ways. The manager will need to find common ground with the council or board on which to develop a vision for the community as well as strategies for achieving that vision over the short and long term. Consensus building, negotiation and mediation, and conflict management skills will be critical, especially with governing bodies seeking to serve diverse community groups and with individual members who have run on single issues or against incumbents in government. From time to time, the manager will also need to play the role of coach, working with members of the governing body to promote understanding of issues and public values, build trust, improve the governing body's policy-making effectiveness, and strengthen working relationships with the professional staff.

The manager will also need to be a convener, broker, and negotiator of interests from both outside and inside the government. Since most important local services require intergovernmental, private sector, or volunteer engagement to be performed successfully, the manager will be both entrepreneur and middle person in government-by-contract arrangements. This role involves identifying opportunities for engagement, bringing diverse groups together, building coalitions, arranging contracts and agreements, monitoring performance, and ensuring that corrective actions are taken. He or she will need to educate the governing board and professional staff on a wide range of matters, including community expectations and issues; regional relationships; state and federal grants, mandates, and regulations; statutory, regulatory, and legal requirements; and the limits as well as advantages of privatization.

In view of citizen confusion over who does what in delivering local services and sometimes unrealistic expectations about the costs and quality of municipal or county services, another dimension of the manager's role as educator is informing the community through websites, public meetings, and citizen academies about the roles and responsibilities of their local government and the division of labor between the governing body and the professional staff. Outreach to prospective volunteers will also be important. In communities where local government has had a tarnished image, marketing and public relations skills will be especially useful to overcome public skepticism and to show how local government works to serve all citizens.

While local managers should not be expected to play the role of lobbyist, in the complex and rapidly changing world of intergovernmental relations, the voice of local government will need to be heard, and thus, managers will increasingly be called on to serve as intergovernmental liaisons. Getting involved in the work of the state league of municipalities, the association of county commissioners, and the city and county manager's association as well as with these groups' national counterparts representing local government interests in Washington, D.C.—the National League of Cities, the U.S. Conference of Mayors, the National Association of Counties, and the ICMA—will be an important way for managers to bolster their local officials' efforts to register the needs of their community and increase opportunities for financial assistance. Managers will need to be politically astute (but not politically involved) professionals.

In the contemporary local government environment, sound management knowledge, skills, and abilities are important, but they will not be sufficient to deal with the political, ideological, intergovernmental, and community-building needs associated with globalization, the new economy, and the information age. In this respect, the manager of the present and future will be looked to as a local leader, an organizational capacity builder, and a community change agent.

The chapters that follow explore more fully the challenges affecting local governments and county and municipal managers. Our hope is that the contents will prove helpful both in preparing students who aspire to careers in local management as well as in motivating current local government professionals who seek to become county or municipal managers.

REFERENCES

Stenberg, C. W. (2007). Meeting the challenge of change. In C. W. Stenberg & S. L. Austin (Eds.), *Managing local government services* (pp. 1–28). Washington, DC: International City/County Management Association.

Svara, J. H. (2004). Achieving effective community leadership. In C. Newell (Ed.), *The effective local government manager* (3rd ed., pp. 27–40). Washington, DC: International City/County Management Association.

U.S. Census Bureau. (2012). *2012 U.S. census of governments*. Retrieved from March 8, 2017, from https://www.census.gov/govs/cog/

Wood, J. (1893). *Dictionary of quotations from ancient and modern English and foreign sources*. London, England: Frederick Warne and Company. Retrieved March 30, 2017, from http://www.gutenberg.org/files/48105/48105-h/48105-h.htm

U.S. LOCAL GOVERNMENTS IN HISTORICAL CONTEXT

The city is recruited from the country.

—Ralph Waldo Emerson (2009, p. 346)

Today, we look at a great American city and we see a giant metropolis the size of a small country with a varied and global economy and people who come from many places. But, as a relatively young country, the cities of the United States are also young. The United States did not begin as a country of urban dwellers, yet today, more than 80% of Americans live in an urban area (U.S. Census, 2010). Many local governments in the United States, both municipalities and counties, exist as a subcomponent of a large, interconnected metropolitan system. This chapter examines how the United States transitioned from rural to metropolitan and how those transformations laid the groundwork for modern local government systems. This transition was not easy or fast, and the people who inhabited early American cities experienced a very different way of life than that of today. Early cities suffered from endless maladies—limited infrastructure, lack of sanitation, substandard housing, political corruption—but these problems were growing pains that paved the way toward major change and reform in the early 1900s.

EARLY DEVELOPMENT OF AMERICAN CITIES: 1700–1900

The early American economy was dependent on agriculture. Early towns were developed to foster mutual protection and came to serve as business centers, collecting and exporting agricultural projects from the region (Schlesinger, 1940). Since land was

17

plentiful in the West, the population spread out, leading to low densities and a mostly rural population (Lemon, 2001). By 1900, nearly 94% of the population lived in rural areas (U.S. Census Bureau, 1998).

Early local government was borrowed and adapted from the European countries that originally colonized North America. Prior to the American Revolution, a royally appointed governor led many colonial governments. Initially, political subdivisions were called *townships*, *towns*, or *parishes*. Counties were created as combinations of these subunits (Lemon, 2001). After the American Revolution, most former colonies relocated their state capitals to more central locations (Martis, 2001).

Cities, as early centers of concentrated population, were only found near transportation hubs. The largest early cities were located near ocean ports (Schlesinger, 1940) or large rivers to facilitate trade in natural resources and agricultural production between rural and urban areas and between the U.S. and other nations. As the Industrial Revolution took hold, population in these early cities exploded. Between 1700 and 1800, Boston's population increased from 7,000 to 25,000; New York from 5,000 to 118,000; and Charleston from 2,000 to 13,000 (Nash, 1987).

Railroad hubs became influential in the location of new cities after the 1830s (Monkkonen, 1988). Cities in the Midwest and West were founded and grew rapidly as the railroads reached them. Chicago's population, a mere 4,470 in 1840, grew to over a half million by 1880 (U.S. Census Bureau, n.d.). Likewise, in St. Louis, the population increased by more than 300,000 in that time period. In New York, the Erie Canal was completed in 1825, providing a link from the Great Lakes to the Atlantic Ocean and increasing the populations of Albany and Buffalo. Towns along the Mississippi River also experienced population growth.

Overall, however, cities remained at low population levels relative to modern cities until a boom in the late nineteenth century. The nation's population increased from about 17 million in 1840 to 76 million by the end of the nineteenth century, and much of this growth was in large cities. The U.S. population exceeded that of Britain by 1820 (Lemon, 2001). New York reached over 1 million residents by 1880. By 1900, Chicago and Philadelphia had joined New York at the over 1 million population mark (U.S. Census Bureau, 1998).

Technological improvements in intracity transportation during the nineteenth century led to geographic and physical growth expansion in cities. Wealthier residents sought to distance themselves from some of the unpleasant conditions that existed in early American cities. Cities were crowded, dirty, and often lacked paved streets or sidewalks, greenspace, and other amenities that we take for granted today. Initially, moving away from the center city by only a mile or two was sufficient to escape urban ills; however, development pushed people further and further out (Hayden, 2003).

Beginning in the 1870s, the installation of new streetcar lines coupled with land speculation led to development beyond the periphery of the cities (Hayden, 2003). These developments were often hastily and haphazardly planned with modest single-family homes being the primary residence type (Hayden, 2003). Precursors to the modern suburb, today, they are often incorporated into the central city.

URBAN POPULATION GROWTH

As the nineteenth century came to an end, population growth in the cities continued to intensify. These population increases had two primary drivers: Improvements in public health led to lower mortality rates and massive waves of immigrants provided growth from other countries.

Before the twentieth century, disease rates were very high in the cities. Living near one another, sharing polluted water sources, and eating tainted food led to death rates frequently exceeding birth rates. Epidemics of cholera and yellow fever were common. Urban mortality exceeded rural mortality until about 1920 (Haines, 2001).

With high infant mortality rates and low life expectancies for city residents, much of the unprecedented growth in the U.S. population in the nineteenth century was due to immigration (see Table 2.1). The 1840s marked the

TABLE 2.1 ■ Total U.S. Population and Foreign-Born Population and Percentage, 1850–1990			
Year	Total Population	Foreign-Born Population	Percentage Foreign Born
1850	23,191,876	2,244,602	9.7
1870	38,558,371	5,567,229	14.4
1890	62,622,250	9,249,547	14.8
1910	91,972,266	13,515,886	14.7
1930	122,775,046	14,204,149	11.6
1950	150,216,110	10,347,395	6.9
1970	203,210,158	9,619,302	4.7
1990	248,709,873	19,767,316	7.9

Source: Gibson & Jung, 2006.

beginning of a period of mass immigration in the U.S. Cities were the destinations for most of these immigrants (Ward, 2001). Industry was the primary driver, offering employment for the new immigrants. By 1920, the U.S. population exceeded 100 million.

The United States has become increasingly more urbanized over time. Until 1930, residents were more likely to live in rural areas than urban areas. In 1820, there were only 12 places designated by the Census Bureau that had more than 10,000 residents. By 1880, the number had increased to 212, and by 1970, there were more than 3,000 incorporated places with populations of 10,000 or above.

The transition from rural to urban was a rapid one in the United States (see Figure 2.1). At the first U.S. census, in 1790, only about 5% of the population lived in urban areas. However, the 50% mark was reached before 1930. By 2010, more than 80% of the population lived in urban areas. Urban areas have grown as well. In many parts of the country, multiple municipal borders converge, creating massive, multijurisdictional metropolitan regions. However, to reach this level of complexity, cities first had to grow—and to grow, they had to cope with problems that had become commonplace for urban dwellers.

FIGURE 2.1 ■ U.S. Urban Population Percentage: 1790–2000

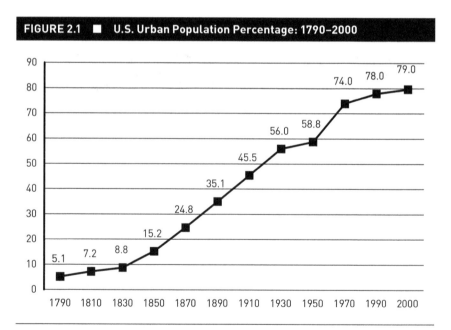

Sources: Gibson & Jung, 2006; U.S. Census Bureau, 1975.

THE PROGRESSIVE ERA

Living Conditions in the Cities

Rapid urbanization and government corruption in the nineteenth and early twentieth centuries led to critical dysfunctions in American cities. These problems included poor-quality housing, dangerous working conditions, and local government systems that barely functioned due to bribes and patronage. As Progressive reformers drew attention to these issues, the need for well-run cities became apparent. Problems of early urban living were numerous. While living conditions were miserable for the lowest-income residents, even the wealthy endured a lower quality of life than is common in modern cities.

Many streets were unpaved or poorly paved, making traversing a city challenging. Early pavement included cobblestones, granite blocks (Belgian block), and wood— but significant swaths of the average city had no pavement at all through the 1800s. The largest cities fared the best with pavement (see Table 2.2) but even by 1890, out of the ten largest cities at the time, only Boston boasted fully paved streets.

Early city streets were muddy, filled with holes, and littered with animal waste. Asphalt did not come into use until the late 1800s (Hart, 1950). These poor conditions

TABLE 2.2 ■ Ten Largest Cities' Percentage of Paved Streets, 1890		
City	Population	Percentage of Paved Streets
New York	1,515,301	62.3
Chicago	1,099,850	30.7
Philadelphia	1,046,964	65.2
Brooklyn	806,343	57.4
St. Louis	451,770	39.8
Boston	448,477	100.0
Baltimore	434,439	58.8
San Francisco	298,997	56.1
Cincinnati	296,908	56.5
Cleveland	261,353	14.9

Source: Billings, 1890.

Street sanitation was nonexistent in nineteenth-century New York, as this picture from 1895 shows.

led to problems with commerce and sanitation. Ideally, pedestrians could walk on sidewalks to avoid the conditions of the streets, but sidewalks were not typically built by city governments. Instead, property owners paid for the installation of sidewalks, so they were only found in the wealthy areas of town in most cities.

Horses remained the primary form of transportation for both people and goods throughout the nineteenth century; but horses created problems as well. Each horse deposited 30–50 pounds of manure per day, and large cities had many thousands of horses (Rosner, 2010). Although most cities had street cleaning or sanitation departments in the early 1800s, local government corruption meant that little was done. Human waste, dead animals, manure, and other trash were simply thrown on the streets. When trash was collected, it was either disposed of in a waterway or an open dump (Louis, 2004).

Pollution from industrialization also contributed to low quality of life in early American cities. Coal was the most commonly used fuel for heating and factory energy production (Gonzalez, 2005). The resulting smoke and soot led to low air quality and dirty cities. Some cities were dark, even during the day. When burned, the coal produced coal ash, another form of solid waste that early sanitation departments were incapable of disposing of properly. Industries that produced pollution of all kinds typically dumped their refuse into the nearest waterway. Industrial sites were located immediately next to low-income residential buildings, meaning residents could not escape the noxious fumes or waste.

Another aspect of urban quality of life in which there were vast discrepancies between the wealthy and lower-income families was housing. The most common early urban dwelling buildings for low-income families were called *tenements*. Tenements served as the homes for new immigrants arriving from other countries. Many tenements had once been single-family homes that were subdivided into small apartments. Due to the overcrowding, poor ventilation, and lack of indoor plumbing, tenements were substandard housing. Tenements that were built as new dwellings typically suffered from shoddy construction techniques and poor building materials, due to the developers' interest in keeping costs low.

The Tenement House Act, passed in 1867 by the New York legislature, required fire escapes, a window in every room, and a minimum of one toilet per 20 residents. However, enforcement of the law was lax and loopholes in the law were exploited. In 1890, Jacob Riis, photographer and author, published *How the Other Half Lives*, a book that exposed the horrible conditions of tenement life. Public outcry caused by the book's revelations led to a series of amendments to New York state law and calls for nationwide housing reform.

Poor sanitation, overcrowded housing, low food quality, and pollution had severe public health outcomes for the population of cities during the Industrial Revolution. Most cities drew their drinking water from the same water source used for sewage disposal and industrial runoff, leading to high waterborne disease rates. Overcrowding in the tenements meant that communicable diseases spread rapidly. Cholera, typhoid, and yellow fever were particularly pernicious infections. Nearly 10% of Memphis's population was lost to yellow fever in 1873 (Melosi, 2005). New York City lost more than 3,500 residents to cholera in 1832, when the population of the city numbered approximately 250,000 (Wilford, 2008).

Exacerbating the issues in housing, public health, and waste management was the fact that many early urban governments were plagued by corruption and patronage. Political machines, with power based in segments of immigrant groups, sought private gain for its leaders through graft and bribes. Contracts with private companies for services such as street cleaning were padded with bribes for office holders. There was little oversight of early municipal contracts.

Internally, hiring was based on loyalty to the machine rather than qualifications for a job. A survey in 1890 found that 70% of the 30 largest cities conducted hiring based on patronage (Reid & Kurth, 1992). Men who delivered votes did so in expectation of getting jobs in the government. Due to machine influence and the lack of professionally trained staff, city services were inadequately and inequitably provided.

Early New York Department of Sanitation workers wore white to give an image of cleanliness and professionalism.

Political machines manipulated the political process through corrupt acts and by exploiting weaknesses in the existing electoral system. While political machines did serve the new immigrant populations by assisting them with housing and work, they did so at a significant cost of waste and inefficiency in local governance (Reid & Kurth, 1992).

Progressive Era Social Reforms

In the late nineteenth and early twentieth century, muckrakers (journalists who exposed many of the ills of urban society), social reformers (including the Catholic church), and government reformers made up primarily of business elites began to draw the public's attention to these problems. Each of these groups sought reform for different reasons, but the unlikely coalition around reform led to significant changes during the Progressive Era.

Socially, reforms were directed at the daily quality of life of the urban population. Labor reforms were intended to make working conditions safer and to place limits on child labor. Food and drug laws were passed to make the food supply safer and remove harmful patent medicines from the market. Housing reforms were passed at the state level. Engineers applied their skills to sanitizing water and removing waste from the cities.

Progressive Era Political Reforms

Although the social reforms helped ameliorate some of the worst issues related to public health and living conditions, these reforms would do little to improve the day-to-day lives of urban residents if the local government system could not improve. Political reforms during the Progressive Era set the stage for greater professionalism in local government and a weakening of political machines and the patronage system. The Australian ballot, which allowed citizens to vote in secret, was adopted throughout the United States by 1892. However, nationally, it was not illegal to pay another person to vote for a candidate until 1925 (18 U.S. Code § 597).

At the national level, the merit system was introduced to reduce patronage under the Pendleton Act of 1883. States and cities gradually shifted away from the patronage system as the power of political machines ebbed. Prior to this shift, local government employees were selected based on who they knew or who they were loyal to, not what they knew.

Much of the initiative behind transforming local government to more professional, businesslike organizations was taken by good government organizations funded by ultra-wealthy benefactors. Advocates working in these organizations sought to create more efficient and effective local government systems through training, research, and advocacy (Hopkins, 1912; McDonald, 2010). The first and most well-known of these organizations was the New York Bureau of Municipal Research. After its founding in 1906, financed by Andrew Carnegie and John D. Rockefeller, similar organizations were created in Chicago, Philadelphia, and Dayton (Hays, 1964).

One area of research these organizations undertook was an exploration of how structural changes to municipal governments might affect performance. Two new forms of government became the focus of advocates for structural reform—the commission and council–manager forms of government. Both of these reform models of government were instituted to improve local government efficiency by borrowing techniques from the private business sector (Bernard & Rice, 1975).

The commission form of government, first instituted in Galveston, Texas, as a means to deal with the massive rebuilding effort from the 1900 hurricane that devastated the island city, quickly grew to become the most popular form of government in the country (Rice, 1975). Under the commission form, elected members of the legislative body—the commission—would also each be tasked with overseeing an administrative department of the local government. Despite its rapid rise in popularity, the plan's weaknesses became quickly apparent. Elected officials, when charged with the responsibilities over a single department, quickly identified with that department, looking out for the interests of the department and its personnel. This almost inevitable result under commission government meant that it was difficult to reach consensus on decisions, since commissioners would put their departments above the city as a whole. Because of these problems with the commission form, adoptions of the plan dropped precipitously after 1920 (Rice, 1975) and the other reform model, the council–manager plan, quickly eclipsed it.

In 1906, Staunton, Virginia, adopted a form of government unlike that found in any other city. The city council created the position of *general manager*, a title that was quickly transformed by the press to the title *city manager* (Grubert, 1954). Staunton had suffered from mismanagement for years, resulting in a significant public outcry over lack of street pavement. Due to both tradition and state legal requirements, Staunton operated under an inefficient bicameral legislative system of 22 elected officials and 30 committees (Grubert, 1954). The manager position was created to handle the administrative duties that were previously conducted by committee. Under the new plan, Staunton was to be viewed as a business corporation and therefore was to be administered as such. This person would be directly responsible to the council. The first general manager, an engineer by training, was appointed in 1908 (Grubert, 1954).

The city manager may have remained an oddity had it not been for the work of Richard Childs. Childs's conception of the council–manager plan was a marriage of Staunton's general manager with the commission form of government (Hirschhorn, 1997). At a meeting of the National Municipal League in 1915, when the council–manager form was used as the basis for the model city charter, Childs proclaimed he was "the minister who performed the marriage ceremony between the city manager . . . in Staunton, and the commission plan in Des Moines" (Childs, 1916, p. 210). He believed that the council–manager form would be the most closely related to a private corporation management structure with a board (council or commission) appointing and directing a chief administrative officer—the city manager. The manager would then direct the day-to-day operations of government.

The first charter adoption of the council–manager plan occurred in Sumter, South Carolina, in 1912. One year later, Dayton, Ohio, became the first large city to adopt the plan. Publicity from these adoptions and reports of early successes with the plan led to widespread adoption throughout the United States. Today, the council–manager form is found in more municipalities than any other form.

POST-PROGRESSIVE ERA METROPOLITAN DEVELOPMENT

The Progressive Era began a wave of initiatives to professionalize local governments. This professionalization led to increases in efficiency and the implementation of technological innovations in urban services that allowed cities to continue to grow

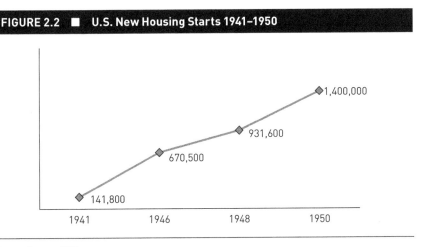

FIGURE 2.2   ■   **U.S. New Housing Starts 1941–1950**

Source: Carney, 1959.

rapidly throughout the twentieth century. However, many of the negative aspects of urban living meant that the borders of the cities were constantly being pushed outward, eventually leading to rapid suburban development.

Forces That Shaped Suburban Development

Pre–World War II, suburban development was modest. The early streetcar suburbs had, in most cases, been subsumed by the central cities. Suburban enclaves, planned communities designed to resemble European estates, were out of reach for most Americans (Hayden, 2003). However, after the war, a number of forces and federal programs led to the development of suburbs for the growing middle class. These forces both drove demand for new housing and facilitated the development of large-scale housing developments further outside cities than was possible before.

A key piece of federal policy that allowed for the construction of massive middle-class suburban developments was the GI Bill. Passed in 1944, financing from the Department of Veterans Affairs allowed military members and retirees to borrow 100% of the value of a home (up to $2,000) with no down payment (Hanchett, 1994). This created a demand for housing that was not satisfied by existing urban housing development.

Demographic changes also fed increasing housing demand. Beginning in 1946, birth rates in the United States grew substantially and remained at elevated levels until the beginning of the 1960s. The total size of the baby boom cohort (those born between 1946 and 1964) was 72.5 million (Colby & Ortman, 2014).

Growth in the American population exacerbated the existing housing shortage. Due to economic decline in the Depression and the subsequent need to devote industry to the war effort, virtually no homes were built during the 1930s and 1940s in the United States.

New housing starts numbered fewer than 200,000 in 1941 but quickly increased after the war (see Figure 2.2). Initially, homebuilding technology was not advanced enough to build the necessary housing needed due to the baby boom. To replace deteriorating housing and provide homes for the growing population at the time, between 1 million and 1.5 million new homes were needed per year (Checkoway, 1980). The United States did not meet that production level until 1950.

The largest and perhaps best-known postwar mass-produced suburban development was Levittown, New York. Located 25 miles from New York City, Levittown would grow to have more than 17,000 homes (Ross, 2014). Levitt built the homes using an assembly line style, allowing the houses to be priced below traditional builder prices. Soon, other builders across the country were replicating Levitt's methods.

In order to build these houses at affordable prices, land needed to be acquired at low cost. However, low-cost undeveloped land lay far outside the city limits. Were it not for federal highway policy and the rise of the automobile for transportation, the modern suburb would not have been created.

As with other industries, the production of cars rapidly increased after the war. Mass production dropped prices to make them more affordable for average families and changes in financing allowed for payments over time. Construction of the interstate highway system provided high-quality roads to feed suburban residents into the cities for work.

Unintended Consequences of Suburbanization

Affordable homes with green space and a system of roads to make commuting to the city quicker and easier led to rapid suburbanization in the United States but also to decline of the central city. The same highways that made transportation to the cities fairly easy for suburban residents often split cities in half, harming healthy neighborhoods. Urban housing, primarily that of minority residents, was destroyed to accommodate the new roads. However, dislocation was seen as an acceptable cost to revitalize blighted areas.

Racial discrimination occurred in several forms. Suburban developers put restrictive covenants in place that prohibited minorities from buying homes. Real estate appraisers devalued homes in predominantly minority neighborhoods (a practice called *redlining*). Mortgage discrimination also made it more difficult for African American families to purchase homes. These forces led to urban populations that were predominately minority and suburban populations that were predominately

FIGURE 2.3 ■ Percentage of U.S. Population Living in Central Cities versus Suburbs

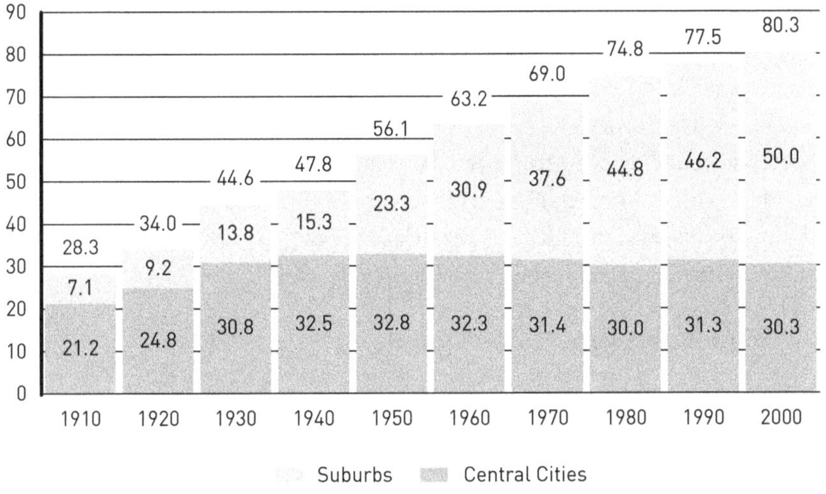

Source: Hobbs & Stoops, 2000.

white. So, the population shift to the suburbs was primarily white. This "white flight" has had lasting implications for inner cities.

Economically, central cities were hit hard. Suburban malls replaced downtown retail areas. Both property and sales tax revenue collections for cities declined due to population shrinkage. As cities experienced revenue decline, they delayed improvements to infrastructure. This led to a general worsening appearance of central cities and a long-term period of urban decline (Banfield, 1968).

Federal housing policy that called for revitalization of blighted urban areas often destroyed healthy neighborhoods (Housing Acts of 1949 and 1954). More low-rent homes were destroyed than were built (Checkoway, 1980). Urban revitalization projects replaced low-rent homes with luxury housing or commercial space. Another federal policy choice served as a further push of population away from central cities: Federal funding for Federal Housing Administration (FHA) mortgage insurance favored suburban housing over urban housing, and Congress began reducing funding for public housing in 1951 (Checkoway, 1980). By 1980, the percentage of the U.S. urban population that lived in suburbs exceeded the percentage living in central cities (see Figure 2.3).

Central cities were not the only localities to suffer from unchecked suburban development. As people moved further and further from the central cities, seeking fresh air, large yards, good schools, and more affordable housing, metropolitan areas increasingly became victims of sprawl. Factors that set sprawl apart from simple urban population growth include low-density development, automobile dependency for transportation, leapfrog subdivision development, and segregated land uses (U.S. Department of Housing and Urban Development, 1999).

Sprawl caused a host of problems for a region (Bhatta, 2010; Johnson, 2001). Higher dependency on cars for transportation led to water, air, and noise pollution. Automobile dependency also led to heavy traffic in a region. The increase in paved surfaces surrounding suburban space, both for roads and the parking lots, meant that much of the rainwater falling in the suburbs became runoff. Other environmental impacts of sprawl included the significant use of green space, loss of farmland, and loss of environmentally fragile land, such as wetlands.

The Beginnings of the Metropolis

When the central city and its surrounding suburbs are viewed as a region, it is called the *metropolitan area*. Today, the U.S. Office of Management and Budget defines a metropolitan area as a core urban area of 50,000 or more people that includes adjacent counties with a high percentage of people who commute to work to the core urban area.

As suburbs evolved from places to live into places to work as well, they expanded geographically, sometimes becoming substantially large cities in their own right. Inner-ring suburbs, the oldest of the suburbs, were often incorporated into the central city while aging middle-ring suburbs developed the problems of the central cities (Orfield, 2002).

As sprawl resulted in population outgrowth away from central cities, central city borders often touched or came close to touching what were once distant suburban municipalities, creating a *metropolis*. In some cases, multiple metropolitan areas abutted, creating a mega-metropolitan area, the *megalopolis*.

The historical legacy of metropolitan America has led us from tiny port towns to megacities. What were once highly disorganized and inefficient local governments are today run professionally and efficiently. While there are a number of problems in the metropolis that will be discussed in other parts of this book, the system of local governments in the U.S. is able to provide high levels of services to the citizens, most of whom do not have to think about whether their trash will be picked up or whether the tap will have clean water.

LOOKING FORWARD

The profession of city and county management is at a crossroads. As the next chapter will describe, the historical legacy of urban and suburban development has led to a level of structural complexity not seen in other nations around the world.

The municipal or county manager plays a key role in a community's success in this complex environment.

REFERENCES

18 U.S. Code § 597

Banfield, E. C. (1968). Why government cannot solve the urban problem. *Daedalus, 97*(4), 1231–1241.

Bernard, R. M., & Rice, B. R. (1975). Political environment and the adoption of progressive municipal reform. *Journal of Urban History, 1*(2), 149–173.

Bhatta, B. (2010). *Analysis of urban growth and sprawl from remote sensing data.* Berlin, Germany: Springer-Verlag.

Billings, J. S. (1890). *Report on the social statistics of cities in the United States at the eleventh census: 1890.* Washington, DC: U.S. Government Printing Office.

Carney, M. F. (1959). *Nonfarm housing starts 1889–1958, bulletin #1260.* Washington, DC: U.S. Department of Labor. Retrieved March 9, 2017, from http://babel.hathitrust.org/cgi/pt?id=uiug.301 12069788310;view=1up;seq=5

Checkoway, B. (1980). Large builders, federal housing programmes, and postwar suburbanization. *International Journal of Urban and Regional Research, 4*(1), 21–45.

Childs, R. (1916). Professional standards and professional ethics in the new profession of city manager: A discussion. *National Municipal Review, 5*(2), 195–210.

Colby, S. L., & Ortman, J. M. (2014). *The baby boom cohort in the United States.* Washington, DC: U.S. Census Bureau.

Emerson, R. W. (2009). *The essential writings of Ralph Waldo Emerson.* New York, NY: Random House.

Gibson, C., & Jung, K. (2006). Historical census statistics on the foreign-born population of the United States: 1850–2000 (Working Paper No. 81). Washington, DC: U.S. Census Bureau.

Gonzalez, G. A. (2005). *The politics of air pollution: Urban growth, ecological modernization, and symbolic inclusion.* Albany: State University of New York Press.

Grubert, W. A. (1954). *The origin of the city manager plan in Staunton, Virginia.* Retrieved March 9, 2017, from http://www.icmaml.org/wp-content/uploads/2014/07/Origin-City-Manager-Plan-in-Staunton-VA.pdf

Haines, M. R. (2001). The urban mortality transition in the United States, 1800–1940. *Annales de Démographie Historique, 1*(101), 33–64.

Hanchett, T. W. (1994). Federal incentives and the growth of local planning, 1941–1948. *Journal of the American Planning Association, 60*(2), 197–208.

Hart, V. (1950). *The story of American roads.* New York, NY: Sloane.

Hayden, D. (2003). *Building suburbia: Green fields and urban growth 1820–2000.* New York, NY: Pantheon Books.

Hays, S. P. (1964). The politics of reform in municipal government in the progressive era. *The Pacific Northwest Quarterly, 55*(4), 157–169.

Hirschhorn, B. (1997). *Democracy reformed: Richard Spencer Childs and his fight for better government.* Westport, CT: Praeger.

Hobbs, F., & Stoops, N. (2000). Demographic trends in the 20th century. *Census 2000 Special Reports, Series CENSR-4.* Washington, DC: U.S. Census Bureau.

Hopkins, G. B. (1912). The New York bureau of municipal research. *The Annals of the American Academy of Political and Social Science, 41,* 235–244.

Johnson, M. P. (2001). Environmental impacts of urban sprawl: A survey of the literature and proposed research agenda. *Environment and Planning A, 33,* 717–735.

Lemon, J. T. (2001). Colonial America in the 18th century. In T. McIlwraith & E. Muller (Eds.), *North America: The historical geography of a changing continent* (2nd ed., 119–139). Lanham, MD: Rowman and Littlefield.

Louis, G. E. (2004). A historical context of municipal solid waste management in the United States. *Waste Management and Research, 22,* 306–322.

Martis, K. C. (2001). The geographical dimensions of a new nation, 1780s–1820s. In T. McIlwraith & E. Muller (Eds.), *North America: The historical geography of a changing continent* (2nd ed., 143–164). Lanham, MD: Rowman and Littlefield.

McDonald, B. (2010). The bureau of municipal research and the development of a professional public service. *Administration and Society, 42*(7), 815–835.

Melosi, M. V. (2005). *Garbage in the cities: Refuse, reform, and the environment.* Pittsburgh, PA: University of Pittsburgh Press.

Monkkonen, E. H. (1988). *America becomes urban: The development of U.S. cities and towns 1780–1980.* Berkeley: University of California Press.

Nash, G. B. (1987). The social evolution of preindustrial American cities, 1700–1820. *Journal of Urban History, 13,* 115, 145.

Orfield, M. (2002). *American metro politics: The new suburban reality.* Washington, DC: Brookings Institution Press.

Reid, J. D., & Kurth, M. M. (1992). The rise and fall of urban patronage machines. In C. Goldin & H. Rockoff (Eds.), *Strategic factors in nineteenth century American economic history* (pp. 427–445). Chicago, IL: University of Chicago Press.

Rice, B. R. (1975). The Galveston plan of city government by commission: The birth of a progressive idea. *The Southwestern Historical Quarterly, 78*(4), 365–408.

Rosner, D. (2010). "Spanish flu, or whatever it is . . .": The paradox of public health in a time of crisis. *Public Health Reports, 125,* 38–47.

Ross, B. (2014). *Dead-end suburban sprawl and the rebirth of American urbanism.* New York, NY: Oxford University Press.

Schlesinger, A. M. (1940). The city in American history. *The Mississippi Valley Historical Review, 27*(1), 43–66.

U.S. Census Bureau. (n.d.). *Census of population and housing.* Retrieved March 31, 2017, from https://www.census.gov/prod/www/decennial.html

U.S. Census Bureau. (1975). *Historical statistics of the United States: Colonial times to 1970.* Washington, DC: Author.

U.S. Census Bureau. (1998). *Population of the 100 largest urban places: 1900.* Washington, DC: Author.

U.S. Census Bureau. (2010). *2010 census urban area facts.* Retrieved March 31, 2017, from https://www.census.gov/geo/reference/ua/uafacts.html

U.S. Department of Housing and Urban Development. (1999). *The state of cities 1999: Third annual report.* Washington, DC: Author.

Ward, D. (2001). Population growth, migration, and urbanization 1860–1920. In T. McIlwraith & E. Muller (Eds.), *North America: The historical geography of a changing continent* (2nd ed., pp. 285–306). Lanham, MD: Rowman and Littlefield.

Wilford, J. N. (2008, April 15). How epidemics helped shape the modern metropolis. *New York Times,* p. F4. Retrieved March 9, 2107, from http://www.nytimes.com/2008/04/15/science/15chol.html?_r=0.

RESOURCE LIST/TO EXPLORE FURTHER

Books/Articles

Childs, R. (1965). *The first 50 years of the council–manager plan of municipal government.* New York, NY: National Municipal League.

Hofstadter, R. (1955). *The age of reform.* New York, NY: Knopf.

Jackson, K. (1985). *Crabgrass frontier: The suburbanization of the United States.* New York, NY: Oxford University Press.

Web Resources

Harvard University's Open Collection Program, "Immigration to the United States: 1789–1930," provides a freely accessible list of resources on muckrakers, tenement housing reform, immigration, and urban poverty. Available at http://ocp.hul.harvard.edu/immigration/riis.html

Video

"Industrial New York." *Filthy Cities.* (2016). BBC/PBS. This episode of a documentary provides a vivid picture of life in early twentieth-century New York.

TYPES, FUNCTIONS, AND AUTHORITY OF U.S. LOCAL GOVERNMENTS

Municipal corporations owe their origin to, and derive their powers and rights wholly from, the legislature. It breathes into them the breath of life, without which they cannot exist. As it creates, so may it destroy.

—Justice John F. Dillon (1911, p. 62)

Despite the critical role local governments play in the daily lives of citizens, they are not mentioned a single time in the U.S. Constitution. Over time, the relationships between local governments and the federal and state governments have shifted. While not referenced in the constitution, the federal government has sought to influence policy at the local level. Power and authority of the nation's local governments varies greatly depending on the type of government, the level of jurisdictional fragmentation in a state, and state legal restrictions on local governments. This chapter will examine the level of autonomy and control afforded local governments, types and distribution of local governments nationally, and local government form and structure.

U.S. LOCAL GOVERNMENT AUTHORITY

Local Governments in the Federal System

The American federal system is based on vertical shared authority. Both the states and the federal governments possess powers that are independent from each other and are governed under individual constitutions; this system of shared and independent authority is called *dual sovereignty*. Throughout time, this system of shared authority has shifted to adapt to social, political, and demographic changes.

In contrast to the federal system that exists between the federal government and the states, the relationship between states and the local governments is a unitary system. Instead of a system of shared authority, power is held by the state. As articulated in the quote at the beginning of the chapter, local governments derive their authority from their states. Local governments have no independent authority unless the state grants it to them.

The federal government does not have direct authority over the local governments granted through the Constitution. Despite this lack of authority, there are times when Congress or the President look to municipalities and counties to carry out national policies and priorities. The federal government has both "carrots" and "sticks" it can use for this purpose. When the federal government wants to influence local policy, it can issue grants-in-aid (which often come with rules attached), regulations, or mandates.

Early in the nation's founding, the relationships between the federal government, states, and local governments resulted in distinctive roles for each level of government. Called *dual federalism* or *layer cake federalism*, this period lasted until the Great Depression (Berman, 2003). During this period, there was a strict division between the responsibilities of the federal and state governments. There was no direct relationship between the federal government and local governments.

During the Great Depression, states were unable to provide sufficient support for needs at the local level. The federal government intervened and began providing assistance for public works, housing, unemployment, and other needs. The New Deal period represented the beginning of a new era of federalism, called *cooperative* (or *marble cake*) *federalism*, in which the roles of the three levels of government became less distinct and functional sharing (instead of separation) characterized intergovernmental relationships (Berman, 2003).

This complicated system, which results in overlapping authority between the federal, state, and local governments, is depicted in Figure 3.1 as conceptualized by Deil Wright (1988) in *Understanding Intergovernmental Relations*. Although first articulated in 1978, this model has retained its relevance (Agranoff & Radin, 2015). In the complex intergovernmental system in the U.S., the three levels of government are each afforded some level of independent authority and are constrained in other areas. Where power is shared, each level of government faces some degree of constraint.

Local Government Relations with the National Government

The direct relationship between the federal government and local governments is primarily based upon funding received from the federal grants process, fiscal federalism, and through regulatory mandates. Beginning in the New Deal period, the federal government infused local governments with substantial grants-in-aid for airport development, housing, economic opportunity, neighborhood improvement, and other purposes. The 1970s witnessed the passage of the Community Development Block Grant program (CDBG), which gave local governments considerable discretion and flexibility for using federal funds for their priority needs in this area. Also in the 1970s, the federal government began revenue sharing with state and local governments, a program that would continue until 1986 (O'Toole & Christensen, 2013). Revenue-sharing grants had no restrictions on how the money was spent. Some smaller jurisdictions became somewhat dependent on these funds, accounting for 10% or more of some local government budgets (Berman, 2003). When the spigot was turned off by the Reagan administration, these local governments struggled to find sufficient revenue to cover the gaps.

The 1970s also saw an increase in the number of federal mandates that affected local governments. Many of these regulations were related to environmental safety. Local governments, as the primary providers of drinking water and wastewater

FIGURE 3.1 ■ Deil Wright's Overlapping Authority Model of Intergovernmental Relations

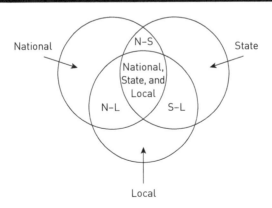

Source: Agranoff & Radin, 2015.

treatment, bore the burden of enforcing and meeting the new requirements. Initially, federal regulations were accompanied by funding to help state and local governments implement them, but increasingly, federal mandates were unfunded (Government Accountability Office, 1994). In 1981, local governments were responsible for 76% of the costs to comply with federal Environmental Protection Agency (EPA) mandates (EPA, 1990).

Courts have been responsible for increasing federal power vis-à-vis the states, primarily through upholding of a concept called *preemption*. In a number of federalism cases, the Supreme Court has determined that federal law supersedes state or local law. When ruling, the court refers to one of two articles in the Constitution (see the box below). The Supremacy Clause states in part that the laws of the United States "shall be the supreme law of the land." The Commerce Clause gives Congress the power to regulate commerce between states. Congress may use preemption to displace existing state or local law.

Total federal preemption occurs when the federal government takes over complete regulatory authority in a given policy area. For example, the federal government mandated that states comply with federal laws under the Equal Employment Opportunity Act of 1972. Under partial federal preemption, the federal government establishes a minimum standard. States are typically required to enforce that minimum standard but are also permitted to implement regulations with more stringent standards. For example, the Clean Water Act of 1977 establishes maximum levels of contaminants that are permitted in drinking water, but states can require lower levels of contaminants than required by federal law (U.S. Advisory Commission on Intergovernmental Relations, 1992, p. A121).

EXCERPTS FROM THE U.S. CONSTITUTION RELATED TO PREEMPTION

Supremacy Clause, Article VI, Clause 2: This Constitution, and the laws of the United States which shall be made in pursuance thereof; and all treaties made, or which shall be made, under the authority of the United States, shall be the supreme law of the land; and the judges in every state shall be bound thereby, anything in the Constitution or laws of any State to the contrary notwithstanding.

Commerce Clause, Article I, Section 8, Clause 3: The Congress shall have the power . . . to regulate commerce with foreign nations, and among the several states, and with the Indian tribes.

Local Governments and Their States

State governments exert a high level of influence on their local governments. As the quote that leads the chapter succinctly points out, local governments are created by their states and therefore, it is the state's right to impose restrictions on its local governments. The level of authority of a local government may vary from nearly no discretionary autonomy to nearly unlimited discretion. Level of authority is dependent on state law but often also varies within states, according to population size (local government classification) and type of government (municipal or county). The term *home rule* is used to apply to local governments that are granted powers of self-government by their state. Generally, states that do not grant home rule are called *Dillon's Rule* states.

Dillon's Rule

In 1868, the Iowa Supreme Court heard the case, *City of Clinton v. Cedar Rapids and Missouri Railroad Company*. Disturbed by some of the municipal investment practices at the time, Justice John F. Dillon based his decision on the idea that state control would limit financial misconduct by disallowing local governments from engaging in private market functions (Krane, Rigos, & Hill, 2001). Dillon wrote,

> Municipal Corporations owe their origin to and derive their powers and rights wholly from the legislature. It breathes into them the breath of life, without which they cannot exist. . . . They are, so to phrase it, mere tenants at the will of the legislature. (*City of Clinton v. Cedar Rapids and Missouri Rail Company,* 1868)

Later, writing in a legal text, Dillon expanded on his opinion by explaining the powers accorded to local governments:

> It is a general and undisputed proposition of law that a municipal corporation possesses and can exercise the following powers, and no others: first, those granted in express words; second, those necessarily or fairly implied in or incident to the powers expressly granted; third, those essential to the accomplishment of the declared objects and purposes of the corporation—not simply convenient, but indispensable. Any fair, reasonable, substantial doubt concerning the existence of a power is resolved by the courts against a corporation, and the power is denied. (Dillon, 1911, p. 48)

By delineating the three categories of local government authority and stating that disputes between localities and their states should be decided in favor of the states,

Dillon had laid out a template for future courts. Thirty-nine states apply Dillon's Rule to at least some of their local governments (Richardson, Gough, & Puentes, 2003).

Dillon's Rule does not preclude a state from providing expansive autonomy to its local governments. However, in the absence of state legislation that grants autonomy, most courts will employ Dillon's Rule to evaluate a conflict between a state and its local governments. Those states that wish to expand local government discretion usually do so through a constitutional amendment or state statutes granting home rule.

Home Rule

When fully realized, home rule establishes a relationship between the state governments and their local governments that closely resembles the relationship between states and the federal government (Moreira, 2015). Home rule does not mean that local governments are free from state oversight. Also, home rule is not a uniform grant of powers from state to state. For example, states that implement home rule may choose to grant it to only some of their local governments or they may choose to grant very limited powers under their so-called home rule charters.

To evaluate home rule authority for a given local government, three areas of local discretion should be considered: structural, functional, and fiscal home rule. Structural home rule is the most common area of home rule in the United States (Krane et al., 2001). Under structural home rule, a local government will be able to choose its form of government. Structural home rule also includes whether local governments are permitted to choose the size of their governing board and the election method and terms of board members. Forty states grant structural authority to municipalities, and 24 states provide this authority to counties.

Another area where local governments differ in discretionary authority is the types and number of services they are permitted to offer. In many states, counties have expanded the number of services they provide to such a degree as to be indistinguishable from the menu of services provided by municipalities (Krane et al., 2001). In states with functional home rule, municipalities and counties can choose the services they wish to provide to their residents. Functional home rule also considers the level of authority a local government has over land use.

Although local government leaders may value having the ability to modify their structure and add or remove service offerings, the area of discretion that is most prized is fiscal. Local governments with fiscal discretion can choose from various tax options, issue debt with few limits, and implement creative methods for generating new revenue (i.e., red light cameras, impact fees) without first seeking the permission of the state legislature. Some states that offer generous structural and functional home rule may retain high levels of control in the fiscal arena. Massachusetts is a case in point. Amendment 89 to the Massachusetts constitution was passed in 1966, allowing local governments to exercise any power not precluded by the constitution or laws of the state. However, later in the amendment, the state reserves sole authority to levy taxes and borrow money (issue debt). By severely curtailing a local government's ability to generate revenue, the state also limits a local government's ability to provide new services. Another method for checking the discretion of local governments, in both home rule and non–home rule states, is the use of tax and expenditure limitations (TELs; discussed in the next section). So, although some state constitutions and statutes provide generous grants of power to their localities, no local government in the U.S. is truly independent and autonomous.

Emerging Issues in State–Local Relations

Tensions appear to be escalating in the relationship between states and their local governments. Recently, both scholars and the popular press have asked whether states are at war with their local governments (Bowman & Kearney, 2011; Greenblatt, 2016; Robertson & Fausset, 2016). From the implementation of TELs to removing specific powers from local control, there appears to be a trend toward limiting the discretionary authority of local governments.

Bowman and Kearney (2012) surveyed city managers, state legislators, and directors of state municipal leagues and county associations to assess whether there was a shared perspective of declining local government autonomy. Perhaps not surprisingly, state legislators were less likely to report that local government authority was declining and that state mandates were negatively affecting local governments. City managers reported a loss of power and an increasing burden of state mandates. Some of this loss in discretionary authority has come in the form of TELs.

In 1978, the citizens of California passed Proposition 13. Proposition 13 placed significant limitations on local property tax levies: Property tax levies were rolled back to 1976 values, increases in property tax were capped at no more than 2% per year until the property was sold, and state lawmakers were granted authority to allocate property tax revenues among local jurisdictions. While Proposition 13 forever changed the local government revenue stream in California, it also led to a wave of TELs throughout the country.

Today, 46 states impose some form of statutory or constitutional TEL on their local governments. Nearly half of the TELs in use today were adopted after 1977 (Mullins & Wallin, 2004). TELs primarily involve property tax rate and/or levy limits, revenue or expenditure increase limits, truth in taxation rules, or limits on assessment increases (Joyce & Mullins, 1991). These restrictions will have lasting effects as local governments recover from the Great Recession. Cities that operate under significant TELs will not achieve prerecession revenue levels for at least a decade (Scorsone & Plerhoples, 2010).

Aside from limiting local governments' ability to tax and spend, in several states, legislatures have taken actions that appear to be targeting their cities. Some reports conclude that conservative-leaning legislatures are intentionally moving to reduce power in cities dominated by Democrats (Greenblatt, 2016). Since 2011, the North Carolina general assembly has passed legislation to limit annexation by municipal governments, remove local government authority to levy a business privilege license, and turn over the Asheville water system and the Charlotte airport to regional authorities run by legislative-appointed boards. When asked about the restrictions, legislators reported that they believed city councils were overregulating (Robertson, 2016). More recently, the legislature passed the controversial bill HB2 to disallow local governments from passing antidiscrimination ordinances that are more restrictive than that of the state and to prevent local governments from allowing transgender people from using public bathrooms for the gender with which they identify.

North Carolina is not alone, however. According to a survey by the National League of Cities, in 2016, 24 states barred municipalities from setting a higher minimum wage than that at the state level, while 37 preempted local authority over ride sharing, 17 over municipal broadband, and 17 over paid leave (DuPuis, Langan, McFarland, Panettieri, & Rainwater, 2017, p. 3). As of 2017, eight states have prohibited local governments from outlawing the use of plastic bags in grocery stores.

What is behind this trend? In the states that have most aggressively taken action against city authority, Republicans hold the legislatures and usually the governorship. Large urban centers continue to be controlled by Democrats. Cities have lost some of their lobbying power in these states, since Republicans do not need the votes of urban citizens to be elected. This leads to a mismatch between what the big cities want and what the state legislators want. Whether this trend will continue has yet to be seen.

LOCAL GOVERNMENT TYPES AND DISTRIBUTION

State governments have authority to create and structure local governments as they deem appropriate. This results in high levels of variability in the types and number of local governments throughout the United States. States also vary in how central-ized or decentralized the local structure is and how service provision responsibility is distributed among the various types of local governments.

There are more than 90,000 local governments in the United States (U.S. Census Bureau, 2012). The most basic way to categorize local governments is by the number of services they provide. Those entities that provide a range of services are called *general-purpose governments*. Cities, counties, towns, and many townships are designated general-purpose governments. In contrast, some local governments provide only one function or a very limited number of functions; these are called *special-purpose governments*. School districts are the most common form of special-purpose government, including school districts. As of 2012, there were 38,910 general-purpose and 51,146 special-purpose governments in the United States. (U.S. Census Bureau, 2012; see Table 3.1).

Townships are just one type of the many local governments in Pennsylvania.

The Midwest has a greater number of local governments than other regions of the country. The region with the lowest number of local governments is the South. As opposed to the South, the Midwest is more likely to have independent school districts (ISDs) and other types of special-purpose governments than other regions,

| | | | Town/ | Special | Independent School |
Year	Total	County	Municipal	Township	Districts	Districts
2012	90,056	3,031	19,519	16,360	38,266	12,880
1952	116,807	3,052	16,807	17,202	12,340	67,355

TABLE 3.1 ■ Number and Type of Local Governments in the U.S.

Source: U.S. Census Bureau, 2012.

particularly the South. There has been a decrease in school districts with the consolidation of smaller districts, although this does not mean that public education is less likely to be organized separately from general-purpose local governments since 1952 (see Table 3.1). During this period, however, the number of other special districts (not including school districts) has increased by more than 210% (U.S. Census Bureau, 2012). General-purpose governments have to coordinate activities with far more special-purpose governments than in the past.

Counties

County governments were the earliest unit of general-purpose government in the United States. States created counties to administer state policies uniformly throughout the state. The number of counties has declined slightly since the 1950s due to consolidation and dissolution. Counties are found in all states except Connecticut and Rhode Island. In Alaska, counties are called *boroughs*; in Louisiana, they are called *parishes*.

New England's primary unit of government is the *town*. Geographically, the New England states are very small, so there is limited unincorporated land, if any, in many of those states. County governments primarily serve those residents who live outside of incorporated areas. For these reasons, counties in New England have limited or no governing responsibilities relative to other states throughout the country.

In other parts of the country, counties vary in the level and types of services they provide to residents. In some cases, such as Georgia and Maryland, counties are empowered to provide a full array of services generally associated with municipalities. Regional patterns of county service distribution exist, which will be discussed in the next section.

Municipalities

Municipal governments are incorporated general-purpose units of government. They may be called *cities*, *villages*, *towns*, *boroughs* (except in Alaska), or *townships* (in some cases). A town in one state may be identical to a city for legal purposes. In New England, the town is a separate, independent, incorporated municipality. State law determines the services that may be provided at the municipal level.

Some states, such as Washington, Indiana, and Minnesota, classify their municipalities according to population. Often, these classifications are tied to specific statutory requirements or restrictions that affect only a given class of municipality. For example, only towns in Indiana can use the council–manager form of government. If a town transitions to a city, it must adopt a different form of government. Towns in Indiana can have any population limit, but to become a city, a town must reach a minimum population of 2,000.

Special-Purpose Governments

Special-purpose governments vary a great deal by function and authority level. Generally, they can be divided by whether they have taxing authority (taxing districts) or not (public authorities). Taxing districts are permitted to levy a property tax. Public authorities receive revenue through user fees, grants, and revenue bonds (Foster, 1997).

There are more than 12,000 ISDs in the United States. California, Texas, and Illinois have the largest numbers of ISDs (U.S. Census Bureau, 2012). Some states have a combination of ISDs and dependent school districts. States in which all school districts are dependent either on the state, county, or municipal government include Alaska, Hawaii, Maryland, and North Carolina.

Illinois is the state with the greatest number of special districts. At 3,227, it has 13% more than the next closest and geographically much larger state of California. Special-purpose governments are created to serve many purposes. The majority of special districts (33,031 out of 38,266) perform a single function. As Table 3.2 illustrates, many were created to address environmental concerns: flood control, soil conservation, and water conservation, for instance. Some special districts take on functions that are more typically performed at the municipal or county level, such as parks and recreation and libraries.

TABLE 3.2 ■ Distribution of Single-Purpose Special Districts by Function	
Function	Percentage of Districts
Fire Protection	17.8
Water	10.7
Housing and Community Development	10.4
Drainage and Flood Control	9.8
Soil and Water Conservation	7.8
Sewer	5.8
Libraries	5.2
Cemeteries	5.1
Hospitals, Health, and Welfare	5.1
Other Natural Resources	4.6
Other	4.4
Parks and Recreation	4.3
Highways	3.3
Other Utilities	1.8
Airports	1.5
Solid Waste Management	1.4
Education (Not Schools)	0.5
Other Transportation (Ports, Parking, Water Transport)	0.5

Source: Stephens & Wikstrom, 2007.

REGIONAL MODELS OF LOCAL GOVERNMENT STRUCTURE

Analyzing how the types, number, service distribution responsibilities, and authority of local governments differ by state leads to a classification of state systems of local governments (SSLGs) (Stephens & Wikstrom, 2007). Arrangements of the state–local system may be highly centralized or decentralized and may be simple or complex. State governments seem to be pursuing greater centralization. The number of local governments is declining, primarily through voluntary consolidation of school districts. However, New Jersey, New York, Indiana, Michigan, and Illinois have attempted to promote local government consolidation, and North Carolina's general assembly established a commission in 2014 to explore school district mergers.

Stephens and Wikstrom (2007) identify five types of SSLGs (see Table 3.3). Hawaii and Alaska each has a unique type. Hawaii's SSLG is called the *state–county* type. With no independent municipal governments, three counties, and one consolidated city–county (Honolulu–Oahu), Hawaii has the most centralized system, with the state providing services that are the purview of local governments in other states. Alaska (the *state–municipal* type) is also highly centralized, having only 14 county governments (called *boroughs*), 144 municipalities (many of which have very low populations and provide limited services), and four consolidated city–boroughs. Given the geography and low population density, many services are provided by the state government.

States with the *southern system* have large general-purpose governments (counties) that provide the majority of services to residents. ISDs are rare or nonexistent, and there are no townships or other minor civil subdivisions. The county typically administers the school districts and provides libraries and other recreational services as well as standard county functions.

New England states rely on towns to fulfill most local service delivery needs. Counties (which no longer exist in Connecticut or Rhode Island) have limited responsibilities. In addition to providing services of both municipal and county-type services, many towns also run school systems.

What Stephens and Wikstrom call the *conventional system* is found in half the states. This system has many layers of local government—general purpose and special purpose. ISDs are the norm in this system. The boundaries and service offerings of these governments often overlap. There may be townships, but unlike in New England, they typically provide a limited number of services.

The remaining states have an arrangement that *combines* features of two of the systems. Three states (New Jersey, New York, and Pennsylvania) have the town/township as municipal government and elements of the conventional system. Ten other states (see Table 3.3) use the Southern system but have ISDs.

This complex network of local governments, with huge variability between and among states, makes generalizing about local government authority or service provision difficult. However, the variability in local government does not stop at the way states structure local governments and assign service responsibility. Local governments themselves differ in their form of government.

TABLE 3.3 ■ State Systems of Local Government (2012)

Type	State(s)	Counties	Municipalities/ City–Counties	Towns/ Townships	Special Purpose	Independent School Districts (ISDs)
State–County	Hawaii	3	1	0	17	0
State–Municipal	Alaska	14	148	0	15	0
Southern	Maryland	23	157	0	167	0
	North Carolina	100	553	0	320	0
	Tennessee	92	345	0	465	14
	Virginia	95	229	0	193	1
New England	Connecticut	0	30	149	447	17
	Maine	16	22	466	237	99
	Massachusetts	5	53	298	417	84
	New Hampshire	10	13	231	131	166
	Rhode Island	0	8	31	90	4
	Vermont	14	33	237	153	291
Conventional	Alabama	67	461	0	548	132
	Arkansas	75	502	0	740	239
	California	57	482	0	2,861	1,025
	Colorado	62	271	0	2,392	180
	Delaware	3	57	0	260	19
	Idaho	44	200	0	806	118
	Illinois	102	1,298	1,431	3,227	905

Type	State(s)	Counties	Municipalities/ City-Counties	Towns/ Townships	Special Purpose	Independent School Districts (ISDs)
	Indiana	91	569	1,006	752	291
	Iowa	99	947	0	535	366
	Kansas	103	626	1,268	535	366
	Michigan	83	533	1,240	443	576
	Minnesota	87	853	1,784	610	338
	Missouri	114	954	312	1,854	534
	Montana	54	129	0	763	319
	Nebraska	93	530	417	1,269	272
	New Mexico	33	103	0	631	96
	North Dakota	53	357	1,313	779	183
	Ohio	88	937	1,308	841	668
	Oklahoma	77	590	0	635	550
	Oregon	36	241	0	1,035	230
	South Dakota	66	311	907	547	152
	Texas	254	1,214	0	2,600	1,079
	Washington	95	281	0	1,285	295
	Wisconsin	72	596	1,255	765	440
	Wyoming	23	99	0	628	55
Combined Township–Conventional	New Jersey	21	324	242	234	523
	New York	57	614	929	1,174	679
	Pennsylvania	66	1,015	1,546	1,756	514

(Continued)

49

TABLE 3.3 (Continued)

Type	State(s)	Counties	Municipalities/ City-Counties	Towns/ Townships	Special Purpose	Independent School Districts (ISDs)
Southern with ISDs	Arizona	15	91	0	326	242
	Florida	66	410	0	1,079	95
	Georgia	153	535	0	510	180
	Kentucky	118	418	0	628	174
	Louisiana	60	304	0	96	69
	Mississippi	82	298	0	439	164
	Nevada	16	19	0	139	17
	South Carolina	46	270	0	279	83
	Utah	29	245	0	307	41
	West Virginia	55	232	0	317	295

Source: Stephens & Wikstrom, 2007.

LOCAL FORMS OF GOVERNMENT

Today, there are four forms of municipal government in the United States: the earliest forms (town meeting and mayor–council) and the reformed types (council–manager and commission). Chapter 2 explained the history behind the council–manager and commission forms of government; this chapter will focus on the authority and structure of local government forms. Of the four, the council–manager and mayor–council forms vastly outnumber the other two (see Table 3.4). In the smallest (under 5,000 population) and largest municipalities (over 250,000 population), the mayor–council form is the most common (International City/County Management Association, 2011). Excluding the town meeting and commission forms, nearly 60% of municipalities with populations over 250,000 use the mayor–council form of government.

Local governments are not always able to freely choose their form of government. As with all local government authority, form choices are dictated by the amount of discretion afforded local governments by their states. In states with home rule charters or that grant structural home rule, the form can be customized for some or all municipalities and counties. Some states provide some local governments with the ability to freely modify their form, but others do not (California is an example). In states such as New Jersey, local governments have many choices for the form of government, but they are all described, in detail, in the state statutes. There are also states that limit the form of local government to only a couple of choices (North Carolina) or that prohibit certain forms either entirely or for certain classes of government. For example, Indiana towns may use the council–manager form, but cities may not.

TABLE 3.4 ■ U.S. Municipal Form of Government*				
	2000		2012	
	Number	Percentage	Number	Percentage
Council–Manager	1,640	55.14	1,804	55.08
Mayor–Council	1,117	37.56	1,258	38.41
Commission	48	1.61	47	1.44
Town Meeting/ Representative Town Meeting	169	5.68	166	5.07

*Population 10,000 or above.

The town meeting (and its cousin, the representative town meeting form) is only found in the New England states. As discussed earlier, the New England town is the primary local government that serves citizens in that region of the country. Under the town meeting form, the citizens of the town meet annually as a legislative body to vote on the budget and make other legislative decisions. The town meeting is an example of true direct democracy. In the representative town meeting form, not all of the citizens vote. Instead, a body of citizens is elected to represent the entire population.

Commission municipalities are found throughout the United States, but today are mostly in smaller communities. Portland, Oregon, is the exception; it is the largest city that continues to use the commission form. Citizens elect commissioners who serve as both legislators and department heads. There is also usually an elected mayor who typically coordinates the activities of the commissioners but does not have a considerable amount of additional authority. Although the commission form was once very popular, in practice, its weaknesses were quickly revealed. Commissioners begin to identify and protect the turf of their departments. This makes consensus decision making difficult, and it is also less likely that commissioners will have a broad perspective on what is best for the community as a whole.

In much more widespread use are the mayor–council and council–manager forms of government. There is extensive variability in the features often associated with the two primary forms of local government. Therefore, the generalizations about which characteristics are associated with a given form (described in the remainder of this section of the book) are not universal. Many of these variations result from state legislative requirements (for example, some states require that all mayors be elected, regardless of form); others are due to the customization by the local government itself.

The mayor–council form is the original form of municipal government in the United States. It remains the form found in most of the long-standing large U.S. cities, such as New York, Philadelphia, and Chicago, as well as large cities that emerged in the early twentieth century, such as Los Angeles and San Francisco. Under the mayor–council form of government, the mayor is elected at-large to serve as the chief executive officer (CEO). Council members serve an exclusively legislative function. Therefore, executive–legislative separation of powers exists in mayor–council cities as it does for the national government and the states.

The mayor–council form can be structured with a weak or strong mayor. *Weakness* refers to the level of formal authority a mayor possesses. Formal authorities of the mayor include (but are not limited to) the power to appoint and remove department heads, draft the budget, and veto legislation. In some states, such as North Carolina, a community can only choose between the council–manager form and what is generally considered a weak mayor–council form, although most of these cities have a city administrator appointed by the entire council. Mayors in North Carolina mayor–council communities are limited in formal powers to those similar to other members of council, although they do preside at council meetings. In other states, such as Illinois, ordinances can be used to approximate a council–manager form while legally remaining a mayor–council form. The mayor is still considered the CEO, but powers are transferred to the manager.

More than 65% of mayor–council communities with populations over 10,000 appoint a chief administrative officer (CAO); (Nelson, 2010). The existence of a CAO position does not necessarily imply that the mayor's authority is weaker. If the mayor retains control over the hiring and firing of the CAO and directs the duties of the CAO, the mayor remains a *strong* mayor. If the council has the power to appoint and remove and the charter dictates the duties of the manager, excluding the mayor from day-to-day operations, the mayor has been weakened by the installation of a CAO.

Councils in the mayor–council system are typically independent of the mayor, preserving the separation of powers. In municipalities with full separation, the mayor attends council meetings, but does not participate. However, in many communities, the mayor has some role on council, which may include presiding but not voting. Mayors in the mayor–council form usually have veto power. In the past, mayor–council form was associated with district elections for council members. Today, district, at-large, or a combination of at-large and district seats occur with nearly equal frequency in municipalities over 10,000 in population (Nelson, 2010). Elections in the mayor–council form are more likely to have partisan ballots than in the council–manager form, but state law usually governs that choice.

This contrasts with the council–manager form of government that is hallmarked by unified executive and legislative powers. Council members are elected and form, with the mayor, the governing body of the municipality. Initially, the mayor was selected from council, but since 1965, the majority of council–manager mayors have been directly elected (Childs, 1965). Currently, in cities above 10,000 in population in the United States, 63% of the council–manager cities have an elected mayor, and 81% of these cities over 100,000 in population elect the mayor (Nelson & Svara, 2010). The mayor can be an important visionary and facilitative leader who helps to ensure that all parts of the government structure work together effectively and pursue a shared mission (Svara, 2008). Although the council–manager form tended to be found in smaller, homogeneous communities before World War II, it has spread to cities of all types. The number of council–manager cities over 100,000 in population is growing and represents 58% of the total. Some cities with the council–manager form have grown to be among the largest in the United States, such as Phoenix, Arizona; Dallas, Texas; and San Jose, California.

The council holds executive authority, which it delegates to a professional manager who is hired by the council. In a few municipalities, the mayor has a more significant role in the selection process than other members of council. Council members in council–manager form may be elected at-large or by district; the at-large variation is the most common. The council and mayor, acting as a body, choose the policy vision and direction for the community. In municipalities using the council–manager form, the mayor presides over council meetings and votes (at least to break ties), and the manager is hired based on his or her professional qualifications to provide professional advice about issues and long-range plans, implement the will of the council, and run the day-to-day operations of the government.

Counties use forms of government similar to municipalities, but there are some distinct differences between counties and municipalities. The traditional form of government for counties is the commission form, but it is not equivalent to the commission form in municipalities. In counties, the commission form of government has an elected legislative body that oversees the county government, typically through a committee process. In 2009, nearly 44% of counties retained this form of government (see Table 3.5). There is no data on county election methods, but both at-large and district election of county commissioners occurs in the U.S.

Increasingly, counties are moving toward forms that are similar to the council–manager and mayor–council plans in municipal governments. The commission with an elected executive is found in more than 20% of counties, and the commission with an administrator or manager is found in approximately 34% of counties. Since its 2009 report, the National Association of Counties (NACo) conducted a new analysis and found that 43% of counties (1,322) have an appointed administrator (NACo, 2016).

TABLE 3.5 ■ County Government Structure, 2009

Form	Number	Percentage
Commission*	1,346	43.97
Commission with Elected Executive (Mayor)	649	21.20
Commission with Administrator/Manager	1,022	33.39
Charter (No Details)/Other	9	0.29
Manager Plan/Council–Manager	18	0.59
City–County Consolidation	17	0.56

*The elected legislative body is called the *commission, council, board of supervisors, assembly,* or other names, depending on the state.

Source: Murphy, 2009.

Managing a county is considerably different from managing a municipality, given the structure of county governments. In counties, several executive officials are independently elected from the county commissioners. The sheriff, tax assessor, auditor, clerk of court, and register of deeds may all be independently elected. Further complicating county administration are boards that are given authority over different aspects of the government, such as mental health, public health, and social services. In many counties, schools are also separate. The person in charge of government administration, the manager or the elected executive, does not have authority over these parts of the organization. Under these conditions, running the organization involves skills in coordination, facilitation, and diplomacy.

The complexity of intergovernmental relations in the United States makes generalizing nationally very difficult. To understand the environment that an individual local government operates within, it is important to consider the state system of local government, the level of autonomy granted individual local governments, the form of government, and the number of local governments with overlapping authority. As regional forms of metropolitan government become more prevalent, some reevaluation of those states with many layers of local government will be necessary. New models of regional government will need to be considered, such as those discussed in Chapter 4, to address the wicked problems and fragmented nature of the American metropolis.

For local government managers, this fragmented system means that a substantial portion of their time will be devoted to building relationships and finding ways to coordinate and collaborate with other local governments in the region. Leaders from the individual entities have individual interests they are trying to serve; it will often be the manager's job to help the local governments in the region find common ground to form a starting point to work from.

REFERENCES

Agranoff, R., & Radin, B. A. (2015). Deil Wright's overlapping model of intergovernmental relations: The basis for contemporary intergovernmental relationships. *Publius, 45*(1), 139–159.

Berman, D. R. (2003). *Local governments and the states: Autonomy, politics, and policy.* New York, NY: M. E. Sharpe.

Bowman, A. O'M., & Kearney, R. (2011). Second-order devolution: Data and doubt. *Publius, 41*(4), 563–585.

Childs, R. S. (1965). *The first 50 years of the council–manager plan of municipal government.* New York, NY: National Municipal League.

Dillon, J. F. (1911). *Commentaries on the law of municipal corporations* (5th ed.). Boston, MA: Little, Brown.

DuPuis, N., Langan, T., McFarland, C., Panettieri, A., & Rainwater, B. (2017). *City rights in an era of preemption: A state-by-state analysis.* Washington, DC: National League of Cities.

Environmental Protection Agency. (1990). *A preliminary analysis of the public costs of environmental protection: 1981–2000.* Washington, DC: Author.

Foster, K. A. (1997). *The political economy of special-purpose government.* Washington, DC: Georgetown University Press.

Government Accountability Office. (1994). *Federal Mandates (HEHS-94-110R).* Washington, DC: Author.

Greenblatt, A. (2016, March 25). Beyond North Carolina's LGBT battle: States' war on cities. *Governing.* Retrieved March 10, 2017, from http://www.governing.com/topics/politics/gov-states-cities-preemption-laws.html

International City/County Management Association. (2011). *Most prevalent form of local government in specific population ranges (2011): Council–manager (CM) vs. mayor–council (MC).* Retrieved March 31, 2017, from http://icma.org/Documents/Document/Document/9364

Joyce, P. G., & Mullins, D. R. (1991). The changing fiscal structure of the state and local public sector: The impact of tax and expenditure limitations. *Public Administration Review, 51*(3), 240–253.

Krane, D., Rigos, P. N., & Hill, M. B., Jr. (2001). *Home rule in America: A fifty-state handbook.* Washington, DC: CQ Press.

Moreira, J. (2015). Regionalism, federalism, and the paradox of local democracy: Reclaiming state power in pursuit of regional equity. *Rutgers Law Review, 67*(2), 501–542.

Mullins, D. R., & Wallin, B. A. (2004). Tax and expenditure limitations: Introduction and overview. *Public Budgeting and Finance, 24*(4), 2–15.

Murphy, K. (2009). *County government structure: A state-by-state report.* Washington, DC: National Association of Counties.

National Association of Counties. (2016). *An overview of county administration: Appointed county administrators.* Washington, DC: Author. Retrieved March 11, 2017, from http://www.naco.org/sites/default/files/documents/06.23.15_SuperFINAL_KeyFindings_ProfAdminv2_NEW%20LOGO.pdf

Nelson, K. L. (2010). State-level autonomy and municipal government structure: Influence on form of government outcomes. *The American Review of Public Administration, 41*(5), 542–561.

Nelson, K. L., & Svara, J. H. (2010). Adaptation of models versus variations in form: Classifying structures of city government. *Urban Affairs Review, 45*(4), 544–562.

O'Toole, L. J., Jr., & Christensen, R. K. (2013). *American intergovernmental relations: Foundations, perspectives, and issues* (5th ed.). Thousand Oaks, CA: CQ Press.

Quinton, S. (2015, July 13). States battle cities over minimum wage. *Stateline.* Retrieved March 10, 2017, from http://www.pewtrusts.org/en/research-and-analysis/blogs/stateline/2015/07/13/states-battle-cities-over-minimum-wage

Richardson, J. J., Gough, M. Z., & Puentes, R. (2003). *Is home rule the answer? Clarifying the influence of Dillon's Rule on growth management.* Washington, DC: Brookings Institution.

Robertson, C., & Fausset, R. (2016, April 15). Southern cities split with states on social issues. *New York Times*. Retrieved March 10, 2017, from http://www.nytimes.com/2016/04/16/us/southern-cities-move-past-states-on-liberal-social-issues.html?_r=0

Robertson, G. D. (2016, April 9). Halting LGBT rules, N Carolina lawmakers again rebuff cities. *Associated Press*. Retrieved March 10, 2017, from http://bigstory.ap.org/article/d00b636d0280428 fa33be2a80c8d98ec/halting-lgbt-rules-n-carolina-lawmakers-again-rebuff-cities

Scorsone, E. A., & Plerhoples, C. (2010). Fiscal stress and cutback management amongst state and local governments. *State and Local Government Review, 42*(2), 176–187.

Stephens, G. R., & Wikstrom, N. (2007). *American intergovernmental relations: A fragmented federal polity*. New York, NY: Oxford University Press.

Svara, J. H. (2008). *The facilitative leader in city hall: Reexamining the scope and contributions*. Boca Raton, FL: CRC Press.

U.S. Advisory Commission on Intergovernmental Relations. (1992). *Federal statutory preemption of state and local authority: History, inventory, and issues*. Washington, DC: Author.

U.S. Census Bureau. (2012). *2012 Census of Governments*. Retrieved March 10, 2017, from https://www.census.gov/govs/cog/

Wright, D. S. (1988). *Understanding intergovernmental relations* (3rd ed.). Pacific-Grove, CA: Brooks-Cole.

RESOURCE LIST/TO EXPLORE FURTHER

Books/Articles

Burns, N. (1994). *The formation of American local governments*. New York, NY: Oxford University Press.

Stephens, G. R., & Wikstrom, N. (2007). *American intergovernmental relations: A fragmented federal polity*. New York, NY: Oxford University Press.

Web Resources

National Association of Counties. (2015). *NACo county explorer: Mapping county data*. Available at http://explorer.naco.org/

National League of Cities. (2016). *Local government authority*. Available at http://www.nlc.org/local-government-authority

U.S. Census Bureau. (2017). *Federal, state, & local governments*. Available at https://www.census.gov/govs

WORKING ACROSS BOUNDARIES

Cooperation is "an unnatural act among nonconsenting adults."

—Beverly Cigler (2007, p. 3)

For many years scholars, public officials, civic groups, and reformers have debated the fragmented structure of local government and the blurred boundaries in relationships among local units as well as between localities and their state government. This chapter reviews the mismatch among structures, boundaries, and problems confronting localities. Practical approaches to regional collaboration and promising innovations that municipal and county managers can use to work across boundaries to address problems are examined, and the states' role in local restructuring is explored.

STRESSED LOCAL STRUCTURE

As discussed in Chapter 3, there was a net decline of 26,700 local units, from 116,807 to 90,056 between 1952 and 2012. Meanwhile, the number of nonschool special districts—90% of which provided a single function in a single jurisdiction or part of it—more than tripled between 1952 and 2012, from 12,340 to 38,266 (U.S. Census Bureau, 2012).

As local structures became more fragmented, the problems local officials confronted and the needs their citizens expected to be addressed increasingly crossed over jurisdictional boundary lines. It has become difficult to identify local services over which counties, municipalities, or other general-purpose units exercise control without significant policy, financial, administrative, or regulatory involvement of neighboring jurisdictions or state or federal authorities. Traditional local functions have become intergovernmentalized since the 1960s. Basically, there are no longer purely local problems and responses; at the same time, the number of "wicked" problems that ignore jurisdictional and sectoral boundaries have exploded. This trend is especially apparent in the 381 metropolitan areas across the United States.

Problems of Unchecked Development

In addition to the mismatch between boundaries and problem sheds, in many metropolitan areas, two critical concerns—sprawl and disparities between areas in the same region—have stressed local structure and generated controversy and conflict. Since post–World War II, government mortgage interest subsidies, low-cost land, and transportation improvements have helped spur suburban development. As explained in Chapter 2, the outer suburbs of most metropolitan areas in the United States experienced significant population and job growth as the middle class and many businesses sought the amenities offered by suburban lifestyles. Unfortunately, many of these development choices were made to maximize profit, and the inefficient land use that resulted has led to some unforeseen consequences. Regionally, poorly planned development has resulted in traffic congestion and environmental problems, while the central cities and inner-ring suburbs have become overburdened with concentrations of the poor, infrastructure deterioration, and public service decline. These trends have been countered by support for "smart growth" policies that include planning for orderly and sustainable development, preservation of open space and historic communities, and environmental conservation.

Disparities within Regions

Social, economic, and service disparities in metropolitan areas and between metropolitan and nonmetropolitan areas have widened. The scenario begins with inelastic jurisdictional boundaries caused either by state restrictions on municipal annexation or the incorporation of neighboring communities. This inability to grow physically circumscribes central cities, preventing them from tapping new tax bases and providing services in outlying unincorporated areas while permissive incorporation provisions foster the creation of new suburban units. Central city residents, seeking better services and more space, move to the new suburbs, further eroding the central city tax base. Magnifying the problem of out-migration is the fact that those people who move to the suburbs tend to be middle-income families and individuals, leaving the city with a disproportionate share of poor and minority residents. Finally, businesses follow the higher-income residents, locating or relocating in suburban areas rather than in the central business district. While urban growth controls, sub-urban traffic congestion, and gentrification are important counterpressures, the general pattern described above persists in the central cities and older inner-ring suburbs of many metropolitan areas (Stenberg, 2008).

The stakes in overcoming sprawl and disparities are high. Research by David Rusk has demonstrated a linkage between jurisdictional boundary elasticity and reduction of segregation by race and wealth in metropolitan areas (Rusk, 2013). In other words, municipalities that are able to expand their geographic boundaries to capture property that is developed in the unincorporated areas on the borders are better able to adapt to problems experienced in central cities. Other studies have found an economic connection between the health of the central city and that of the region. In terms of employment, for example, worsening job creation and retention in the central city are reflected in declines throughout the region. Similar connections have been found with respect to population and income. Jurisdictional fragmentation and noncooperation have proven to be disincentives for economic development, as companies are interested in locating in areas where local units and officials work together on common problems. While local governments may compete for residents and employers, they share a common market and need to collaborate in order to achieve and sustain regional economic success (Downs, 1994; Jimenez & Hendrick, 2010; Ledebur & Barnes, 1992; Orfield, 1997; Peirce, 1993).

REFORM PERSPECTIVES

Despite these conditions and concerns, the debate over regional structure continues without resolution. In 2000, David Walker pointed out the following:

> Jurisdictional facts: (1) at least 51 percent (42,565) of all local governments are nonviable, given the population size of their jurisdictions; (2) economies of scale and the provision of merely a majority of the local services their citizens require are not feasible for the 14,669 townships with populations below 5,000, for the 16,868 municipalities with populations below 10,000, and for the 2,257 counties with populations below 50,000; and (3) the same can be said of the 51 percent of all school districts that have fewer than 1,000 pupils. (p. 298)

In these cases, low population and limited commercial development means that the revenue base is insufficient to support a basic level of service provision. These observations are still relevant today and pose significant local management challenges.

In addition, tensions have grown between special- and general-purpose units, and disparities have widened between rich and poor and between large and small jurisdictions. As will be discussed later in this chapter, in states such as New Jersey and New York, governors and legislators attribute high local property taxes to the inefficiencies and duplication inherent in small, fragmented local structures. Increasingly, due in part to declining revenues from the state and federal governments, multiple jurisdictions are relying on the same tax base to fund services.

Reformers usually seek incremental improvement and fine-tuning of local structure and relationships rather than replacement or overhaul, especially given strong political and citizen support for maintenance of the jurisdictional status quo in most communities. Nevertheless, as will be described later in this chapter, bolder reforms have been proposed and adopted by local and state officials.

Scholars and practitioners have agreed on the need for less intergovernmental competition and more collaborative public management. Traditionally, remedial actions to overcome structural constraints have been called *functional* or *pragmatic* regionalism (Zimmerman, 1976). They have been guided by at least five values: efficiency, effectiveness, equity, accountability, and responsiveness. Not only are these values weighted differently depending on the nature of the activity and the perspectives of local officials, they may well compete with one another. For example, as responsibility for performance of a function moves from the local to the regional level, prospects for achieving administrative effectiveness and equity may be enhanced. Economies of scale also may be achieved for some functions to a threshold level when diseconomies occur. However, as the locus of decision making moves to a more distant unit, accountability and responsiveness may be diminished.

Responses to the debate over local structure have been influenced by three schools of thought: consolidationists, choice advocates, and collaborationists (Bish & Ostrom 1973; Jones, 1942; Miller, 2002; Stenberg, 2008). Their views are summarized below.

Consolidation

Consolidationists argue the virtues of structural simplicity achieved by consolidation of all or most general-purpose units under a single county or metropolitan government. According to this perspective, consolidating multiple units of government will lead to greater efficiency and lower costs, primarily through improved economies of scale. Supporters also suggest that consolidation will lead to fewer disparities among residents of the region and will spur economic development through greater collaboration among local governments.

Voters usually have not been persuaded by their arguments. There have been close to 100 consolidation referenda since 1975, but only about one quarter of them were approved. Of the 3,069 counties in the U.S., only 34 represent city–county consolidations (National League of Cities, 2016). The merger of Princeton Borough with Princeton Township, New Jersey, was the most recent case, in 2012. Even successful mergers have excluded some general-purpose jurisdictions and school districts. In some consolidations, such as Nashville–Davidson County, Tennessee, population growth has overrun the boundaries of the original merged area to make the older metro the core of a multicounty metropolitan area. Moreover, research has found that the promises of consolidation advocates to lower taxes, reduce personnel, achieve greater efficiencies, spur economic development, and promote equity have not been achieved (Martin & Schiff, 2011).

Public Choice

Choice advocates take the opposite position, that local structure should be unaltered or, if it is changed, the purpose should be to encourage market competition in order to present multiple jurisdictional choices to citizens who will "vote with their feet" in search of services they desire at tax and fee rates they are willing and able to pay. Also called the *polycentric* model, this view of regional governance is consistent with existing conditions in many parts of the country. Proponents of public choice believe that the market will serve as the mechanism to stabilize the region. Some people will choose their community based on a high service level with a high tax rate and others will choose lower service levels at lower tax rates. The private sector may also be a prominent partner in local service delivery (Ostrom, Tiebout, & Warren, 1961). For example, experience with interdistrict school choice plans in Minnesota and other states demonstrate the values of giving parents options beyond the neighborhood public school and of putting pressure on schools from which students are being transferred to improve their performance. This may mean allowing parents to transfer their children between public schools in the same or nearby districts or using private sector alternatives, such as charter schools and voucher programs (Stenberg & Colman, 1994, pp. 399–413).

Critics of this model argue that residents are not equally mobile. So, even if some wanted to move to another location with a different tax/service mix, they may not be able to do so. Low-income citizens, senior citizens, and people with disabilities may all fit into this category. Further, public choice theory assumes that residents understand the tax/service mix when they may not. In other words, residents may not have the resources or knowledge to make the best choice.

Collaboration

Collaborationists support approaches to service delivery focused on neighborhood, citywide, county-based, and multicounty governance arrangements. They advocate

new regionalism and emphasize the virtues of a multifaceted response to interjurisdictional needs, drawing on the authority of governmental units and networking with the
resources of the nonprofit and for-profit sectors. These approaches offer practical advantages such as cost savings and greater effectiveness as opposed to relying exclusively on
governmental alternatives, and successful regional collaboration enhances regional economic competitiveness. Similar to the choice model, contracts and service agreements
play important roles in implementation, and it is assumed that local governments possess sufficient discretionary authority to carry out their responsibilities (Dodge, 1996,
pp. 239–334; Frisken & Norris, 2001; Savitch & Vogel, 2000; Vogel & Harrigan, 2007).

   While there has been spirited debate among proponents of each view, no single
dominant theory has emerged to guide local reformers, although the collaboration-
ist school of thought has been popular in practice. Scholarly contributions, however,
have been labeled *academic cacophony*. As a result, "the many faces of reform have
produced little real reform at any time" (Walker, 2000, p. 285).

THE MANAGER'S KEY TRANSCENDING ROLE

With respect to the internal dynamics of local structure, as fragmentation grows,
efforts have been undertaken to centralize administrative responsibility and focus
accountability where home rule charters permit. A large part of this effort involves
increasing the professionalism of the day-to-day management of the local government. Especially in large and medium-sized metropolitan municipalities operating
under the mayor–council form of government, chief administrative officers (CAOs)
have been appointed by and serve at the pleasure of the mayor and/or governing
body. The critical need for professional management is underscored by the prevalence of part-time elected officials, technical complexity of problems confronting
localities, and intergovernmentalization and privatization of services.

   George Frederickson argues that while jurisdiction is meaningful to local officials for electoral purposes, the contemporary relevance of borders and boundaries
is limited and diminishing. As intergovernmental "bottom feeders," municipalities are nested with other local units and layered over by regional organizations. To
Frederickson (2005), "The nested or embedded quality of localities situates them in
arrangements of dependency—financial dependency, legal dependency, and dependency for program effectiveness—the opposites of jurisdictional autonomy" (p. 12).
He points out two fundamental paradoxes: (1) Local elected and appointed officials
will need to transcend the boundaries of their community in order to serve their
citizens and have to share power with other players in fragmented metropolitan areas

and (2) interjurisdictional relationships, power-sharing arrangements, and other aspects of democratic governance must be handled by professional administrators (p. 14). So, while officials are elected by and accountable to voters within their jurisdiction, the interdependency of modern metropolitan areas means that broader regional issues are also important. Local government managers serve a crucial role in helping elected officials understand the importance of regional collaboration.

It is not surprising that local elected officials look more inward than outward, since regional citizens cast no ballots and have weak identification with regional organizations (Feiock, 2007). Given these parochial community or electoral-focused vantage points, municipal and county managers will be looked to for leadership in boundary-spanning strategies and initiatives. In this context, their job is to build community in metropolitan settings by "framing issues and processes to deal with diverse interests, to focus on interests rather than positions when problem solving, and to develop collaborative partnerships in policymaking and service delivery" (Nalbandian, 1999, p. 195).

In view of the relative weakness of regional and metropolitan forms of governance, local managers are primarily responsible for holding them together. "Regional and metropolitan authorities are . . . secondary forms of democracy that are generally less effective politically and only effective insofar as they have good professional administration" (Frederickson, 2005, p. 12). According to Eric Zeemering, "Surveys of managers in council–manager cities identify managers as the most extensive intergovernmental actors, as measured by membership in intergovernmental associations and their contacts with other administrative officials" (2008, p. 732). Of course, elected officials are also involved in intergovernmental relations—such as membership on council of government boards and involvement with state municipal leagues and county associations—but more at the policy level than management level.

Somewhat paradoxically, Frederickson observes, nonelected public administrators are responsible for making regional democratic governance work. However, questions have been raised regarding whether academic programs, graduate accrediting bodies such as the Network of Schools of Public Policy, Affairs, and Administration (NASPAA), and professional organizations such as International City/County Management Association (ICMA) have given sufficient attention to developing the skill set needed for horizontal management, network navigation, and collaborative arrangement development (Miller & Cox, 2014, pp. 208–222).

Questions have also been raised about whether local elected officials are as jurisdiction-focused and parochial as the literature suggests. Zeemering, for instance, observes that these officials have at least three interests in interlocal partnerships: identifying problems, negotiating cooperative and collaborative responses, and educating and representing their public. Interlocal cooperation may align with jurisdictional interests and reelection goals if working with others is the most feasible way to address problems and satisfy pressing citizen needs or to carry out capital-intensive projects, such as water and sewer services or transit (Zeemering, 2008, pp. 733–734).

FROM COOPERATION TO GOVERNANCE: SNOW WHITE AND THE 17 DWARFS

A wide range of responses to boundary-crossing problems have been implemented with varying degrees of success, reflecting the reform perspectives described earlier. They have drawn upon an arsenal of legal mechanisms that states have granted municipalities and counties to enable them to address cross-jurisdictional matters. These include formal and informal joint powers agreements, contracts, extraterritorial powers, annexation, and interlocal functional transfers (Dodge, 1996, pp. 243–244). In many metropolitan areas, these institutional and procedural responses have been accompanied by organizational arrangements designed to promote cooperation and collaboration, chiefly councils of governments (COGs) and areawide planning and development commissions. David Miller has classified these approaches into four types of regionalism, which will be considered in this section (2002, pp. 99–124):

- Coordinating (e.g., regional councils and areawide organizations)

- Administrative (e.g., interlocal agreements, special districts, urban counties)

- Fiscal (e.g., tax-base sharing)

- Structural (e.g., annexation, consolidation)

In 1987, David Walker published an article on approaches or tools for achieving metropolitan governance entitled "Snow White and the 17 Dwarfs." In his view, "regionalism is a gold mine for officials seeking to solve local problems, and 17 different miners may be put to work to extract the gold" (p. 135). Walker placed the approaches to closing the gap on a spectrum from easiest to middling to hardest to accomplish (see Table 4.1). In his judgment, "nowhere is this [gap-closing] a bigger problem than in the growing metropolitan areas," where 80% of America's population lives (2000, pp. 283–284).

This section reviews the approaches in each category that offer the greatest promise in striking a balance between the needs for working across boundaries while retaining local identity with the exception of intergovernmental service contracts, private contracting, and the reformed urban county, which will be discussed in Chapter 9. Among the variables affecting the local manager's choice of a particular tool or option are the severity and urgency of the problem, the extent of support from local elected officials for managers to initiate discussions and negotiations with neighboring jurisdictions, the history of collaborative efforts involving both elected officials and administrators, the anticipated benefits and barriers, the rationale behind using particular tools, and the expected outcomes (Foster & Barnes, 2012; Hilvert & Swindell, 2013).

TABLE 4.1 ■ Regional Approaches to Service Delivery
Easiest
1. Informal cooperation
2. Interlocal service contracts
3. Joint-powers agreements
4. Informal and formal interagency collaboration
5. Extraterritorial powers
6. Regional councils/COGs
7. Federally encouraged single-purpose regional bodies
8. State planning and development districts
9. Contracting (private)
Middling
10. Local special districts
11. Transfer of functions
12. Annexation
13. Regional special districts and authorities
14. Metro multipurpose districts
15. Reformed urban county
Hardest
16. One-tier consolidations
17. Two-tier restructuring
18. Three-tier reforms

Source: Walker, 1987.

Easiest Approaches

Informal Cooperation

Experts in local government management (both academic and practitioner) have observed that a critical part of the transcending role of municipal and county managers is to ensure balance between administrative sustainability and political feasibility. As community leaders as well as organizational leaders, managers must find ways to work across boundaries, even though elected officials, citizen representatives, and other local stakeholders may be reluctant to do so, fearing loss of identity, control, and recognition. There also may be long-standing political, philosophical, and cultural differences among local governments in a region that pose additional hurdles. Nevertheless, the nature of contemporary problems requires that local government leaders find win–win regional solutions.

Informal cooperation between jurisdictions is an important first step to building trust and support for more ambitious undertakings. Manager-to-manager conversations to identify, explore, and frame possible joint opportunities often arise during regional managers' meetings or state association conferences. Often, these discussions are below the political radar screen and do not attract attention from elected officials or the media.

One way to test the waters is for managers of two or more communities to "pick low-hanging fruit" around collaborative arrangements. Common examples include sharing capital equipment among local units, loaning information technology staff and equipment, and participating in 911 centers. These informal actions could help establish a foundation for some of the other approaches identified by Walker.

Areawide Planning and Coordinating Bodies

Partly in response to continued fragmentation of local government structure and unwillingness on the part of local officials to develop effective collaborative problem-solving approaches, the federal and some state governments assumed regional leadership roles over 60 years ago. Beginning with a 1959 amendment to Section 701 of the Housing Act of 1954, federal funds were provided to encourage the formation of and support the operation of regional planning commissions and COGs—more generally called *regional councils*—to provide comprehensive planning and technical assistance to local units whose elected officials comprised the majority of the members of COG governing bodies. Nearly all states have enacted statutes enabling or prescribing local participation in regional organizations. In 2013, there were about 700 regional councils across the United States (Whisman, 2015, p. 70). Municipal and county managers are usually actively involved in the staff work of these bodies.

COGs were not intended to be regional service providers, and only a few have taken on this role. They were established primarily to serve as impartial data collectors and information providers, catalysts and conveners for interlocal communications between elected officials, comprehensive planners for future development in the region, reviewers of and commentators on proposed projects against the contents of these plans, and providers of technical assistance to member jurisdictions. A 2013 national survey of regional council directors found that their organization's work commonly involved transportation planning, information technology or geographic information systems (GIS), emergency management, and workforce training and development. The directors indicated that their most important work involved providing technical assistance (Whisman, 2015, pp. 72–73). According to the National Association of Regional Councils (NARC) website, other contemporary COG functions include being designated as economic development districts, serving as clearinghouses for federal and state aid applications, engaging in land use planning, assisting in allocating federal and state revolving loan funds for wastewater and drinking water facilities, and providing services to the elderly.

Studies of regional councils have concluded that they have played a key role in serving as a neutral forum to help local members build trust and develop a sense of shared purpose. This usually means that controversial issues on which local elected officials are divided are not on the agenda. One director characterized his organization's role in dealing with conflicts as "managing expectations in a way that does not end in a fistfight" (Whisman, 2015, p. 73). Nevertheless, occasionally friction occurs between members over dues rates, voting arrangements, or members trying to protect their local interests from regional interference (Dodge, 1996). There also is considerable variation in the effectiveness of and member support for regional councils, but many have the potential to "mature into institutions that coordinate the new metropolitan region" (Miller & Cox, 2014, p. 192).

Many COGs serve as one of the more than 400 metropolitan planning organizations (MPOs) that have been established to fulfill federal and state metropolitan transportation planning requirements in areas with 50,000 or more population. MPO structure differs considerably throughout the country. MPOs may also be independent government organizations, such as the metro in Portland, Oregon, or a municipality or county may take on the MPO role. Some of these independent organizations serve a large region and also tackle issues such as regional land use planning and revenue redistribution. For example, the Chicago Metropolitan Area Planning (CMAP) organization is an MPO, land use planner, and regional issue advocate for the seven-county area around Chicago.

Single-purpose functional planning and regulatory organizations also have been formed in metropolitan areas as a result of federal "carrots and sticks." During the

1970s, these bodies proliferated, covering functions such as environmental protection, law enforcement, health care, and economic development. They were responsible chiefly for planning activities, but grant coordination, standard setting, and regulation also were among their tasks. In many cases, these organizations were separate from regional councils. MPOs established under the Intermodal Surface Transportation Efficiency Act (1991) and its successors—the Transportation Equity Act for the 21st Century (1998); the Safe, Accountable, Flexible, Efficient, Transportation Equity Act: A Legacy for Users (2005); and the Fixing America's Surface Transportation Act (2015)—together with air-quality districts organized pursuant to the Clean Air Act (1990) are currently the most visible and authoritative of the federally supported regional agencies.

During the 1960s and 1970s, many states organized their own areawide planning and development districts (APDDs) for state purposes to meet federal grant review requirements under the Intergovernmental Cooperation Act of 1968 and to provide technical assistance to localities within their boundaries. Most of these organizations focused on planning, economic development, and transportation. The extent to which the APDDs were freestanding regional bodies or piggybacked existing COGs varied from state-to-state. Despite their collaborative and coordinative benefits, multiple federal and state initiatives to create and support areawide organizations added to the layer of substate governmental units and to structural fragmentation in some metropolitan areas.

Middling Approaches

Local Special Districts

Special districts and public authorities are pragmatic and popular. Since these organizations are frequently able to avoid the legal restrictions of general-purpose governments, they are relatively easy to create and do not have the same debt limits. Another reason for their popularity is their ability to draw boundaries around problem sheds. Special districts have been especially popular for areas that needed expensive repairs to their water or wastewater systems but did not have sufficient revenue to pay for the upgrades. The figures on the growth of special districts since the 1950s underscores their popularity.

However, special districts have been criticized as being "invisible" or "shadow" governments in that their boards of directors have a low profile with the voters and thus rate poorly on citizen accountability and transparency values. Most special districts provide a single service to a single jurisdiction, making it difficult to undertake comprehensive, well-coordinated approaches to problems. Illustrative of the wide range of functional importance are hospitals and fire protection at one extreme and mosquito abatement and cemetery maintenance at the other.

Transfer of Functions

Localities have been active in pursuing functional regionalism. Interlocal contracts are one form of service sharing, while transfer of functions is a second. A 1975 national survey of municipalities with more than 2,500 in population conducted by Joseph Zimmerman found that 31% of the respondents (51% of central cities, 30% of suburbs) had voluntarily transferred full or partial functional responsibility to another municipality, county, special district, state, or regional council (Zimmerman, 1976, pp. 120–121). An example is found in Morrisville, North Carolina, a small town that has transferred its traffic signals, water, and sewer systems to its larger neighbor, the town of Cary. More recently, states have taken on or assumed responsibility for or mandated shifts of functions to geographically larger units in such functional areas as transportation, courts, corrections, welfare, and mental health. Another well-established trend, discussed in Chapter 9, is privatization of local functions.

Although functional transfers are a more permanent approach to service sharing, they confront a number of external and internal barriers. The former include mistrust between potential partners, interjurisdictional financial disparities, and concerns about loss of control and lack of accountability. The latter include local staff resistance, time and patience limits, and absence of senior management or elected official support (Collins, 2006).

Liberalized Annexation

The easiest and most middling approaches may not go far enough. In the view of some experts, bolder and more creative approaches are in order (Miller & Cox, 2014; Peirce, 1993; Rusk, 1999). One long-standing innovation that offers promise for changing the regional landscape is liberalized annexation of unincorporated territory. As David Rusk advocates, liberalized annexation involves permitting municipalities to initiate proceedings as well as respond to landowner petitions and authorizing governing body action to determine the fate of the proposal in lieu of a public referendum (Rusk, 1993). While appealing to scholars, liberalized annexation has not spread across metropolitan areas or been strongly endorsed by public officials and citizens. Liberalized annexation is not even an option in many metropolitan areas, given the lack of land that remains unincorporated.

Regional Special Districts and Public Authorities

Despite the proliferation of special-district governments, the number of these bodies serving more than one jurisdiction or providing more than one service is relatively small. Areawide and multipurpose districts and authorities are not common. Only about 9% of the 38,266 special districts in existence in 2012 performed more than one function, chiefly water and sewerage, and 13% were areawide or multicounty (U.S. Census Bureau, 2012). About two thirds of the areawide districts covered two counties (Wikstrom & Stephens, 1998).

Regional special-purpose districts or authorities are not restricted by existing local boundaries in defining their problem shed. They provide a single function—such as mass transportation, schools, water supply, sewage treatment, solid waste disposal, public housing, libraries, and hospitals—to localities or directly to citizens within their territory on a pay-as-you-go basis and are not subject to debt limits and other financial constraints on general-purpose local units. The functional scope could be expanded if local officials agree on what services could best be provided by such an areawide body, but this rarely happens. While providing a mechanism for addressing interlocal concerns and realizing economies of scale, the single-function "silo effect" impedes coordination and raises administrative costs. As a result, according to Hal Wolman (2016), compared to general-purpose local governments, "empirical research is nearly unanimous that, despite any gains derived from achieving economies of scale, service delivery by special districts results in *higher* total government expenditures without any improvement of quality" (p. 3).

The regional district or authority is not a government with directly elected areawide council members. Board members are usually appointed by constituent local governments. The limited regional single-service or multiservice districts are creatures of the local governing bodies that created them, which appoint their board members, determine how votes are apportioned, approve their budgets, and review plans and projects. Similar to local special districts, their governance structures raise accountability and transparency concerns.

Hardest Approaches

Walker (2000) considers one-tier consolidation, two-tier restructuring, and three-tier reforms to be the hardest approaches because "all three involve the creation of a new areawide level of government, a reallocation of local government powers and functions, and as a result a disruption of the political and institutional status quo" (pp. 294–295). Since these efforts involve a formal transfer of authority (and often major personnel changes), they are also the least-common regional efforts. One-tier consolidation was discussed earlier—city–county consolidation and city–city consolidation are two types. As previously mentioned, recent efforts to consolidate general-purpose governments have rarely been successful.

The best American example of two-tier restructuring is Metro Dade County, serving the Miami, Florida, region. Narrowly approved by referendum in 1957, a home rule charter features a sorting out of areawide and municipal functions with little overlapping. Unlike the incremental approach represented by the reformed or urban county, from the outset, a wide range of areawide functions and related powers were authorized to the county. Services typically associated with municipal governments, such as law enforcement and sanitation, are provided countywide by Miami-Dade County government, while most municipalities in Miami-Dade County provide their own policing, planning and zoning, and fire protection. The metropolitan mayor is directly elected, and he or she appoints a CAO (Miller & Cox, 2014, p. 158; Walker, 2000, pp. 294–295). Examples of the three-tier—municipal–county–multicounty—model will be examined in the next section.

STATE RESTRUCTURING INCENTIVES

The paucity of significant local actions and innovations to alter the jurisdictional status quo has generated interest in state incentives for local restructuring and collaboration. The capacity of local governments to overcome a fragmented regional structure and deal with problems and needs that ignore their boundaries and stress their structures through regional collaboration is constrained by state law and the limited authority of local governments. State constitutional or statutory provisions outline how much collaboration can occur without state legal intervention. In addition, local governments may not have the legal authority to create formal agreements with other local governments. As noted earlier, local officials have advocated removal of state restrictions and empowerment of their jurisdictions as a fundamental first step toward working across boundaries. State "carrots and sticks" have been used to accelerate regional collaboration and decision making (Krane, Rigos, & Hill, 2001; Miller & Cox, 2014, pp. 193–207). Minnesota and Oregon provide two historic examples of how states have facilitated authoritative metropolitan governance.

Minnesota and Oregon Three-Tier Experiments

Perhaps the boldest approach in Walker's spectrum of regional options is modeled on the experiences of two states. The Minnesota legislature established the Twin Cities (Minneapolis–St. Paul) Metropolitan Council in 1967 as the "authoritative regional coordinator, planner, and controller of large-scale development for its region," now covering 16 counties and the municipalities of St. Paul and Minneapolis (Walker, 2000, p. 295). There are 17 council members appointed by the governor to review and approve plans, projects, and budgets of constituent regional special districts (called *commissions*). The council also directly provides urban services such as transit and wastewater operations and management (Miller & Cox, 2014, pp. 183–184). According to its website, the council's 2017 operating budget was $1.017 billion and there were 4,250 staff members (Metropolitan Council, n.d.).

In 1971, the Minnesota legislature enacted a pioneering tax-base growth-sharing plan for the Twin Cities region. The legislature sought to reduce fiscal disparities in the Twin Cities metropolitan area by establishing a fund into which 40% of the new property tax revenues generated by industrial or commercial property development would be pooled and distributed to all general-purpose local units within the region, with the remaining tax revenues going to the jurisdiction within which the industry or business is located. According to Miller and Cox (2014), "The program covers $2.5 million people, 7 counties, and 200 local jurisdictions, and involves $200 million in tax proceeds" (p. 137).

While the concept of tax-base sharing makes sense and the scope of Minnesota's program is impressive, only a handful of metropolitan areas have adopted tax sharing. In Allegheny County, Pennsylvania, a Regional Asset District uses proceeds from a 1% countywide sales tax for cultural facilities such as the zoo, parks, libraries, and the Pittsburgh Steelers football stadium. Dayton, Ohio, has adopted a voluntary tax-base sharing program to provide funding for economic development projects and achieving greater regional financial equity. And Denver, Colorado, has established a Scientific and Cultural Facilities District that distributes a portion of regional sales tax revenues—one tenth of 1%—to support the zoo, museums, a performing arts center, and botanic gardens, among other civic attractions, while another tax district raised funds to build and operate a stadium for the Denver Rockies baseball team (Miller & Cox, 2014, pp. 139–142).

In 1978, a Portland Metropolitan Service District (MSD) was established by the state legislature to provide areawide planning and limited services (e.g., zoo, solid waste disposal) in the metropolitan area encompassing three counties, 24 municipalities, and one half of the state's total population. The legislature intended the MSD to be a flexible structure that could assume other responsibilities desired by Portland area citizens or state legislators.

In November 1992, a home rule charter was adopted by citizens of the metropolitan area, consolidating MSD with the regional council of governments and making "Metro" the only directly elected regional government in the country. Seven members serve on the nonpartisan council for four-year terms with an executive officer elected at-large. In addition to its core planning responsibility, described in the charter as the primary function, Metro is responsible for a wide range of functions, including solid waste collection, recycling, and disposal; air and water quality; operation of the Washington Park Zoo; management of the Oregon Convention Center; allocation of federal highway funds; and oversight of the regional transportation system. As part of its regional land use planning and growth management responsibilities, Metro also is authorized to resolve inconsistencies between local plans and its regional framework plan/land use standards and to establish the urban growth boundary for the region (Cisneros, 1995, pp. 23–25; Miller & Cox, 2014, p. 184; Rusk, 1993, pp. 99–100). According to its website, Metro's 2016–2017 budget was $636 million and the full-time equivalent staff numbered 855.

Creation of a third-tier unit similar to those in the Twin Cities and Portland regions does not require consolidation or restructuring of existing local governments that are nested below it. Instead, it is an extension of the metropolitan special-district proposal, but with a clearly defined multifunctional charge, capacity to handle regional equity issues, and emphasis on public accountability. Voters select a charter that specifies the powers and functions of the regional organization and that can be expanded or contracted by the electorate or state legislature. Regionally elected or state-appointed officials are visible and can be held accountable, in contrast to the largely invisible nature of traditional special districts and public authorities with governing bodies appointed by local officials.

But similar to tax-base or growth-sharing arrangements, the sparse adoption record indicates that this proposal has limited political appeal and that it takes time to develop elected official comfort with it and citizen understanding of it. Initiatives to establish a three-tier system could easily be miscast by opponents as a hostile takeover of communities by metropolitan government. Other high political hurdles have to be overcome, including voter distrust of "big government," racial minority group fears that their political strength in the central city will be weakened, and unwillingness of leaders of municipalities and counties to share visibility and prestige with regional elected officials. While a large multipurpose organization may give the region more clout in dealing with the governor, legislature, and state agencies, it could also fuel state opposition to Metro. With respect to political feasibility in other states, not to be overlooked here is the underrepresentation of urban and metropolitan interests in many state legislatures. As Miller and Cox (2014) point out,

> The states are rarely seen as active or positive contributors to the resolution of metropolitan issues. To be more blunt, it is the interests and concerns of

suburban legislators, whom in many states seem as disinterested in urban and metropolitan issues as their rural-dominated counterparts that controlled state politics into the 1950s that dictate the legislative agenda. (p. 206)

This point was illustrated by the April 2016 cover of *Governing* magazine, which read, "We Interrupt This Program . . . Some states will step in to cut off local government actions any chance they get."

Carrot and Stick Approaches

The Minnesota and Oregon examples illustrate the boldest of the bottom-up or "carrot" approaches to state leveraging, greater interlocal collaboration, and authoritative action by giving localities greater discretionary power to work across jurisdictional and public–private boundaries to forge strategies and build relationships for delivering services more efficiently, effectively, and equitably. This approach is sometimes called *second order devolution* (Bowman & Kearney, 2011). Examples of actions taken in a bottom-up approach are listed in Table 4.2.

A second approach is more directive than facilitative. The top-down or "stick" approach involves governors or legislators taking steps to induce realignment of local services or structures through legislation and other actions, such as those shown in Table 4.2.

A 2013 review of research reports featuring news of relevant state initiatives and surveys of the executive directors of state municipal leagues and county associations revealed a range of leveraging examples embracing the approaches undertaken during and since the Great Recession (Morse & Stenberg, forthcoming). Noteworthy initiatives were taken in recent years in 11 states, with two states—New Jersey and New York—going the furthest. Their actions are summarized below.

New Jersey

Governor Chris Christie and his predecessor, Jon Corzine, criticized the fragmented structure of local government in their state—featuring 21 counties, 566 municipalities, 523 school districts, and 234 special districts in 2012—claiming that the layering of bureaucracy contributed to high property-tax burdens. But the governors had been unable to muster political support to mandate or induce top-down changes. In 2007, the legislature passed the Uniform Shared Services and Consolidation Act to help reduce property taxes by promoting greater government efficiency through shared services, regionalism, and consolidation. The act recodified existing laws that authorized local units to enter into agreements to provide or receive services by adopting a resolution and to contract for services.

TABLE 4.2 ■ Bottom-Up and Top-Down Approaches

Bottom-Up Approaches	Top-Down Approaches
expanded authority for local governments to enter into service sharing, transfer, or consolidation agreements	imposing limits on local revenues and the creation of new local units
facilitation of local management improvement practices, such as collective purchasing and private contracting arrangements	strengthening the authority and capacity of counties to serve as regional governments, expanding their scope of authorized services, and sorting out and mandating transfer of functional responsibilities between counties and municipalities
authorization to use regional COGs or state areawide districts to provide local services	transferring financial and/or administrative responsibility for a service to the state
liberalization or standardization of procedures for initiating annexation, downsizing governing boards, changing forms of government, and consolidating or dissolving jurisdictions	creating metropolitan authorities to provide services on an areawide or regional basis, as in Portland, Oregon
state funding to support local planning studies for charter revisions and other actions to enable shared or consolidated services and merger or dissolution of local units	mandating interlocal or regional cooperation in service delivery
strengthening the power of voters to compel service or jurisdictional mergers	mandating regional consolidation of a local service
designating a state office to provide technical assistance to local government service sharing or merger initiatives and structural reform efforts	eliminating or reducing the number of nonviable units—such as some townships, rural school districts, and small general-purpose local units—that have very limited size and functional responsibilities, weak own-source financial bases, or heavy dependence on state and federal aid
incentives in state aid formulas for regional collaboration or local unit consolidation	curtailing or terminating state aid or local revenue authority to units that fail to meet effectiveness criteria (size, cost-savings, etc.)
establishing a statewide benchmarking system to provide the public and policy makers with information about local productivity and progress	

The Senate president, a Democrat, introduced legislation in the 2012–2013 session that embraced a more punitive "stick" approach than the 2007 act. Under the bill, New Jersey's Local Unit Alignment, Reorganization and Consolidation Commission, established in the Department of Community Affairs, would conduct studies of the structure and functions of counties, municipalities, and schools to determine whether consolidation would produce greater efficiencies and tax savings. The commission's consolidation or shared services proposals were to be transmitted to the governor and legislature and put before the voters of the affected jurisdictions at the next general election. Voters would be asked to approve shared or consolidated services that were recommended, but any town that does not pass the recommended changes would lose state aid equivalent to the projected cost savings. The New Jersey State League of Municipalities and American Federation of State, County, and Municipal Employees opposed the bill and it has not been enacted.

A third noteworthy New Jersey initiative was taken in 2011 to promote local accountability, sound management practices, and transparency. A Local Best Practices Checklist of budgeting, management, and cost-control tools was developed by the Division of Local Government Services. Each local government was required to fill out and certify the survey annually in order to receive its December 1 state aid payment, which represents the final 5% of its total annual aid allocation. A sliding scale of up to 5% of total aid could be withheld by the division for municipalities failing to reply "yes" or "not applicable" to fewer than 40 of the 50 questions on the survey. The Best Practices Inventory categories are general management (including shared services), finance and audit, procurement, budget preparation and presentation, health insurance, and personnel.

New York

Service sharing and local restructuring have been on the agendas of five recent New York governors. Similar to Governor Christie, the current incumbent, Andrew M. Cuomo, has linked the large number of local governments in the state with high property taxes. Incentives to promote local efficiency and reduce the costs of the 1,607 general-purpose local governments through cooperation and consolidation are key components of achieving his agenda.

The New York Department of State's Division of Local Government Services currently administers the main incentive programs under the Local Government Efficiency (LGe) portfolio (Local Government Efficiency Grant and Local Government Citizen's Reorganization and Empowerment Grant programs). The department also provides training and technical assistance to local governments to help control costs, promote efficiencies, and coordinate joint provisions of state services.

Planning grants were made available to study opportunities to achieve cost savings through cooperative agreements and shared or consolidated service initiatives as well as for municipal or county charter revision studies that covered functional consolidation, service sharing, mergers, or dissolution. In addition to these planning grants, implementation grants were made available to help defray costs such as capital, equipment, and transitional personnel.

A 2014 summary of all LGe projects included education, utilities, public safety, and transportation among the general functional reorganization categories. Examples of other specific shared services for which awards were made included GIS and information technology, office space, zoning and code enforcement, records management, health insurance, courts, and parks and recreation. Between 2006-2014, 161 shared services studies and projects were approved, and 92 functional consolidation studies and 27 consolidation implementation projects have been funded. Fifty-two dissolution studies and 12 implementation projects have been undertaken, mostly involving villages and amounting to less than $50,000 apiece. According to the New York Department of State, since 2005 the LGe program has resulted in more than $600 million in savings to taxpayers from $85 million invested in 466 shared services and consolidation projects" (New York State, n.d.).

Another LGe restructuring component was the 2010 New N.Y. Government Reorganization and Citizen Empowerment Act, establishing uniform procedures for the consolidation or dissolution of local government units, except for school districts and some special-purpose districts. In 2012, a Citizen's Reorganization and Empowerment Grant (CREG) program was established to implement the municipal restructuring provisions of the Act, including provisions for citizens to petition their town or village to vote on consolidation or dissolution. Grants may be used for reorganization plan studies or implementation and may not exceed $100,000.

In summary, both New Jersey and New York State have a long tradition of bipartisan gubernatorial and legislative support for local collaboration. But most of the targets have largely been noncontroversial, involved lower-cost services, and concerned small units, such as villages and school districts. Providing funds to undertake consultant studies, seed start-up costs, and promote citizen understanding of referenda are important ways for the state to leverage change. But questions remain about whether the amount of state incentive funds is sufficient to attract jurisdictions that otherwise would not pursue such opportunities and to encourage the consideration of costly and controversial reorganizations, such as police force consolidation and jurisdictional mergers. Official backing has also wavered and been inconsistent, while opposition from local representatives and unions has been strong.

Across the country, a few states have moved ahead to facilitate or mandate dramatic changes in local service and structural arrangements, but the majority have not done so. Most efforts are modest in scope and not part of a larger, strategic agenda to influence fundamental changes in how local governments do business. So the states' role as regional catalyst has not been widely realized, and states are often perceived by local officials as being adversaries instead of partners. Nevertheless, local managers play important roles as intergovernmental liaisons and should capitalize on opportunities to work with state officials to identify "carrots" that could promote and facilitate their strategies to work across boundaries.

REGIONAL COOPERATION: LOOKING FORWARD

There is no formula to ensure that the next stage in the evolution of local structure and relationships within and outside metropolitan areas will be successful. As Beverly Cigler observes in the opening of this chapter, regionalism remains "an unnatural act among consenting adults." Problems such as sprawl, tax-base disparities, deteriorating services, and environmental degradation are formidable, and the weapons that local officials have in their arsenal are not very powerful relative to the severity and persistence of these problems. Substantial obstacles to regional collaboration and governance also must be overcome, especially local official parochialism and coveting of home rule, political resistance by suburban voters, state reluctance to intervene in local affairs, racial and economic disparities, and citizen distrust of big government and new layers of bureaucracy. Citizen desires to retain their community's lifestyle and sense of place also are important hurdles.

Local government managers play critical roles as barometers, planners, educators, and communicators with respect to regional collaboration. They must identify win–win opportunities and mutual benefits and sense when the timing is opportune for joint ventures. A survey of 22 Florida city and county managers and department heads identified the following eight lessons from their collaborative experiences: (1) clarify expectations; (2) communicate, communicate, communicate; (3) be transparent; (4) expect a lengthy process; (5) realize that not all plans will work as anticipated; (6) find possible solutions in the experiences of other organizations; (7) seek out personnel and agencies with common interests; and (8) keep the big picture at the forefront (Lee & Hannah-Spurlock, 2015).

As Walker's "Snow White and the 17 Dwarfs" research indicates, local government officials have several tools at their disposal to tackle tough problems and needs crossing their boundary lines. The preceding discussion highlights five tools (informal cooperation, COGs, single-purpose regional bodies, state planning and development districts, and local special districts) that are being used or could be readily implemented to work across boundaries and three others (functional transfers, liberalized annexation, and regional special districts) that may be more challenging to undertake. The discussion does not include three of the most popular, pragmatic, and politically acceptable tools (informal cooperation, interlocal contracts, and private contracting) or relationships with county governments, which will be covered in Chapter 9.

These and other political realities suggest that new and renewed strategies for working across local boundaries will be essential. Local managers and elected officials will need to bring both vision and patience to the task and will need to exercise strong and skillful leadership in building networks to advance transcending strategies. Above all, they will need to keep the three *T*s at the forefront of their efforts: Regional collaboration requires participants to put aside *turf* concerns; achieving results takes *time*, often several years; and building and maintaining *trust* with peers, staff, elected officials, and citizens is crucial to successful outcomes (Lamontagne, Poore, & Tupper, 2016).

REFERENCES

Bish, R. L., & Ostrom, V. (1973). *Understanding urban government: Metropolitan reform reconsidered.* Washington, DC: American Institute for Public Policy Research.

Bowman, A. O'M., & Kearney, R. (2011). Second-order devolution: Data and doubt. *Publius, 41*(4), 563–585.

Cigler, B. (2007). Post-Katrina emergency management: Forum overview. *The Public Manager.* Fall. p. 3.

Cisneros, H. G. (1995). *Regionalism: The new geography of opportunity.* Washington, DC: U.S. Department of Housing and Urban Development.

Collins, S. (2006). Interlocal service-sharing agreements. *IQ Report, 38*(3).

Dodge, W. R. (1996). *Regional excellence: Governing together to compete globally and flourish locally.* Washington, DC: National League of Cities.

Downs, A. (1994). *New visions for metropolitan America.* Washington, DC: Brookings Institution.

Feiock, R. C. (2007). Rational choice and regional governance. *Journal of Urban Affairs, 29*(1), 47–63.

Foster, K. A., & Barnes, W. R. (2012). Reframing regional governance for research and practice. *Urban Affairs Review, 48*(2), 272–283.

Frederickson, H. G. (2005, November). Transcending the community: Local leadership in a world of shared power. *Public Management,* 8–15.

Frisken, F., & Norris, D. F. (Eds.). (2001). Regionalism reconsidered. *Journal of Urban Affairs, 23*(5), 467–478.

Hilvert, C., & Swindell, D. (2013). Collaborative service delivery: What every local government manager should know. *State and Local Government Review, 45*(4), 240–254.

Jimenez, B. S., & Hendrick, R. (2010). Is government consolidation the answer? *State and Local Government Review, 42*(3), 258–270.

Jones, V. (1942). *Metropolitan government.* Chicago, IL: University of Chicago Press.

Krane, D., Rigos, P. N., & Hill, M. B., Jr. (2001). *Home rule in America: A fifty-state handbook.* Washington, DC: CQ Press.

Lamontagne, A., Poore, N., & Tupper, N. (2016). Working together regionally: How Maine communities are collaborating on service delivery. *Public Management, 98*(11), 12–15.

Ledebur, L., & Barnes, W. (1992). *City distress, metropolitan disparities and economic growth.* Washington, DC: National League of Cities.

Lee, R., & Hannah-Spurlock, S. (2015). Bridging interests on local government collaboration. *Public Management, 97*(7), 15–17.

Martin, L. L., & Schiff, J. H. (2011). City–county consolidations: Promise versus performance. *State and Local Government Review, 43*(2), 167–177.

Metropolitan Council. (n.d.). [Website]. Retrieved April 1, 2017, from https://metrocouncil.org/

Miller, D. Y. (2002). *The regional governing of metropolitan America.* Cambridge, MA: Westview Press.

Miller, D. Y., & Cox, R. W., III. (2014). *Governing the metropolitan region: America's new frontier.* Armonk, NY: M.E. Sharpe.

Morse, R. S., & Stenberg, C. W. (forthcoming). *Pulling the lever: The states' role in catalyzing local change.*

Nalbandian, J. (1999). Facilitating community, enabling democracy: New roles for local government managers. *Public Administration Review, 59*(3), 187–197.

National League of Cities. (2016). *Cities 101—consolidations.* Retrieved March 11, 2017, from http://www.nlc.org/resource/cities-101-consolidations

New York State. (n.d.). *Department of state, division of local government services.* Retrieved April 1, 2017, from https://www.dos.ny.gov/lg/

Orfield, M. (1997). *Metropolitics: A regional agenda for community and stability*. Washington, DC: Brookings Institution Press/Lincoln Institute for Land Policy.

Ostrom, V., Tiebout, C. M., & Warren, R. (1961). The organization of government in metropolitan areas: A theoretical inquiry. *American Political Science Review, 55*(4), 831–842.

Peirce, N. R. (1993). *Citistates: How urban America can prosper in a competitive world*. Washington, DC: Seven Locks Press.

Rusk, D. (1993). *Cities without suburbs*. Washington, DC: Woodrow Wilson Center Press.

Rusk, D. (1999). *Inside game, outside game: Winning strategies for saving urban America*. Washington, DC: Brookings Institution.

Rusk, D. (2013). *Cities without suburbs: A census 2010 perspective* (4th ed.). Washington, DC: Woodrow Wilson Center Press.

Savitch, H. V., & Vogel, R. V. (2000). Paths to new regionalism. *State and Local Government Review, 32*(3), 158–168.

Stenberg, C. W. (2008). Fragmented structures and blurred boundaries: Strategies for regional governance. In I. W. Morgan & P. J. Davies (Eds.), *The federal nation: Perspectives on American federalism* (pp. 83–101). New York, NY: Palgrave MacMillan.

Stenberg, C. W., III, & Colman, W. G. (1994). *America's future work force: A health and education policy issues handbook*. Westport, CT: Greenwood Press.

U. S. Census Bureau. (2012). *2012 census of governments*. Retrieved March 11, 2017, from https://www .census.gov/govs/cog/

Vogel, R. K., & Harrigan, J. J. (2007). *Political change in the metropolis* (8th ed.). New York, NY: Pearson/Longman.

Walker, D. B. (1987, January/February). Snow White and the 17 dwarfs: From metropolitan cooperation to governance. *National Civic Review, 76*, 14–28.

Walker, D. B. (2000). *The rebirth of federalism: Slouching toward Washington* (2nd ed.). New York, NY: Chatham House Publishers.

Whisman, H. (2015). Can we work together? Regional councils and the challenges they face. *Municipal year book 2015* (p. 70). Washington, DC: International City/County Management Association.

Wikstrom, N., & Stephens, G. R. (1998). Trends in special districts. *State and Local Government Review, 30*(2), 129–138.

Wolman, H. (2016). *Learning from abroad: Multi-purpose special districts in British Columbia as a possible model for governance innovation for local governments in the United States*. Phoenix, AZ: Alliance for Innovation.

Zeemering, E. S. (2008). Governing interlocal cooperation: City council interests and the implications for public management. *Public Administration Review, 68*(4), 731–741.

Zimmerman, J. F. (1976). *Pragmatic federalism: The reassignment of functional responsibility*. Washington, DC: U.S. Advisory Commission on Intergovernmental Relations.

RESOURCE LIST/TO EXPLORE FURTHER

Books/Articles

Agranoff, R. (2001). Managing within the matrix: Do collaborative intergovernmental relations exist? *Publius, 31*(2), 31–56.

Hamilton, D. K. (2014). Governing metropolitan areas: Growth and change in a networked age (2nd ed., pp. 187–317). New York, NY: Routledge.

U.S. Advisory Commission on Intergovernmental Relations. (1962). *Alternative approaches to governmental reorganization in metropolitan areas*. Washington, DC: U.S. Government Printing Office.

Web Resources

The following web resources are examples of regional governance in the U.S.:

Chicago, IL: http://www.cmap.illinois.gov

Portland, OR: http://www.oregonmetro.gov

San Diego, CA: http://www.sandag.org

Twin Cities, MN: https://metrocouncil.org/

THE CAREER OF THE LOCAL GOVERNMENT MANAGER

I look upon my profession as city manager in exactly the same way that a minister of the gospel looks upon his mission. I believe that as a city manager endeavoring to make the city for whose administrative affairs I am responsible better in every way for every man and woman I am doing the work of the Master.

—Louis Brownlow (1922, p. 151)

Although the profession of the local government manager only recently reached the age of 100, it has a rich and storied history. The profession is one that has evolved over time, yet the roles managers play in their communities have remained mostly consistent. Today, the majority of local governments, both municipal and county, have chief executive officers who are professional managers. As the complexity of communities increases and the problems those communities face become more "wicked," the value of professional management is increasingly clear.

In this environment of challenging issues facing local governments and increasingly complex relationships with states—when professional managers will be needed most—there is evidence that the pipeline of educated and experienced future managers will not be sufficient. A wave of manager retirements and a narrow pipeline of graduate students pursuing training in local government management could lead to difficulty finding qualified people to run local governments. However, the career of the local government manager can be immensely rewarding. This chapter describes the local government management career and the people who have chosen to spend their professional lives running the communities Americans call home.

LOCAL GOVERNMENT MANAGER PROFILES

PAMELA ANTIL
ASSISTANT CITY ADMINISTRATOR, SANTA BARBARA, CALIFORNIA

Twenty-five years ago, I transitioned from a job in state government to my first position in local government and have never looked back! I have been a career assistant city manager and love my role as the "chief operating officer" of the city. In this role, I have managed all aspects of the day-to-day operations in public works, police, fire, planning, airport, library, finance, IT [information technology], parks and recreation. I am so proud of the work I have done with six really unique cities across the nation. I can't think of a better way to have fulfilled my desire to use my MPA [master of public administration] to make life better for people through service to my community.

Education

At the time of the birth of the profession of local government management, the United States was in the midst of the Industrial Revolution. While substantial changes occurred in private industry during this time, it also marked a period of rapid population growth in urban centers. In response, towns and cities faced the daunting task of creating and sustaining a system of infrastructure—water and sewer systems, roads, and public safety—to support that population growth. As adoption of the council–manager form spread throughout the nation, elected boards chose managers who they believed could best address this challenge.

It is for this reason that so many early city and town managers were trained in engineering (Stone, Price, & Stone, 1940). Generally, managers were tasked with overseeing large public works projects. "City after city adopted the plan because it was thought a manager would more quickly build paved streets, sidewalks, sewers, and other public works" (p. 56). Early managers were not required to have college diplomas, and many communities sought people with experience directing public works projects rather than a specific educational background.

Although today the most popular degree for local government managers is public administration, until after World War II, it was uncommon for managers to have a graduate degree in public administration (and such programs were scarce). Table 5.1 shows the level of education of local government managers from 1935 to 2000. In the 1930s, very few managers had advanced degrees. By 2000, more than 60% held graduate degrees. The reverse is true of managers holding high school diplomas or less. In the 1930s, close to 40% had no education beyond high school. As municipal and county governments grew in size and complexity—adding more services to satisfy more people—greater capacity in leading and expertise in managing a large organization became necessary.

TABLE 5.1 ■ Education Level of Local Government Managers, 1935–2000

	1935	1964	1974	1984	2000
High School or Less	39%	14%	6%	2%	2%
Some College, No Degree	24%	22%	18%	10%	9%
Bachelor Degree	35%	41%	38%	30%	26%
Graduate Degree	2%	23%	38%	58%	63%
Number Reporting	449	1,582	1,646	2,348	3,175

Sources: City Management Intl., 1996; ICMA, 1984, 2001; Nolting, Arnold, & Powers, 1965; Ridley & Nolting, 1940.

Adoption of the council–manager form increased considerably after World War II (Nelson & Svara, 2014a), partly in response to the increasing complexity in local governance. Also in this period, the degree focus shifted away from engineering and toward the social sciences.

Age

The average age of the local government manager is increasing (see Table 5.2). While the percentage of managers over 60 had remained below 10% since the 1970s, in 2012, it ballooned to over 20%. Two thirds of managers are now 50 and over. These figures are not surprising, as they represent the baby boom generation. However, the low percentage of managers in the 40-and-under category indicates that the pipeline to replace retiring managers may not be sufficient.

In 2013, the International City/County Management Association (ICMA) conducted a survey of its members to gather data on retirement and succession planning. All members currently in service received the survey (3,742) and 1,080 members responded for a response rate of 35%. The retirement numbers are sobering. More than 60% of respondents have been working in local government for 20 years or more. This figure is consistent with the age data found in the 2012 State of the Profession survey that is summarized in Table 5.2.

TABLE 5.2 ■ Age of Local Government Managers, 1974–2012				
	1974	1984	2000	2012
40 & under	42%	49%	18%	11%
41–50	31%	26%	40%	26%
51–60	22%	20%	37%	40%
Over 60	6%	5%	5%	23%

Sources: ICMA, 1975, 1985, 2001, 2013.

The pending wave of retirements at the local government chief administrative officer (CAO) level coupled with reports that enrollments of master of public administration (MPA) students interested in local government are down means that there will likely be a significant gap between the number of open CAO positions and people available to fill them. Some local governments have begun investing in developing a future cadre of senior managers. However, succession planning is rare. Fewer than 2% of the respondents to the 2013 ICMA retirement survey reported that they had a succession-planning program. Nearly 45% reported that they have no programs in place to recruit or retain future senior managers.

Gender and Racial Diversity

Concerning diversity, municipal and county managers are not representative of the U.S. population. People of color and women continue to be starkly underrepresented in the profession. According to the ICMA 2012 State of the Profession survey (ICMA, 2013), more than 90% of local government CAOs are white and close to 85% are men.

Women now make up approximately 15% of CAOs in U.S. municipalities and counties (Nelson & Svara, 2014b), but that ratio has changed very little in the past 40 years, and it is far from reflective of the U.S. population. Today, women manage some of the largest council–manager communities in the nation (i.e., Las Vegas, Nevada; San Antonio, Texas; Mecklenburg County, North Carolina). However, these are limited exceptions to the general rule that most municipal and county managers are men and that approximately 50% of female managers serve in jurisdictions under 10,000 in population, compared to 40% of men (Nelson & Svara, 2014b).

In 2012, the ICMA formed a task force on women in the profession. Upon completion of their work, the task force made a set of recommendations to the ICMA executive board to aid in the promotion of women in the profession. These recommendations ranged from improving the data and research to explain issues of gender inequality in the profession to partnering with state associations and municipal leagues on recruitment initiatives. Unfortunately, research is limited that investigates why female local government CAOs remain in low proportion to male CAOs. However, there is speculation that elected boards may be discriminating and that women are choosing to stay in the assistant manager position to ensure greater stability for their families. The position of assistant manager is less likely to be subject to some of the politics experienced in the CAO position, which makes a longer tenure more certain than as a manager. To some degree, efforts to promote local government management to women are conducted without full information about the roots of the problem.

Racially, the profession is also not representative of the population. According to the 2012 ICMA State of the Profession survey (ICMA, 2013), more than 90% of local government CAOs are white. Given that many professionally run communities are majority–minority and that minority managers should be accepted in all communities, this discrepancy is problematic when seeking *bureaucratic representativeness*. A bureaucracy is representative when its members are demographically similar to the citizens they serve, particularly in race and gender. According to the theory of representative bureaucracy, administrators who have characteristics in common with the population being served are better able to understand and meet the interests of the public.

WORKING AS A LOCAL GOVERNMENT MANAGER

The recruitment and selection process for managers is different from other local government positions. Local governing boards usually select and hire the manager as a body. The mayor's role may be more significant than that of other members of the board; this additional authority will be outlined in the charter. In medium and large communities, search firms are often hired to handle the recruitment process, but many smaller communities use in-house resources.

PETER AUSTIN
COUNTY MANAGER, MCHENRY COUNTY, ILLINOIS

As I was nearing completion [of] my undergraduate degree [at the University of Iowa], I attended a graduate school fair and was introduced to the MPA degree [at Northern Illinois University] and the profession of local government management. I immediately had a clear career path and I have never looked back. For me, the opportunity to serve the public in a professional, respected, dynamic environment was exactly what I was looking for and it remains both challenging and rewarding today.

Job Requirements for a Local Government Manager

In most cases, local elected boards have the authority to select the municipal or county manager with few restrictions. Advertisements for positions as local government managers usually specify at least three categories of requirements: education, experience, and residency. Local ordinances or charters may mandate a minimum level of experience and/or education and will speak to whether or not residency within the community is a requirement. Local governing boards may choose to exceed the education or experience minimums when advertising for the positions.

As discussed earlier, the majority of current managers have graduate degrees. Although a bachelor's degree is often listed in the local government code as a minimum requirement, job announcements for city and county managers increasingly seek a master's degree. The degree field is rarely limited to public administration.

Local government charters and ordinances (and in some cases, state statutes) provide limited guidance about the minimum qualifications for the position of city or county manager. The language used in Rio Rancho, New Mexico's home rule charter is fairly standard:

The city manager shall be appointed solely on the basis of executive and administrative qualifications. The city manager need not be a resident of the City or State at the time of appointment, but may reside outside the City while in office only with the express prior approval of the Governing Body. (Rio Rancho, 2016, Charter Article III, Section 3.04)

Some charters are more specific about the education requirements of the prospective manager, such as this excerpt from Cedar Rapids, Iowa:

The city manager shall be appointed solely on the basis of his or her education, experience, and fitness of the person to serve in that capacity without regard to political or other affiliation. The manager need not be a resident of the city or state at the time of appointment but shall reside within Cedar Rapids unless residence outside of the city is approved by the council. (Cedar Rapids, 2016, Article IV, Section 4.01)

Bixby, Oklahoma, mandates a minimum education of bachelor's degree but also stipulates that the university must be accredited.

County codes referencing the minimum qualifications of the county manager are similar to those of municipal governments. Sullivan County, New York, requires candidates to have a master's degree in public administration (or a similar degree) and five years of government employment. Lyon County, Nevada's code provides considerable detail on minimum qualifications:

Be chosen upon the basis of knowledge and skills in public administration, demonstrated administrative ability and knowledge of public budgeting, personnel, finance and organization. This requirement may normally be met by a combination of education and experience equal to a bachelor's degree in business or public administration and at least five (5) years of administrative experience, preferably in government or public administration and involved management responsibilities. (2016, Title 1, Chapter 7, 1.07.03)

Given the somewhat general language used in the local laws, governing boards have considerable discretion in selecting their top candidate for the job. Therefore, experience may come from a variety of sources, not solely from previous local government work. And the degree field may be less important than the degree itself. Recent research suggests that boards make a distinction between graduate education in public administration and other advanced degrees. "We find that an advanced degree in public administration is valued more than other educational backgrounds by city councils, and this value is independent of social and economic characteristics of cities and traits of individual managers" (Vanderleeuw, Sides, & Williams, 2015, p. 453). However, the narrower pipeline of traditional candidates for local government has led to a diversification of the career paths of municipal and county managers.

Career Paths and Patterns

Local government managers attain CAO positions through several potential career paths. More than 60% of respondents to the 2013 ICMA retirement survey have worked their entire careers in local government. Although there is limited data to provide percentages, the most common career path for a professional local government manager is through the attainment of an MPA degree and progressively greater experience. This is demonstrated in the 2013 ICMA retirement and succession planning survey, in which more than 56% of respondents reported that their first exposure to local government was through an internship or fellowship during or immediately following their MPA studies. Some new MPA graduates proceed immediately into the management of a small town (2.4% in the ICMA survey). However, the majority of graduating students attain junior management positions in a local government, working their way up both in progressively larger communities and jobs with greater responsibility and authority. Common entry-level jobs for new MPA graduates seeking to become local government managers include management analysts, financial analysts, management fellows, and assistant to the city/county manager. Later, they will progress into jobs as assistant department heads or managers. Ultimately, if they choose to take that path, they are more likely to become CAOs of a municipality or county.

As the number of retiring managers has increased, local elected bodies may consider hiring managers from less-traditional paths. It is becoming more common to see managers who once worked in the private sector, including nonprofits, or who have a military background. Although the appeal of the nontraditional candidate may be evident to elected officials, these potential new managers typically have no training in public budgeting and finance, personnel, or the dynamics of the local government system. They will also have a limited understanding of how local governments work or how local governments fit into the broader system of government.

Former police and fire chiefs are also being hired as managers; this used to be an atypical progression. Department heads who are more likely to become managers are finance, public works, and economic or community development. Hiring managers with a background in public safety may be an indication of the community's concern over crime or other public safety issues.

What happens to local government managers after they take a CAO position in a municipal or county government? Watson and Hassett (2004) identify one of four career paths once a manager reaches the CAO position. A small percentage of managers essentially remain in one community as the manager for most of their career. These are long-serving managers who have found their niche in a stable community. Lateral movers make up another group, moving from place to place but staying in smaller-sized jurisdictions. Watson and Hassett suggest that these managers are often fired or forced to resign due to political issues. Another group of managers have worked their way up through the same organization. They hold a number of jobs within a single government, moving into positions with increasingly higher levels of authority. Finally, the fourth group of managers moves up by taking positions in communities with progressively larger populations.

Job Satisfaction and Turnover

Concerns about job stability are a perennial question among managers and those interested in becoming managers. Local government CAOs work at the will of their elected bodies and/or mayors and may have little or no warning before being dismissed or encouraged to resign. Some communities place a moratorium on management changes in the first few months following an election, but this is uncommon. When council members run on an agenda for change, change in the manager may be the primary goal.

A number of studies have been conducted to explore the tenure of the local government manager. Data shows that the average tenure of a city manager is short, less than seven years (Renner, 2001). However, this is an increase from the average stay of 3.5 years in 1965 (Watson & Watson, 2006). Most of the research has been confined to municipal governments. Generally, the factors that affect whether a manager stays or goes can be divided into two categories—those that push the manager out and those that pull the manager to another jurisdiction. Those factors that push a manager out are generally political in nature, while the pull factors deal with career advancement. Research indicates that both categories of factors are influential in manager turnover (DeHoog & Whitaker, 1990).

At the local level, the political environment is frequently fraught with conflict and potential instability. Political conflict may result from disagreements among council members, making it difficult for the manager to determine consensus. Therefore, the manager may be seen as taking sides. Research shows that political conflict and uncertainty are related to managers' turnover (McCabe, Feiock, Clingermayer, & Stream, 2008; Tekniepe & Stream, 2012; see Photo 5.1). Managers may be asked to resign under these circumstances or may decide to seek a job with a more supportive political environment. Conversely, cities with greater stability among the elected officials have lower probability of manager turnover (Renner & DeSantis, 1994).

Issues in the community may reach a level that also creates an inhospitable environment for the manager. Generally, research has identified community conflict as a contributor to manager turnover (Feiock & Stream, 1998). Other issues that may impact turnover include fiscal stress (Tekniepe & Stream, 2012) that may be blamed on the manager, public safety problems, or economic development strains.

Local government managers can be dismissed without cause.

Not only can community turmoil over an issue affect the tenure of a given manager, it can have implications for the success of the form of government more generally. In 2005, the Supreme Court ruled in *Kelo v. City of New London, CT,* that economic development is a legitimate public purpose and therefore, private property can be seized and redeveloped for economic development. This decision was very unpopular in the city of New London, particularly because the primary developer backed out of the project, leaving vacant property where private homes had once stood. In 2007, voters elected through referendum to modify New London's charter, changing from the council–manager form to the mayor–council form.

Pull factors relate to managers' competitiveness for other jobs and their openness to seeking other positions. There is some evidence that higher levels of education both make it more likely that a manager will seek employment advancement elsewhere (DeHoog & Whitaker, 1990) and that higher education provides some safeguard against being asked to leave (Feiock & Stream, 1998; Tekniepe & Stream, 2012). As the field has grown more professionalized, there is some evidence to suggest that careerism leads to managers holding more positions than in the past (Nalbandian, 1991; Renner, 1990).

Other factors that have been found to have an association with manager turnover cannot be classified as push or pull. For example, research in large counties found that managers who were hired from within had a longer tenure than those hired externally (Tekniepe & Stream, 2012). Some managers report that they seek positions with greater stability for their family's sake (Hassett & Watson, 2002).

Generally, managers' decisions to stay in a community or go elsewhere depend on whether the managers are experiencing satisfaction with the job. Research has shown that external motivators such as salary level do matter to managers but so do intrinsic motivators (Zhang, Yao, & Cheong, 2011). In surveys, managers report having greater satisfaction when they have policy-making influence, a positive relationship with members of council, and a belief in the effectiveness of council (DeSantis, Glass, & Newell, 1992; Zhang et al., 2011).

ROLES OF THE LOCAL GOVERNMENT MANAGER

MICHAEL BAKER
ASSISTANT MANAGER, DOWNERS GROVE, ILLINOIS

I have found a career in local government management to be rewarding in many ways. It's professionally challenging, deeply connects me to my local community and offers tremendous opportunities for growth and development. As a Deputy Manager, I am able to take on substantial responsibilities that help to leave a legacy of strong professional management in the community.

Local government managers differ in how they spend their working time. These differences are the result of a number of factors, including the size of the community, the engagement level of the elected body, the size of the staff, the culture of the organization, and the leadership style of the manager and mayor.

Policy versus Administration

Perhaps the key consideration a manager needs to make is how much time to devote to the policy process versus administrative tasks. The question of how to strike the correct balance between politics and administration has been an ongoing one since the inception of the profession. (See Chapter 6 for a discussion of the politics–administration dichotomy from the elected official perspective.)

A key debate in the field has concerned whether or not there should or could be a dichotomy between politics and administration. A dichotomy would mean that the manager does not engage in any political or policy activity and elected officials do not intervene in administrative duties. Conceptually, this would mean the manager is able to remain neutral, relying on his or her professional expertise, and does not provide opinions or have an active role in the policy process.

While this concept may have sounded good in the abstract—meaning managers stay out of policy decisions—it is not consistent with the theory of the council–manager plan nor is it realistic in practice. Research of documents related to this question dating back to the early 1900s show that the endorsers of the council–manager plan in the National Municipal League and early local government managers realized that the manager has a critically important role in the policy process (Nelson & Svara, 2014a).

The influential work of James Svara on the relationship between policy and administration in local government suggests that the relationship between elected officials and managers is a complementary one (Svara, 2002). According to Svara, "The complementarity of politics and administration is based on the premise that elected officials and administrators join together in a common pursuit of sound governance" (p. 179). Their responsibilities and roles overlap at times, but ideally, they will work in partnership toward a better government.

Svara argues that the relationship between politics and administration in local government has always been one of complementarity. Although a number of scholars assert that there once existed a dichotomy in the council–manager profession, research on the early papers of the profession show that was not the case (Nelson & Svara, 2014a). There is evidence that the manager has always served an advisory role to the council in the policy process. In addition, the manager has always played a role in the broader community. Moreover, Nelson and Svara did find evidence that the community role has grown from being directed to information sharing and actively seeking citizen engagement.

Role Differences between Local Government Managers and Chief Administrative Officers

Professional management of local governments is not confined to the council–manager form. Municipalities and counties using the mayor–council, commission, and town meeting forms of government often have the option to add a CAO to the organization. The level of authority and independence granted the CAO can vary vastly from one community to the next.

A mayor–council government can have a strong mayor with a CAO. In that case, the mayor would be the person who appoints and directs the work of the CAO. There are, however, two other ways to appoint the CAO that provide greater potential interaction with the city council. In some mayor–council cities, the council must approve the appointment of the CAO, and in others, the mayor and council jointly make the appointment. In some communities, the appointed CAO has power and authority that is equivalent to that of a manager under the council–manager form. In states such as Wisconsin and Illinois, municipalities can use ordinances to approximate the council–manager form while switching to the statutory council–manager form, which requires a referendum. Therefore, it is much easier to institute a mayor–council with CAO form and delegate similar powers to the CAO that would normally be assigned to the manager than it is to have an official council–manager form of government. However, because statute or charter does not protect the powers and position of the manager, the council can alter the position through a simple ordinance, providing the CAO with less stability and certainty about the position.

When considering whether a job as a CAO in the mayor–council form is equivalent to the top job in a council–manager community, a prospective candidate should consider both the list of duties assigned to the CAO and how those duties are assigned. If the assignments are determined by the mayor, the CAO is, in effect, an extension of the mayor's office. If the duties and authority are delineated in ordinances, they are more definitive, although they can be modified by the council as a whole through the normal council procedure for instituting ordinances. In contrast, if the duties are specified in either charter or state law, the method for modifying those duties is a more complex procedure that will take much longer to take effect. Even if the ordinances contain a provision that states that the changes will not apply to the sitting CAO, a significant reduction in the authority through ordinances sends a disappointing message to the administrator.

David Ammons (2008) conducted a study to determine how roles of CAOs and managers differ by surveying people who have held both types of positions. One question asked them to estimate the percentage of time they spent engaged in management, policy, and political activities as both managers and CAOs. While they rated the amount of time spent on management time as roughly equivalent in the two positions, they rated the CAO job as spending more time on political activities while rating the manager as spending more time on policy activities.

Respondents were also asked to evaluate which characteristics were more closely associated with the council–manager than the city administrator positions. The majority (81%) of respondents rated the managers as having more authority to direct the management team; 75% said that the manager had greater responsibility, too.

However, when asked which position had more influence on budgetary matters, only 47% identified the manager as having greater influence. The majority (52%) said that it was about equal. Ammons states that conclusions that the CAO brings the same level of professionalism to mayor–council governments that managers bring to theirs are overstated.

In a survey of managers and CAOs in 1997, Svara (1999) found similar results. City managers rated their influence in decisions about the budget and economic development higher than did the CAOs. In the mayor–council cities, the method of appointing the CAO made a difference. Those appointed by the council perceived their influence to be greater than those appointed by the mayor. Differences in the structure of the two systems and variations in the mayor–council form led to differences in how power, authority, and role expectations were perceived.

The profession of the local government manager is an exciting one. Managers rarely remain in the same community throughout their careers. While this can be unsettling to some, especially those moves that result due to firing or forced resignations, it can also provide a sense of excitement and new challenges to the managers. Given the opening up of the field due to pending retirements, the next generation of managers will have new opportunities not seen for a generation.

Managers are tasked with counseling elected officials regarding the identification of issues and alternative policy options and with the day-to-day running of a local government as well as shaping its planning for the future. To carry out these tasks, they must also be leaders who are able to create a bridge between the policy directives of elected officials, the needs and aspirations of their communities, and the skills and abilities of their staff.

MANAGERS AS LEADERS

Leadership of a public organization is necessarily more complex than that of a private organization, and perhaps no public sector leadership environment is as complex as that of the local government manager. Public sector organizational leaders must contend with multiple competing interests, an environment that is infused with politics, and a level of transparency to both the media and the citizens that is unmatched in the private sector or at other levels of government. At the local level, all of these factors are heightened further by the smaller size of the organization and constituency being served, bringing the managers and elected officials in closer proximity to the people they serve. Services provided by local governments have the greatest impacts on the day-to-day lives of citizens.

KIMIKO GILMORE
ASSISTANT CITY MANAGER, KANSAS CITY, MISSOURI

My career in local government was not a path that I chose, it chose me. After receiving my MPA, I was working for a presidential campaign and after it concluded, a new councilman asked me to work with him. That was when I fell in love with local government. Crafting legislation at the local level was truly a civic engagement activity. Citizen input emanating from town halls, kitchen table talks, calls, letters and e-mails were all used to ensure that the constituents received what they needed. I began to understand the almost immediate impact that local government action has on communities.

Years later, after a successful run in nonprofit management and a period working for a U.S. Senator, an opportunity at the city to work for the city manager came my way. Without hesitation, I applied for the position and was fortunate to be offered the job. Since that time, my appreciation for local government has grown. Working for a city, county, town, or village is a tremendous responsibility. Every aspect of what makes communities work is implemented by local government officials who have expertise in many areas. Engineering, social work, law, science of all types, finance, architecture—most professions have a place in local government.

The level of professionalism that is demonstrated daily by these individuals may go unnoticed, which is a very good thing. It's when a crisis occurs and is not managed in a reasonable amount of time that one understands the value of local government leadership. When it's done right, when management invests in the professional development of their team in order that they can offer the highest level of service to residents, the result is a community where people want live, work and grow.

Local government managers have two primary leadership roles: leader of the local government organization and community leader. The role of the manager as the chief administrator, the person who controls day-to-day operations and short- and long-term planning, is the one that is probably foremost in most people's minds when they think of the job of a local government manager. However, the increasingly complex interorganizational and intergovernmental environments that exist in the modern metropolis have led to the community leadership role taking on additional importance.

The choice to add a professional manager to a local government is one that brings benefits to both the organization and the community. Most managers have training and education that allows them to improve both the governance of the organization and the relationships with citizens and other stakeholders. The ICMA's Task Force on Professionalism developed an inventory of the ways that managers add value to their communities and to their organizations (Keene, Nalbandian, O'Neill, Portillo, & Svara, 2007).

One of the key values they discuss is the input managers provide during the public policy process, which results in more quality policies and positive results for their communities. Unlike elected officials, local government managers' tenure typically runs longer than the electoral term and is not representing a single district, so this provides the local government with someone in leadership with a long-term, community-wide perspective. Through their training, managers are taught how to evaluate performance and promote innovation as well as to produce greater efficiency and effectiveness.

The local government management profession is also grounded in a code of ethics that will be discussed in more detail later in the chapter. Managers are committed to personally adhering to ethical standards and promoting ethical behavior in their organizations. More broadly, the values that local government managers support lead them to engage in community building and promotion of the democratic process. Likewise, professional managers take measures to implement equitable processes within their organizations and to seek fair outcomes through the provision of local government services.

Management versus Leadership: What's the Difference?

Some assume that leadership and management go hand-in-hand. But, in fact, a person can be a manager without being a leader. Leadership is not automatically assigned through position in the organization. Instead, leadership comes from leaders interacting with their followers.

There exist many definitions of leadership. As Stodgill pointed out in 1974, "There are almost as many different definitions of leadership as there are persons who have attempted to define the concept" (p. 7). While most people believe they know leadership when they see it, defining it is difficult, given the many dimensions of leadership. A selection of definitions includes the following:

- "A process of motivating people to work together collaboratively to accomplish great things" (Vroom & Jago, 2007, p. 18).

- "A process whereby an individual influences a group of individuals to achieve a common goal" (Northouse, 2016, p. 7).

- "Leadership involves a relationship between people in which influence and power are unevenly distributed on a legitimate basis" and "in order for there to be a leader, there must be a follower" (Ott, Parkes, & Simpson, 2008, p. 33).

Distilling the overlapping elements of the three definitions above leads to the conclusion that leadership is a process that involves the interaction of individuals—the leader and the follower(s)—toward the pursuit of goals.

However, these definitions do nothing to distinguish between the concepts of *leadership* and *management*. One key difference between the two is that managers achieve their status through their position in an organization. A leader can emerge from anywhere in an organization's hierarchy. So, in addition to the fact that a person can be a manager but not a leader, a person can also be a leader without being a manager.

One of the earliest attempts in public administration to describe the functions of a manager was the seminal work by Gulick and Urwick, *Papers on the Science of Administration* (1937). A good manager must handle the daily tasks of running an organization and must do so efficiently. As discussed in Chapter 10, Gulick and Urwick developed the acronym POSDCORB to succinctly describe the functions of the manager.

These functions, when done well, allow a large organization to be run effectively on a day-to-day basis. However, these tasks do not constitute leadership. Although the manager must select staff and direct them, a leader does more than simply direct people.

Just as leadership theorists have struggled to develop a single definition of leadership, so has the question of distinguishing between leadership and management been a perennial one. Bennis (2009) created a list of 12 differences between leaders and managers. Bennis argues that leaders are more innovative, forward thinking, and independent than managers. While not universally flattering, and perhaps a negation of management's importance that goes too far, Bennis's list does point out that management tends to be defined more by daily tasks, while leadership, especially transformational leadership, means acting as a visionary.

Table 5.3 summarizes the distinctions between leadership and management from some of the most well-known leadership experts. The legitimacy of the manager comes from his or her position in the organization, whereas leaders use their skills in inspiring people to gain their cooperation, regardless of their formal level of authority. In the case of local government managers, it is essential that the CAO be both a skilled leader and a skilled manager to optimally run the organization.

TABLE 5.3 ■ Leadership versus Management		
Leadership	**Management**	**Source**
Do things right	Do the right thing	Bennis, 2009
Getting people to want to do what needs to be done	Getting people to do what needs to be done	Bennis, 1994
Innovate	Administer	Carter-Scott, 1994
Effectiveness	Efficiency	Covey, 2004
Long-term thinking	Short-term thinking	Gardner, 1990
Coping with change	Coping with complexity	Kotter, 1999
Guide to new and unexplored territory	Handle things; maintain order, organization, and control	Kouzes & Posner, 2012
Architect	Builder	Mariotti, 1998
Persuading	Commanding	Weathersby, 1999

THE LOCAL GOVERNMENT MANAGER AS ORGANIZATIONAL LEADER

The management tasks of the local government CAO are key to achieving a high-functioning organization. Good management makes organizational leadership easier to achieve. A key aspect of leading a local government is being able to facilitate the political–administrative relationship (Whitaker & Jenne, 1995). Managers

BILL HORNE
CITY MANAGER, CLEARWATER, FLORIDA

I was drawn to the city manager profession out of my sense of call to public service. I retired from the United States Air Force with 27 years of wonderful service and had the privilege of performing an assignment very similar to what a city manager does outside of Tokyo, Japan. This experience confirmed what I wanted to [do] post retirement and [I] was very fortunate to be in the right place at the right time in local government [in Clearwater]. I have been able to use all of my accumulated leadership and management experience to serve a local community and its leaders that want to be the best it can be.

connect the elected board to the departments of the local government. Accepting that politics at the local level is unavoidable for the manager leads to the understanding that the manager will play a key role in enabling the relationship between staff and elected officials.

Elected officials must trust that the manager and the staff are professional experts. However, managers and staff should also have an understanding that they take direction from the elected officials. Managers must have good relationships with elected officials for the government to operate efficiently and effectively.

Unique Challenges to Leading in Local Government

Local government organizations possess unique management and leadership challenges not found in the private sector. Jim Collins, author of *Good to Great* (2001), wrote a monograph for the social sectors that explains that public organizations should not seek to run themselves as businesses. Not all businesses are great, but all organizations should seek to be great.

When public sector organizations seek greatness, the traits that set them apart from private organizations can present challenges. For example, Collins describes how power is diffused in public sector organizations. In local governments, the CAO does not have unilateral authority. The CAO takes policy direction from the elected officials. The elected officials themselves share authority, so consensus is not always possible. This leaves the managers in situations without clear direction. Choosing one policy alternative over another can be interpreted as the manager taking sides. Because power is so diffuse, Collins argues that public sector leaders must draw on legislative leadership. Since no one person has sufficient power to make significant unilateral decisions, legislative leadership draws on the powers of "persuasion, political currency, and shared interests" (Collins, 2001, p. 11).

Another issue that is particular to government is that hiring and firing of staff is constrained by the civil service system. Rules that were put in place to encourage merit hiring today may limit the choices of managers when dealing with issues with staff. Collins argues that it is just as important to be able to "get the wrong people off the bus" as it is to get the "right people on the bus" (Collins, 2011, p. 44). In government, civil service protections and due process regulations can make it difficult to dismiss employees who do not perform well. City and county managers typically have considerable discretion when making hiring and firing decisions. However, rules and regulations vary by state and jurisdiction, so there may be more or less autonomy regarding staffing, depending on the state and the organization.

The differences between public and private organizations highlighted by Collins leads to the conclusion that local government managers have to be creative in the ways they lead and motivate within their organizations. Most studies on how leadership quality affects organizational performance deal with private industry alone. However, research in local governments has found that those managers who are perceived as high-quality leaders are able to create organizations that are more innovative (Gabris, Golembiewski, & Ihrke, 2000; Gabris & Nelson, 2013). High-quality local government leadership is also associated with local governing boards that experience less dysfunctional conflict (Nelson & Nollenberger, 2011). Other studies have found high-quality leadership in local government to be associated with the use of performance measures (Moynihan, Pandey, & Wright, 2012)—an example of management supporting leadership.

Manager Fit with the Community

Another part of the equation that may determine the success of managers as organizational leaders is whether the fit between the manager and the community is a good one. Unlike private sector jobs, in local government management, the person hired as CAO must not only be compatible with the organization itself but with the elected board and with the community. If a manager's personality does not fit with existing expectations of the elected officials or with the culture of the organization, it will likely mean a short tenure for the manager.

One study that examined manager fit found that although the literature in city and county management promotes the idea of the manager as a transformational leader—visionary, mission driven, and high achieving—it is the manager who is perceptive, inwardly driven, and not high achieving who has the longest tenure (Hanbury, Sapat, & Washington, 2004). Their research provides evidence that managers keep their jobs longer if they keep their heads down. The research fails to consider, however, that managers who are active in pursuing goals and innovation in one jurisdiction may be likely to pursue a vacancy in another jurisdiction that offers new opportunities, challenges, and rewards. Consequently, these managers will have a shorter tenure because they choose to move. Furthermore, it is likely that a transformational manager will be successful if that is what the elected officials expect of him or her.

A recent example of this disconnect occurred in Charlotte, North Carolina. In 2016, the city council chose not to renew the contract of Ron Carlee, city manager since 2013. Carlee was Charlotte's first outside hire for city manager since 1981, having previously worked as Arlington, Virginia's county manager and later for the ICMA. When hired, council members indicated they wanted an effective spokesperson for the city. The mayor was arrested for public corruption shortly after Carlee began working as manager, and Carlee spoke to the press about how the council–manager form provided protection against bribery and other forms of corruption. Carlee also took a public role in the city's effort to prevent a state takeover of the airport and the city's defense in a potentially racially divisive police shooting. However, despite the encouragement of the council for Carlee to take a public role when they first hired him, according to news reports, some council members believed Carlee had become too outspoken (Harrison, 2016), and this was ultimately behind the pressure he received to resign. Carlee acted as a transformational leader, being out front on several key issues facing the city and making substantial changes to the organization, but it was controversy over this role that contributed to his short tenure.

Part of the problem with assessing manager fit to a community is determining the expectations of all involved. Even managers differ in what they consider the best leadership style (Fairholm, 2006). Some managers try to adhere to a very task-oriented, management-only style. At the other end of the spectrum, some managers believe in a whole-soul leadership style—leadership as a spiritual endeavor. Because people have different perspectives on what constitutes leadership, there may be conflict about whether or not a person is doing a good job. When this occurs, it is likely that the manager's tenure will be a short one.

When looking for a CAO position, prospective managers should seek to determine the culture of the community and the organization. They should also be familiar with the leadership style of their predecessor (if there was one) and determine whether that style was one that the elected officials were happy with. Candidates should be honest with themselves about their own leadership style and not believe that they can adapt to a setting that does not fit with their personality.

Other aspects of managing a municipality or county, particularly a smaller one, make fitting in with the community critical. Some managers describe their jobs as "leading in a fishbowl" (Morris et al., 2008). Managers live in the communities they serve. Their positions tend to be ones of greater visibility, compared to other jobs. For the manager, this means that he or she is often recognizable to a large number of residents—the manager is rarely completely off duty. They have to assume that people recognize them and behave accordingly. In addition, the job can affect the manager's family—whether it is a conflict of interest with a spouse's employment or the manager's children being confronted by schoolmates about something happening in town, the family is likely to be affected in some way.

Being a city or county manager is not easy. In addition to living in a fishbowl, the manager is always faced with multiple, competing interests (Beets, 2011). These competing interests lead to a set of leadership challenges. While managers are tasked with recommending good public policy, there are always political considerations to be made. The best policy option may be the least popular from the perspective of citizens. Another challenge is that the manager must be both authoritative and a consensus builder. Dealing with various levels of staff, the manager must act with authority. But managers are also asked to build consensus with community members. Switching gears is not always easy to do.

Managers must also balance efficiency and equity concerns. While trying to provide services at the lowest cost and highest quality possible, managers must also ensure that the procedures and outcomes of the policy are fair. Efficiency and effectiveness are not sufficient to ensure fair treatment of individuals when implementing policies. If an individual or group is negatively and disproportionately affected or positively rewarded through a policy, the manager should seek to mitigate the inequity.

THE MANAGER'S CODE OF ETHICS

SCOTT LAZENBY
CITY MANAGER, LAKE OSWEGO, OREGON

The city manager's ability to make a real difference in a community can be deeply satisfying. As with other professions, a job well done is its own reward. But the city manager's close physical connection with the local community, and close personal connection with individuals in the community provide immediate and tangible evidence of the city manager's influence in a way that is reflected in few other professions.

The tremendous variety the city manager's job brings can also be exhilarating for individuals who thrive on change.

How to ensure accountability of public sector managers and staff in an environment of diffuse power and limited direct supervision has been an open question in public administration since the field was founded. Local government managers are not elected, so they cannot draw their authority directly from the voters. In the early 1940s, the debate between Carl J. Friedrich and Herman Finer set the stage for the basic question of public administrator accountability. Friedrich argued that traditional methods of accountability, primarily direct oversight, were unnecessary for public administrators because their professionalism, knowledge, and expertise serve as internal checks on accountability. Finer counterargued that despite greater professionalism, oversight by elected officials was still necessary to ensure that the democratic process would be intact (Jackson, 2009).

Dunn and Legge (2000) argue that the relationship is more complicated than either Friedrich or Finer would allow, that local government managers look to their profession when defining their responsibilities but to their elected officials when considering new policy options. This perspective is consistent with the council–manager form of government. Municipal and county managers rely a great deal on their professional training to handle oversight of government operations. However, when considering the suggestion of policy alternatives, they must also consider, to some degree, how the various options will fit with the goals of the elected body.

It is not possible for the elected officials to exercise daily direct oversight of the municipal or county manager. In addition to training and education, managers who are members of ICMA adhere to a strict professional code of ethics. The ICMA Code of Ethics (see Appendix 1) provides a set of 12 tenets with guidelines to aid managers when making decisions. The Code has been in place since 1924 and it has evolved over time as the profession has changed. Members of the organization sign a statement affirming their adherence to the Code. One of the most important aspects of the ICMA Code of Ethics is the enforcement provisions that back it up. When an ethics complaint is filed against a member, a peer review body called the ICMA Committee on Professional Conduct reviews the complaint and determines whether or not sanctions are warranted. Sanctions vary from a private censure to a lifetime membership ban. In 2014, ICMA reviewed 19 ethics complaints against its members. Of the 19, five resulted in public censures, five resulted in private censures, and nine cases were closed. Common offenses that result in public censure include driving under the influence, misuse of public funds, political activities, and personal relationships with subordinates. Those resulting in private censure are usually related to employment searches and tenure, for example, staying on a job for less than two years (ICMA, 2014).

Some local government managers who choose not to join ICMA may instead join state managers' associations or the American Society for Public Administration (ASPA). ASPA recently amended their code of ethics and has also adopted enforcement provisions. Codes of ethics may be adopted at the local level as well. State chapters of ICMA often have their own codes of ethics with enforcement provisions. Increasingly, cities and counties are adopting their own codes of ethics for both elected officials and staff.

Ethical dilemmas—a case in which a decision may not be clear from a single ethical perspective—are common in government. James Svara (2007) argues that in these cases, public sector leaders rely on an "ethics triangle" to guide their decision (see Figure 5.1). The ethics triangle is built around four ethical philosophies: duty, principle, virtue, and consequences.

FIGURE 5.1 ■ Svara's Ethics Triangle

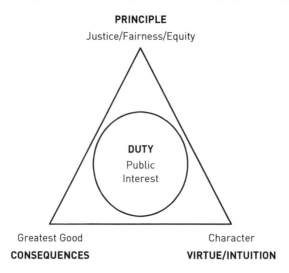

PRINCIPLE
Justice/Fairness/Equity

DUTY
Public
Interest

Greatest Good
CONSEQUENCES

Character
VIRTUE/INTUITION

Source: Adapted from Svara, James H., 1997, "The Ethical Triangle: Synthesizing the Bases of Administrative Ethics." *Public Integrity Annual*, 1997. Used with permission.

Duty is the responsibility a public sector employee or manager has to serve the public interest. Public servants are entrusted as stewards of the public interest. They are to put the public interest above their interests as individuals.

A decision that is ethical based on *principle* is one that is fair. It is considered just and equitable. Rules and laws are based on the principle basis of ethics. Certain actions are judged right or wrong by law.

The qualities that define whether a person is good or bad determine *virtue*. This form of ethics is based on the character and integrity of the individual. People have difficulty making choices that violate their own personal conceptions of right or wrong.

Finally, when making a decision, the manager may try to assess the *consequences* of the decision and seek to provide the greatest good for the greatest number of people. Alone, each of these sources of ethics provides some guidance as to how to act, but in some cases, a problem or situation may not be clear-cut. When using multiple perspectives, the manager gains a fuller perspective of the various elements of right and wrong in the situation.

Svara (2007) uses hypothetical cases to illustrate examples using the ethics triangle. One of these cases describes a candidate for city manager who is asked by the council to agree to fire one of the department heads and is told that the other candidates have agreed to do the firing. There are beneficial consequences to that decision, primarily that it gives the candidate a better chance at getting the job. The candidate may also believe that he or she is the most qualified for the job and so will be able to make positive changes in the organization and the community. However, these positive consequences are not sufficient to override concerns of duty and principle. As manager, it is his or her duty to make personnel decisions. In principle, the decision to fire the department head at council direction is not fair. Also, if the manager does fire the department head, he or she has established a precedent for encroachment from the council.

Having an established code of ethics does not make the tough choices of a local government manager easy. It does provide managers with guidance, however. Part of the excitement and challenge of a career in local government management is that the job is not the easiest. Every day presents a new opportunity to make a difference in the lives of the residents of communities throughout the country.

MAKING THE CASE FOR A CAREER IN LOCAL GOVERNMENT MANAGEMENT

SEAN STEGALL
TOWN MANAGER, CARY, NORTH CAROLINA

As town manager, I am in the unique position to serve the community with my colleagues while also serving as a coach to help them achieve their professional goals.

In an era where politics often trumps governance at "higher" levels of government, throughout my career, I have experienced the direct opposite at the local level. The vast majority of those council members I have worked for have been driven simply by making their community a better place. As a manager, I have the privilege of working with them to translate that collective goal into actual projects that make the world a better place, one community at a time.

As the testimonials from managers and assistant managers included in this chapter demonstrate, people who choose a career in local government management do so for many different reasons. However, all managers value their role as public servants and their ability to contribute to a better quality of life for the residents of the communities they serve. Perhaps in no other public sector career are administrators able to have such a close and authentic connection to those served by their organization.

The job of a local government manager is not an easy one, but the challenges make it interesting, ever changing, and rewarding.

REFERENCES

Ammons, D. N. (2008). City manager and city administrator role similarities and differences: Perceptions among persons who have served as both. *The American Review of Public Administration, 38*(1), 24–40.

Beets, N. (2011, April). Why being a manager is tough. *Public Management,* 12–14.

Bennis, W. (1994). Leading change: The leader as the chief transformation officer. In J. Renesch (Ed.), *Leadership in a new era: Visionary approaches to the biggest crisis of our time* (pp. 102–110). San Francisco, CA: New Leaders Press.

Bennis, W. (2009). *On becoming a leader.* Philadelphia, PA: Basic Books.

Brownlow, L. (1922). *Eighth yearbook of the city managers' association.* Washington, DC: ICMA.

Carter-Scott, C. (1994). The differences between management and leadership. *Manage, 46*(2), 10–12.

Cedar Rapids. (2016). *Charter of the city of Cedar Rapids, Iowa.* Retrieved April 2, 2017, from http://www.cedar-rapids.org/local_government/about_city_government/home_rule_charter.php#content

City Management Intl. (1996). *The municipal year book 1996* (E. Moulder, Ed.). Chicago, IL: ICMA.

Collins, J. C. (2001). *Good to great and the social sectors: A monograph to accompany good to great.* New York, NY: Harper Collins.

Covey, S. R. (2004). *The 8th habit: From effectiveness to greatness.* New York, NY: Free Press.

DeHoog, R. H., & Whitaker, G. P. (1990). Political conflict or professional advancement: Alternative explanations of city manager turnover. *Journal of Urban Affairs, 12*(4), 361–377.

DeSantis, V. S., Glass, J. J., & Newell, C. (1992). City managers, job satisfaction, and community problem perceptions. *Public Administration Review, 52*(5), 447–453.

Dunn, D. D., & Legge, J. S., Jr. (2000). U.S. local government managers and the complexity of responsibility and accountability in democratic governance. *Journal of Public Administration Research and Theory, 11*(1), 73–88.

Fairholm, M. (2006, October). I know it when I see it: How local government managers see leadership differently. *Public Management,* 10–15.

Feiock, R. C., & Stream, C. (1998). Explaining the tenure of local government managers. *Journal of Public Administration Research and Theory, 8*(1), 117–130.

Gabris, G. T., Golembiewski, R. T., & Ihrke, D. M. (2000). Leadership credibility, board relations, and administrative innovation at the local government level. *Journal of Public Administration Research and Theory, 11*(1), 89–108.

Gabris, G. T., & Nelson, K. L. (2013). Transforming municipal boards into accountable, high-performing teams: Toward a diagnostic model of governing board effectiveness. *Public Performance and Management Review, 36*(3), 473–496.

Gardner, J. W. (1990). *On leadership*. New York, NY: Collier Macmillan.

Gulick, L. H., & Urwick, L. (1937). *Papers on the science of administration*. New York, NY: Institute of Public Administration.

Hanbury, G. L., Sapat, A., & Washington, C. W. (2004). Know yourself and take charge of your own destiny: The "fit model" of leadership. *Public Administration Review, 64*(5), 566–576.

Harrison, S. (2016, February 24). Ron Carlee to step down as Charlotte city manager. *The Charlotte Observer*. Retrieved March 15, 2017, from http://www.charlotteobserver.com/news/politics-government/article62287862.html

Hassett, W. L., & Watson, D. J. (2002). Long-serving city managers: Practical application of the academic literature. *Public Administration Review, 62*, 622–629.

International City/County Management Association. (1975). *The municipal year book 1975*. Chicago, IL: Author.

International City/County Management Association. (1984). *Municipal year book, 1984*. Chicago, IL: Author.

International City/County Management Association. (1985). *The municipal year book 1985*. Chicago, IL: Author.

International City/County Management Association. (2001). *The municipal year book 2001*. Chicago, IL: Author.

International City/County Management Association. (2013). *ICMA 2012 state of the profession survey results*. Washington, DC: Author. Retrieved March 14, 2017, from http://icma.org/en/icma/knowledge_network/documents/kn/Document/305096/ICMA_2012_State_of_the_Profession_Survey_Results

International City/County Management Association. (2014). *ICMA ethics program report 2014*. Washington, DC: Author. Retrieved March 15, 2017, from http://icma.org/en/icma/knowledge_network/documents/kn/Document/307232/ICMA_Ethics_Program_Report_2014.

Jackson, M. (2009). Responsibility versus accountability in the Friedrich–Finer debate. *Journal of Management History*, *15*(1), 66–77.

Keene, J., Nalbandian, J., O'Neill, R., Jr., Portillo, S., & Svara, J. (2007, March). How professionals can add value to their communities and organizations. *Public Management*, 33–40.

Kotter, J. P. (1999). *What leaders really do*. Boston, MA: Harvard Business Review.

Kouzes, J., & Posner, B. (2012). *The leadership challenge: How to make extraordinary things happen in organizations* (5th ed.). San Francisco, CA: Jossey-Bass.

Lyon County, Nevada. (2016). *Lyon County, Nevada county code*. Retrieved April 2, 2017, from http://www.sterlingcodifiers.com/codebook/m_index.php?book_id=536

Mariotti, J. (1998). Leadership matters: So does the soft side of management. *Industry Week*, *247*(6), 70.

McCabe, B. C., Feiock, R. C., Clingermayer, J. C., & Stream, C. (2008). Turnover among city managers: The role of political and economic change. *Public Administration Review*, *68*(2), 380–386.

Morris, R., Enevoldsen, D., Johnson, S., Jordan, R., Sigman, S., & Ward, C. (2008, May). Living in a fishbowl. *Public Management*, 6–14.

Moynihan, D. P., Pandey, S. K., & Wright, B. E. (2012). Setting the table: How transformational leadership fosters performance information use. *Journal of Public Administration Research and Theory*, *22*(1), 143–164.

Nalbandian, J. (1991). *Professionalism in local government*. San Francisco, CA: Jossey-Bass.

Nelson, K. L., & Nollenberger, K. (2011). Conflict and cooperation in municipalities: Do variations in form of government have an effect? *Urban Affairs Review*, *47*(5), 696–720.

Nelson, K. L., & Svara, J. H. (2014a). The roles of local government managers in theory and practice: A centennial perspective. *Public Administration Review*, *75*(1), 49–61.

Nelson, K. L., & Svara, J. H. (2014b). Upholding and expanding the roles of local government managers: State of the profession 2012. In *The municipal year book 2014* (pp. 3–19). Washington, DC: ICMA Press.

Nolting, O. F., Arnold, D. S., & Powers, S. P. (Eds.). (1965). *The municipal year book, 1965*. Chicago, IL: ICMA.

Northouse, P. G. (2016). *Leadership theory and practice* (7th ed.). Thousand Oaks, CA: SAGE.

Ott, J. S., Parkes, S. J., & Simpson, R. B. (2008). *Classic readings in organizational behavior* (4th ed.). Belmont, CA: Thomson Wadsworth.

Renner, T. (1990). Appointed local government managers: Stability and change. In E. R. Moulder (Ed.), *The municipal year book* (pp. 30–41). Washington, DC: ICMA.

Renner, T. (2001). The local government profession at century's end. In ICMA (Ed.), *The municipal year book 2001*. Washington, DC: ICMA.

Renner, T., & DeSantis, V. S. (1994). City manager turnover: The impact of formal authority and electoral change. *State and Local Government Review*, *26*(2), 104–111.

Ridley, C. E., & Nolting, O. F. (Eds.). (1940). *The municipal year book, 1940*. Chicago, IL: ICMA.

Rio Rancho. (2016). *Rio Rancho municipal code*. Code Publishing Company: Seattle, WA. Retrieved April 2, 2017, from http://www.codepublishing.com/NM/RioRancho/html/RioRanchoNT.html

Stodgill, R.M. (1974). *Handbook of leadership: A survey of theory and research*. New York, NY: The Free Press.

Stone, H. K., Price, D. K., & Stone, K. H. (1940). *City manager government in the United States: A review after 25 years*. Chicago, IL: Public Administration Service.

Svara, J. H. (1999). U.S. city managers and administrators in a global perspective. *The municipal year book* (pp. 25–33). Washington, DC: International City/County Management Association.

Svara, J. H. (2002). The myth of the dichotomy: Complementarity of politics and administration in the past and future of public administration. *Public Administration Review*, *61*(2), 176–183.

Svara, J. H. (2007). *The ethics primer for public administrators in government and nonprofit organizations*. Sudbury, MA: Jones and Bartlett.

Tekniepe, R. J., & Stream, C. (2012). You're fired! County manager turnover in large American cities. *American Review of Public Administration, 42*(6), 715–729.

Vanderleeuw, J., Sides, J., & Williams, B. (2015). An advanced degree in public administration—Is it valued by city councils? *Public Administration Quarterly, 39*(3), 453–483.

Vroom, V. R., & Jago, A. G. (2007). The role of the situation in leadership. *American Psychologist, 62*(1), 17–24.

Watson, D. J., & Hassett, W. L. (2004). Career paths of city managers in America's largest council–manager cities. *Public Administration Review, 64*(2), 192–199.

Watson, D. J., & Watson, R. J. (2006). *Spending a lifetime: The careers of city managers.* Athens, GA: Carl Vinson Institute of Government.

Weathersby, G. (1999). Leadership vs. management. *Management Review, 88*(3), 5.

Whitaker, G. P., & Jenne, K. (1995). Improving city managers' leadership. *State and Local Government Review, 27*(1), 84–94.

Zhang, Y., Yao, X., & Cheong, J. O. (2011). City managers' job satisfaction and frustration: Factors and implications. *The American Review of Public Administration, 41*(6), 670–685.

RESOURCE LIST/TO EXPLORE FURTHER

Books/Articles

ELGL. (2014, February 27). *The great debate: City manager vs. assistant city manager.* Available at http://www.elgl.org/2014/02/27/great-debate-city-manager-vs-assistant-city-manager/

Harlow, L. (1977). *Without fear or favor: Odyssey of a city manager.* Provo, UT: Brigham Young Press.

Stillman, R. J. (1977). The city manager: Professional helping hand, or political hired hand? *Public Administration Review, 37*(6), 658–670.

Web Resources

International City/County Management Association. Available at http://www.icma.org

ROLES AND RELATIONSHIPS

City managers everywhere have a preference
for strong and capable political leadership.

—Richard Clay Wilson, Jr. (2016, p. 86)

M ost American local governments operate under the mayor–council or the council–manager form of government.[1] The former is generally found in the largest and smallest jurisdictions, while the latter is popular in medium-sized and suburban communities. This chapter will look at the roles of elected officials and their relationships with managers chiefly through the lens of the council–manager and mayor–council forms of government.[2]

MAYORAL AUTHORITY AND ROLES

Council–Manager Mayors

The mayor's powers under the council–manager plan are quite limited, as the plan is based on the unitary principle of all powers vested in the governing body. This form of government is often equated with the American model of private corporations. A board (council) appoints a professional chief executive officer (manager) to run the day-to-day operations of the organization with broad policy direction from the board.

Frank Polich/Getty Images

Former Chicago Mayor Richard M. Daley gavels the close of his last city council meeting.

As with the mayor–council form, mayors in council–manager jurisdictions are usually directly elected. The mayor might also be the top vote getter in the council election or be chosen by the council from its membership. How the mayor is selected can have a substantial influence on the mayor's informal power. Regardless of the form of government, a mayor who is elected at-large has the power of the bully pulpit and typically has widespread name recognition. When elected at-large, many citizens will perceive the mayor as the key figure in the local government, even if the formal powers for the position are no greater than those of other elected officials. Conversely, mayors who are selected by the other members of council will have less informal power because they do not possess the same level of name recognition. Also, terms are usually shorter when a mayor is selected from among the council's membership.

Sometimes called a weak mayor, the duties of this position are chiefly ceremonial but not inconsequential. The mayor is first among equals but not a strong chief executive. In some communities, the mayor can vote only to break ties; in others, he or she may vote on all matters. The mayor usually lacks veto power, and the manager normally has authority to appoint department heads. Managers also are usually assigned the task of formulating the annual budget; in only a few municipalities does the mayor have the right to see the budget before other members of the council.

The council–manager mayor's informal power should not be trivialized. The mayor is the presiding officer and often looked to by the other council members to efficiently run meetings, ensure members are recognized and provided opportunities to speak, manage public comment periods and hearings, and deal with colleagues who disrupt the conduct of business or are uncivil to others. The mayor and manager work closely to set the agenda for council meetings and work sessions and the items to be covered and time allocations. The mayor is also in the media's spotlight as the spokesperson for the local government. Although gaveling down or expelling unruly members or citizens are tools mayors can use, they rarely do so. Instead, the mayors are expected to be facilitative leaders and skillfully exercise their informal powers and influence.

Mayor–Council Mayors

In municipal governments using the mayor–council form, the mayor is nearly always elected at-large. Unlike the council–manager form, the mayor–council form rests on the separation of powers principle between the mayor and council members. The mayor has executive power, similar to a governor or president, and the council is responsible for legislative responsibilities.

Strong mayors, similar to those seen in the cities of New York and Chicago, have a great deal of formal and informal power. Formally, they oversee daily operations of government, including developing an annual budget and handling most of the hiring and firing of staff and management. Many mayor–council mayors do not preside at the council meetings but do have the authority to veto ordinances. Informally, mayor–council mayors, particularly those in larger communities, have the power of the bully pulpit, which enables them to reach the entire constituency through the media.

Weak mayors may be found in mayor–council governments as well as council–manager governments. As in the latter form, the weak mayor–council mayor primarily holds the authority to convene council and preside at meetings but usually has no hiring and firing authority. Their roles are similar to that of a council–manager mayor, but there may not be a chief administrator. In these cases, much of the work typically done by a mayor or chief administrative officer (CAO) is instead done through board committees and increased reliance on department heads. Mayor–council mayors with limited formal authority must rely on informal powers to accomplish their goals.

In the council–manager form, research has shown that council effectiveness is positively associated with the mayor being perceived as a facilitative leader and with positive interpersonal relationships among council members (Nelson, Gabris, & Davis, 2011). According to James Svara (2009), facilitative leaders are distinguished by their attitudes toward colleagues, styles of interaction, and approach to goal setting and vision setting:

> The leader who uses the facilitative approach is committed to helping other officials accomplish their goals. He or she promotes open communication among officials. The approach to managing conflict stresses collaboration in which the interests of the leader and others are mutually satisfied. The leader shares leadership and seeks to coordinate efforts among officials. Finally, the leader seeks to create a shared vision that incorporates his or her own goals *and* the goals of others, promotes commitment to that shared vision, and focuses efforts of all involved on accomplishing the vision. (p. 11)

BASICS OF COUNCIL–MANAGER RELATIONSHIPS: A NORTH CAROLINA EXAMPLE

North Carolina has a long tradition of using professional managers to assist elected leaders in governing their communities and ensuring that local governments operate efficiently and effectively. In 1929, Robeson County became the first county in the United States to adopt the county–manager form, and in 1930, Durham County became the second. The cities of Hickory and Morganton first adopted the council–manager plan as part of their charters in 1913, just one year after the first charter adoption of the plan in the country by Sumter, South Carolina. By the time the country celebrated the 100th anniversary of the council–manager plan, all 100 of North Carolina's counties employed a county manager, all but one of the 62 cities over 10,000 population operated under the form, and 109 of the 136 municipalities between 2,500 and 9,999 population had professional managers (Stenberg, 2014, pp. 57–58).

North Carolina's laws authorizing the council–manager form of government, similar to those of most states, drew on the provisions contained in the National Civic League's *Model City Charter* (2014). The key provisions of the North Carolina General Statutes relating to municipal and county managers follow.[3]

The Municipal Manager

The powers and duties of the municipal manager are specified in North Carolina's General Statutes 160A-148. In North Carolina, cities and towns are legally identical. The introduction of the statute reads as follows: "The manager shall be the chief administrator of the city. He [or she] shall be responsible to the council for administering all municipal affairs placed in his [or her] charge by them."

Authority

The laws of North Carolina require that the city council appoint a city attorney. A city clerk is also mandated; some charters authorize the council to appoint the clerk, others specify that the manager makes this appointment, and still others are silent on the matter. In all municipalities, the clerk performs duties for the council, but some clerks report to the council and others to the manager. Some clerks are members of the city's management team. The General Statutes provide for the council to appoint the tax collector, if such position exists, although some charters authorize the manager to make this appointment. Otherwise, except for these council appointments, the manager is responsible for the hiring, supervision, disciplining, and removal of all administrative personnel in accordance with human resources rules adopted by the council. Managers consider this authority to be of critical importance, because if the council is to hold them responsible and accountable for the performance of administrative units, they must have hiring and firing authority over personnel directly responsible for the work.

Duties

Among other municipal manager statutory responsibilities are attending all meetings of the council and recommending measures that he or she deem expedient; faithfully executing all state laws, the charter, and ordinances, resolutions, and regulations of the council; preparing and submitting an annual budget and capital program; and annually submitting to the council and making available to the public a complete report on the city's finances and administrative activities as of the end of the fiscal year.

The County Manager

The powers and duties of the county manager specified in North Carolina's General Statutes (153A-82) are typical of those found in most state statutes and are consistent with the general elements of the council–manager plan in municipalities. The introduction and first subsection of the law read as follows:

> The manager is the chief administrator of county government. He [or she] is responsible to the board of commissioners for the administration of all departments of county government under the board's general control and has the following powers and duties: He [or she] shall appoint with the approval of the board of commissioners and suspend or remove all county officers, employees, and agents except those who are elected by the people or whose appointment is otherwise provided for by law. The board may by resolution permit the manager to appoint officers, employees, and agents without first securing the board's approval. The manager shall make his [or her] appointments, suspensions, and removals in accordance with any general personnel rules, regulations, policies, or ordinances that the board may adopt.

Authority

As indicated above, unlike the municipal manager in North Carolina, the county manager does not have automatic statutory authority to hire, fire, and discipline all employees not otherwise appointed by the governing board. The county manager may perform these actions only with the approval of the board of county commissioners, unless the commissioners grant the county manager the power to do so without their approval.

Under the statutes, the county manager is responsible for supervision of county operations in accordance with whatever laws, regulations, policies, direction, and guidance the board of commissioners might decide to provide. The manager "shall see that the orders, ordinances, resolutions, and regulations of the board of commissioners are faithfully executed within the county" (153A-82).

The commissioners' control is meant to be general in nature, leaving the manager to exercise professional judgment as to how to carry out the board's intent. This can be a difficult line to draw, and its actual practice varies from county to county, depending on a variety of factors such as tradition, confidence in the manager, individual personalities and styles, and issues.

As noted earlier, the manager's hiring and firing authority does not extend to administrative officers who are elected by the citizens or to those who are appointed by authorities other than the commissioners, such as the state-appointed directors of the social services, public health, and mental health agencies. In addition, the board appoints the county clerk, the county attorney, the tax assessor, and the tax collector. Thus, county managers preside over an administrative structure in which they have less and sometimes unclear authority of appointment and removal than municipal managers. To be successful, North Carolina county managers have to be more tolerant of ambiguity in their authority and more facilitative in their leadership and management styles than their counterparts in North Carolina municipalities. This is typically the case in other states.

Duties

Statutes require the county manager or his or her designee to attend all meetings of the board of commissioners and recommend any measures that he or she considers expedient. This provision acknowledges that one of the manager's fundamental responsibilities is to give professional advice and counsel to the commissioners in their deliberations to ensure that the board has access to and understands the information it needs to make informed decisions, including options and pro/con assessments. Most managers will try not to miss a board meeting and will secure the concurrence of the chair or the entire board if they must be absent. They will also make sure that an assistant or other designee chosen to act in their place is prepared to provide necessary information and advice.

Under the county–manager form of government, the manager is also the budget officer and is required to prepare a budget for consideration by the commissioners in whatever form and detail the board might specify. This is a recommended operating budget and capital program which the commissioners may modify before adopting the budget ordinance. Further, in addition to the statutorily required annual report on county finances and administrative activities as of the end of the fiscal year, the manager typically makes periodic reports to the commissioners throughout the fiscal year.

REALITIES OF COUNCIL–MANAGER ROLES AND RESPONSIBILITIES

In over 100 years, the main elements of the council–manager plan have changed very little in the design of roles and responsibilities. But significant changes in the political and social landscape of contemporary local government have affected the dynamics of manager–elected official relationships.[4]

In 1993, the International City/County Management Association (ICMA) convened a task force of municipal and county managers to examine council–manager relations in light of the forces and tensions that were affecting the form of government at that time (ICMA, 1993a, 1993b, 1993c). Two important changes in the local environment that the panel identified were that citizens were losing respect for politics, government institutions, and public officials and that the public was fragmenting into organized interest groups with competing narrow agendas and an unwillingness to cooperate. As a result, managers were receiving mixed signals and sometimes faced irresolvable conflicts of expectations from elected officials and citizens. The latter trend was exacerbated in communities where the directly elected mayor viewed the manager as a competitor for local leadership and media attention.

Also in 1993, an article was published in ICMA's monthly magazine, *Public Management,* presenting research findings on council members' perceptions of the council–manager relationship (Mathis, 1993). It identified seven unspoken concerns and beliefs often held by governing body members that can harm the relationships between elected officials and the manager. The first two indicate a lack of trust on the part of elected officials toward the manager: Managers hide money amidst complex budget accounts, arcane language, and detailed provisions and are reluctant to inform governing bodies how much discretionary money is available and managers have personal agendas that they advance, especially when the governing body is divided. Three others indicate actions by elected officials that can lead to a less than high performing council–manager government: Governing bodies will not acknowledge or deal with personality conflicts with their manager; members want to hire their own manager, so newly elected officials may not be committed to the current manager; and governing bodies do not take seriously the task of evaluating the manager, in part because they have not set clear goals and objectives for the community or staff. Finally, elected officials may have unreal and differing expectations about what the role of the local government manager should be: Managers should be out in front of issues that are lose–lose for elected officials, such as tax hikes and service cuts, and elected officials expect the manager to discipline or coach controversial mavericks on the governing body. If the mayor and council members possess perspectives such as these, the council–manager form cannot work as intended.

Another 1993 article bemoaned the reluctance of elected officials to exercise political leadership on social issues, citizen participation, workforce development, and use of volunteers, and the reliance of elected officials on managers to guide their decision making and get the job done:

> Public officials are looking for managers who are willing to "stick their necks out" and take a leadership role without taking all the credit for getting things done. The old axiom "make councils look good, no matter what they do" still is in effect. (Brimeyer, 1993, p. 11)

Since that time, a number of ICMA publications have provided a manager's perspective on challenges they face in building relationships with elected officials (Svara, 2004). Among these, there are three that are particularly common in local government today: the "do more with less" belief, the rise in single-issue candidates, and the increase in elected officials who overstep their role.

An expectation exists among some elected officials that greater efficiencies can always be found that will allow the government to do more with less. In addition to maintaining financial transparency and employing modern management practices to ensure maximum bang for the buck, in this situation, managers must also remind elected officials of the role values play in policy choices. For example, when faced with limited economic development incentive funds, a community may have to choose to invest them in a new Walmart on the fringe of town or in a downtown redevelopment plan. In communities that seek additional sales tax revenue, Walmart may be the best choice, whereas a community that values the social connectedness that comes with a vibrant downtown may choose to invest the money there.

Another common scenario that often strains the elected official–manager relationship is the election of a board member who campaigned on a single issue. Members who are focused on a single issue or policy area may have difficulty making decisions based on the best interests of the community overall. For example, some elected officials believe that many government services could be contracted out to the private sector in order to achieve cost savings for local government. Elected officials who begin their tenure believing that private provision is better may have difficulty accepting staff research that shows an in-house option is better, even if it costs more, due to accountability concerns.

Perhaps the most common stressor on the relationship is the tendency for some board members to micromanage. The council–manager form of government is designed to function with the manager handling day-to-day operations and the board providing broad policy direction. However, some elected officials believe that they have individual authority over staff members and proceed to issue instructions and directives without consulting the manager. This situation may be avoided through an orientation of new board members about the council–manager form of government. In cases where that is unsuccessful, the manager may need to enlist the assistance of the mayor and/or other members of the board.

Policy and Administration

Although the statutes and the ICMA Code of Ethics (Appendix 1) and related guidelines prescribe responsibilities for the manager and the governing body, as seen in the North Carolina example, these are very general and do not describe in detail how these officials should interact with one another in order to be effective in the division of labor set out in the Code's 12 tenets. Many years ago, scholars and ICMA promoted the notion of a strict dichotomy between policy making and administration: The elected body should make policy and the manager should carry it out, each without interference from the other as it performed its functions. However, it is one thing to separate politics from administration; it is another to distinguish policy from administration, especially the initiation and formulation stages.

The manager often has education and training, analytical skills, experience in other jurisdictions, and in-depth knowledge of the county or city and its governmental operations, which can be important assets to the governing body in making policy. He or she may have lived in the community longer than the mayor or some council members and worked with community organizations such as the Rotary Club and Chamber of Commerce for many years. With this professional background and community network, the manager can bring to the attention of elected officials problems and issues that have policy implications that are not on their radar screen. Nalbandian (1991) observed,

> The practical world of city management often suggests a more complicated view [than the dichotomy theory]. The manager is deeply involved in policymaking as well as implementation, responds to a multitude of community forces as well as to the governing body, and incorporates a variety of competing values into the decision-making process. (p. iii)

A realistic relationship between elected officials and managers in policy and administration has been depicted by James Svara (1985), as shown in Figure 6.1.

Svara's depiction recognizes that there is no strict dichotomy; instead, elected officials and managers interact at all levels of policy and administration. The extent of engagement and the responsibility of each party differ depending on the level at which they occur. At the highest level, the governing body is responsible for setting the overall direction, or *mission*, of local government, including its purpose, scope, values, and philosophy. Figure 6.1 indicates that although the governing body has

FIGURE 6.1 ■ Dimensions of Governmental Process

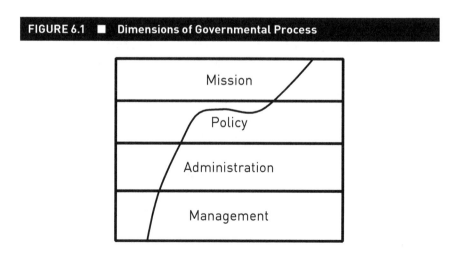

Source: Svara, 1985.

a clearly dominant role in this function, the manager can bring knowledge and experience that enhances the elected official's ability to make informed choices and decisions.

The governing body's legislative role involves enacting policy to achieve the mission that it sets for local government. It does this through functions such as budgeting, capital improvement programming, and strategic planning. Although the governing body has final responsibility for adopting budgets, plans, and ordinances, the manager and his or her staff play a major role in conducting technical studies, developing cost estimates, and analyzing the impact of alternative choices. The manager is a policy advisor, not a policy advocate (Nelson & Svara, 2015, p. 51).

In practice, these kinds of policy-making tasks are a shared responsibility and have characterized manager–elected official relationships throughout the evolution of the form and been accelerated by the political, social, and economic changes since the 1960s and 1970s. In 1997, the then–city manager of Savannah, Georgia, made an observation that is relevant today:

> Managers are no longer viewed as public works specialists by councils. . . . They are no longer passive observers in the policy development process. They actively participate in this process, proposing policy, advising on policy proposals initiated by councils, and supplying information on which policy decisions can be made. (Mendosa, 2006, p. 51)

As noted in a previous chapter, this relationship has been described by Svara as complementary:

> Officials in council–manager governments function as a team to achieve effective governance. A complementary relationship presumes responsiveness and accountability of administrators to elected officials along with independence in identifying problems and proposing policies and a commitment to professional standards and ethics. (Nelson & Svara, 2015, p. 56)

In government, how something is done is often as important to citizens' satisfaction with the outcome as what is done. Consequently, although the manager and the staff are responsible for implementing policies adopted by the governing body, elected officials still have a stake in how those policies are carried out—that is, in administration and management. Their respective roles in execution have been described by Kevin Duggan and Mike Conduff (2016):

The value of the council–manager form of government is most clearly on display in this handoff from desired outcomes to the implementation of activities to accomplish them. . . . The governing body does not have to "help" the CAO accomplish the outcomes; indeed such help is generally a hindrance not a help in implementation. This is not to say the governing body cannot offer advice and counsel or serve as a sounding board for suggested activities. (p. 36)

Some elected officials may feel the need to be intimately familiar with day-to-day aspects of service delivery, while others may concern themselves with administrative matters only when public controversy might be created or when matters may relate to the special interests of their constituents. When constituents complain about the quality of a service or the treatment they receive from local employees, a member of the governing body is unlikely to feel that it is an administrative matter that does not concern him or her.

Elected officials can serve as an important buffer, shock absorber, or safety valve between the citizenry and service deliverers (Svara, 1999, p. 51). For example, after making a decision to build a new community park and budgeting funds for it, the governing body will have a continued interest in the appearance of the facilities and who uses them. Elected officials will be concerned about how well the scheduling of repairs on a downtown street project minimizes disruption of business for merchants and traffic congestion for citizens. They will want to know how increases in public safety spending have impacted reported crime rates and citizen perceptions of safety in their neighborhoods. And they will have an interest in how overall employee morale is affected by human resources management policies developed by the administration.

In addition to identifying necessary performance fine-tuning or corrective actions in policy implementation, elected officials' involvement in administration and management can have other benefits. These include helping to "clarify legislative goals and expectations, develop politically feasible solutions, reduce the gap between policy formulation and implementation, and enhance the overall effectiveness of policy implementation" (Demir, 2009, p. 880).

In summary, Figure 6.1 shows a partnership at each of the four levels of the governmental process, with the governing body shouldering most of the responsibility, authority, and initiative at the mission level, the manager shouldering most of it in internal management and administration, and the two sharing significantly in policy. The line would vary among jurisdictions, within a particular jurisdiction at different times, with the personalities involved, and by the issue. Some governing bodies want managers to take the lead and push aggressively for initiating policies, while others want the manager to stay in the background and respond to their directives.

> The combination of the manager's style and the culture/history of the organization shapes quite different roles for the manager from one community to another. For some managers and in some settings, the manager may play a very visible and active role in the meeting. For other managers in other settings, the manager may appear almost like an interested spectator. (Duggan & Conduff, 2016, p. 81)

The manager's experience and tenure, personality and interpersonal skills, and the degree of trust and confidence in his or her relationship with the governing body also affect where the line is drawn in each of the four roles. Agreement between elected and appointed officials is an essential element of a good working relationship and, because the relationship is dynamic, it needs to be assessed regularly.

CHANGING ROLES AND RELATIONSHIPS

Successful council–manager relationships rest on a partnership between elected officials and managers in leading their communities. Governing body members, presiding officers, and managers are mutually dependent on one another, sharing responsibility for most aspects of local government while dividing some duties to make the form function as intended.

The roles that these key officials play in local government and their interrelations have remained broadly consistent over time. But the nature of those roles and relationships has shifted. For example, managers have always had significant interaction with members of the community. Historically, managers used their interactions to provide information or to stay informed about events, perspectives, and emerging issues. Today, managers take on a more expansive leadership role in the community, serving on boards and speaking publicly.

As shown in Table 6.1, managers and their senior staff play a critical role as go-betweens in the worlds of politics and administration. They translate data, technical information, and staff reports into information that is understandable and politically useful for the elected officials.

TABLE 6.1 ■ Characteristics of Politics and Administration		
Characteristics	**Politics**	**Administration**
Activity	Game/allocation of values	Problem solving
Players	Representatives	Experts
Conversation	"What do you hear?"	"What do you know?"
	• Passion CAO & Senior ⟶	• Data
	• Dream ⟵ Staff	• Plans
	• Stories	• Reports
Pieces	Intangible: interests and symbols	Tangible: information, money, people, equipment
Currency	Power (stories)	Knowledge (deeds)
Dynamics	Conflict, compromise, change	Predictability, cooperation, continuity

Source: John Nalbandian, UNC Public Executive Leadership Academy Presentation, Chapel Hill, NC, July 13, 2016.

The need for this mutual awareness has grown with the complexity of local government. As indicated in earlier chapters, most important public problems, to be successfully addressed, require working across jurisdictional and sectoral boundaries and developing intergovernmental, intersectoral, and interdisciplinary approaches. The impacts of how officials spend their time and set their agendas have not been confined to municipal and county managers and their governing bodies. Departmental leaders, for example, are being called upon to break out of their functional silos and work to identify interdepartmental collaborative opportunities and strategies for closing the gaps identified by Nalbandian.

As managers seek to develop jurisdictional scale capacity to deal with the problems that do not respect boundaries without compromising the core values and identity of their community, their role has expanded to include bridge building with elected officials, community stakeholders, and other organizational representatives. As a result, managers are spending more and more time with their governing bodies, seeking to form and sustain partnerships to enable their jurisdiction to respond to and survive the diverse, divisive, and difficult demands of contemporary governance. Personalities, constituent interests, political and ideological divisions, and polarized positions make building consensus and trust on and with governing bodies quite challenging. In addition to policy making, elected officials and managers have sometimes experienced tension in their efforts to share or divide responsibilities in community leadership.

Community Leadership

Citizens' greatest expectation is that quality public services will be provided reliably and efficiently; they care less about how the service is provided or by whom. They also want to be treated with dignity and respect and feel that local employees practice good customer service. If the administration does not satisfy these expectations, citizens will look to the governing body to take a more dominant role. If citizens' needs are being met routinely, they may be satisfied with elected officials taking a more passive role on a day-to-day basis.

While customer service is important, it is essential for managers as community leaders to distinguish between residents being mainly citizens but also customers. Whether dealing with a store in their neighborhood or with their local government, when citizen/customers do not receive a quality product at a fair price in a timely manner, they tend to blame, complain, and find fault. Elected officials can be both customers and representatives as they and their families make use of local services such as schools, parks, streets, and public utilities. As explained in Chapter 8, the citizen role is critical: "Even though residents are sometimes customers, they are primarily residents with a shared responsibility to help [their] government solve tough problems" (Everett, 2015, p. 24). A major responsibility of the manager is to find ways to tap this resource as a partner in community building.

As indicated previously, some observers of local government bemoan the increase in confrontational politics on the part of constituents, the trend back to district representation on governing bodies, the increasing polarization and declining civility among governing body members, and the growing number of single-issue and antigovernment candidates for local elective office. They argue that these developments undermine the principles of broad representation of the public interest and efficient and effective administration. Others, however, point out that these realities typify constituent politics and make for more transparent, fairer representation of all the diverse interests in the community instead of only the powerful and privileged. They argue that in addition to being organizational leaders, managers must be community leaders.

Nalbandian (1999) has observed the implications for managers as community leaders: "In the future, the legitimacy of professional administrators in local government will be grounded in the tasks of community-building and enabling democracy—in getting things done collectively, while building a sense of inclusion" (p. 189). This is not a new role for managers. In a 1952 revision of the Code of Ethics, ICMA referred to the manager as a community leader.

In summary, both the council–manager and mayor–council forms of government have potential advantages that can be realized if elected officials and managers work together in a good faith effort to navigate a very complex and dynamic relationship. Success depends, ultimately, on the governing body and the manager's ability to establish clear expectations, maintain good communication, and develop a sense of shared vision, trust, and teamwork on behalf of the community.

> Managers know that their job security, how they feel about their job, and their effectiveness in the job all directly relate to the quality of their relationship with their elected officials. Yet managers don't always give the time and effort the relationships need. (Duggan & Conduff, 2016, p. 15)

The next chapter considers strategies managers could take to enhance council and staff effectiveness.

NOTES

1. As mentioned in Chapter 3, there are two other forms of government in the United States: the commission form and the town meeting/representative town meeting form.
2. See Chapter 3 for a more detailed discussion of local government form and structure.
3. Portions of this section have been excerpted from Stenberg (2014, pp. 53–57).
4. Portions of this section have been excerpted from Stenberg (2014, pp. 59–65).

REFERENCES

Brimeyer, J. (1993). Council–manager relations: Time for adjustment, before it is too late. *Public Management, 75*(9), 10–12.

Demir, T. (2009). The complementarity view: Exploring a continuum in political–administrative relations. *Public Administration Review, 69*(5), 876–888.

Duggan, K., & Conduff, M. (2016). *Making it work: The essentials of council–manager relations.* Washington, DC: International City/County Management Association.

Everett, E. (2015). Today's local government management model. *Public Management, 97*(7), 22–25.

International City/County Management Association. (1993a). *ICMA Newsletter, 74*(10).

International City/County Management Association. (1993b). *ICMA Newsletter, 74*(11).

International City/County Management Association. (1993c). *ICMA Newsletter, 74*(13).

Mathis, R. W. (1993). What councils want from managers . . . but do not tell them. *Public Management, 75*(8), 5–10.

Mendosa, A. A. (2006). Year 1977 council–manager relations and the changing community environment. *Public Management, 88*(7), 49–51.

Nalbandian, J. (1991). *Professionalism in local government.* San Francisco, CA: Jossey-Bass.

Nalbandian, J. (1999). Facilitating community, enabling democracy: New roles for local government managers. *Public Administration Review, 59*(3), 187–197.

Nalbandian, J. (2016, July 13). UNC Public Executive Leadership Academy Presentation. Chapel Hill, North Carolina.

National Civic League. (2014). *Model city charter* (8th ed.). Philadelphia, PA: Author.

Nelson, K. L., Gabris, G. T., & Davis, T. J. (2011). What makes municipal councils effective? An empirical analysis of how council members perceive their group interactions and processes. *State and Local Government Review, 43*(3), 196–204.

Nelson, K. L., & Svara, J. H. (2015). The roles of local government managers in theory and practice: A centennial perspective. *Public Administration Review, 75*(1), 49–61.

North Carolina General Statutes. (2016). Retrieved April 2, 2017, from http://www.ncleg.net/gascripts/statutes/Statutes.asp

Stenberg, C. W. (2014). County and city managers. In F. S. Bluestein (Ed.), *County and municipal government in North Carolina* (pp. 53–76). Chapel Hill, NC: UNC School of Government.

Svara, J. H. (1985). Dichotomy and duality: Reconceptualizing the relationship between policy and administration in council–manager cities. *Public Administration Review, 45*(1), 221–232.

Svara, J. H. (1999). The shifting boundary between elected officials and city managers in large council–manager cities. *Public Administration Review, 59*(1), 44–53.

Svara, J. H. (2004). Achieving effective community leadership. In C. Newell (Ed.), *The effective local government manager* (3rd ed., pp. 27–40). Washington, DC: International City/County Management Association.

Svara, J. H. (2009). *The facilitative leader in city hall: Reexamining the scope and contributions.* Boca Raton, FL: Taylor & Francis Group.

Wilson, R. C., Jr. (2016). *Rethinking public administration: The case for management* (2nd ed.). Irvine, CA: Melvin & Leigh Publishers.

RESOURCE LIST/TO EXPLORE FURTHER

Books/Articles

Ehrenhalt, A. (1990, September). The new city manager is: (1) invisible (2) anonymous (3) non-political (4) none of the above. *Governing,* 41–46.

Nalbandian, J. (1994). Reflections of a "pracademic" on the logic of politics and administration. *Public Administration Review, 54*(6), 531–536.

Nalbandian, J. (1999). Facilitating community, enabling democracy: New roles for local government managers. *Public Administration Review, 35*(4), 311–326.

ENHANCING
COUNCIL–MANAGER
EFFECTIVENESS

The most basic issue regarding roles and responsibilities for councilmembers is whether—or maybe when—they will act in their role as representatives of constituencies—customer service representatives—in contrast to acting as "trustees" of the community.

—John Nalbandian (2016, p. 22)

The ideological and political trends discussed in the previous chapter have sometimes produced dysfunctional effects on governing boards. To the extent that elected officials are interested primarily in promoting particular causes or special constituencies, micromanaging administration, and criticizing their colleagues and the staff, prospects for responsible decision making in the public interest are diminished. Tensions on the governing body are exacerbated in such cases by two gaps: the knowledge and experience that separates a full-time professional staff from a body of part-time elected officials and the governing body's preoccupation with political acceptability and the staff's focus on administrative sustainability, identified by John Nalbandian (Nalbandian & Nalbandian, 2002).

The typical lack of government expertise on the part of newer members is compounded by frequent turnover on some councils and boards. In many communities, governing bodies range from five to seven members, so the majority can readily change. Elected officials are amateurs, in the very best sense of the term, who function as civic-minded citizen legislators. Although they may be interested in seeking reelection, the vast majority are not professional, full-time politicians. Most local elected officials do not derive the bulk of their income from serving on governing bodies. They see themselves individually and collectively as local government leaders. Some consider themselves as trustees, delegates, and activists responsible for representing citizens and making public policy to improve their community. However, as indicated in the quote at the beginning of this chapter, they may envision their chief role as customer service representatives. And managers often consider themselves (and are viewed as) community leaders as well as technical experts and policy initiators.

In many communities, these gaps are growing and creating the potential for misunderstanding and conflict. While they are rooted in the differing expectations, styles, and cultures of elected officials and professional managers, finding more common ground would improve the conduct of local government business. What are the attributes of a high-performing decision-making body? How can these gaps be closed, the board or council given the tools it needs to become effective, and a partnership developed with the professional staff? These questions are addressed in this chapter in the context of the council–manager plan, although the key points are also applicable to localities operating under the mayor–council form.

HIGH-PERFORMING HABITS

In view of these gaps, councils or boards can easily get off the track to high performance. Key indicators that this is happening include lack of clarity over who does what in terms of the roles of the governing board and the staff on the four dimensions of governmental process identified by James Svara (1985)—mission, policy, administration, and management—in the previous chapter. With respect to elected officials, disagreement about who is in charge, especially if the presiding officer's authority is limited or if his or her facilitative leadership skills are weak, and clashes among the members that get personal undermine effectiveness. Other indicators of relationship problems include members focusing on their individual campaign positions instead of community interests, disrespecting staff in public, not doing their homework, and feeling overwhelmed by staff reports and data. Micromanagement of staff and operations by elected officials and bypassing the manager to deal directly with staff can create tensions throughout the organization. Another source of friction is member confusion over whether they are primarily trustees of their community or customer service representatives and advocates for their constituencies, or both. With respect to the last factor, Nalbandian (2016) observes, "The interesting challenge is that councilmembers are charged with fulfilling both roles and, unfortunately, there is no common guidance as to when a councilmember should act in one role as opposed to the other" (p. 22).

The International City/County Management Association's (ICMA's) 2012 State of the Profession survey asked city and county managers to rate the effectiveness of their council as a decision-making body. Twenty-six percent responded that their council was highly effective, 28% said it was moderately effective, and 38% stated that it was not effective (Nelson & Svara, 2014, p. 14). Clearly, while the majority of the ratings were positive, there is room for improvement.

Building governing body effectiveness is especially difficult, given the mayor's or chair's limited authority as presiding officer. Regardless of whether members are elected at-large or from a district, they do not owe their electoral success to their governing body colleagues. And they have a mandate from voters to pursue the agenda on which they campaigned. Having been elected, they may consider themselves experts in the art and practice of local government or, at least, in campaigning for office. For the most part, the members are equals, and as a result, no one is really in charge (especially if the presiding officer lacks strong interpersonal and facilitative skills), so power is widely shared.

At least nine habits of a high-performing governing body have been identified: (1) thinking and acting strategically and with a vision for the community's future; (2) respecting the shared constituency with citizens and in their relations with other governments and organizations; (3) demonstrating teamwork; (4) mastering small-group decision making, including adhering to rules of procedure, time allocations, and meeting agendas; (5) honoring the council–staff partnership; (6) using governing body time and effort appropriately in four key areas—goal-setting retreats, study sessions, regular public hearings and meetings, and community relations; (7) having clear rules and procedures for board or council meetings; (8) obtaining feedback and conducting regular assessments of policy and implementation performance; and (9) practicing continuous personal learning and leadership development of individual elected officials (Neu, 2003, p. 10).

In some cases, veteran governing body members can play important roles in building relationships among the members or between the elected officials and the manager or chief administrative officer (CAO). Veterans can also be helpful with the onboarding of new members, especially with respect to how the group conducts itself and interpersonal relationships. But the team-building challenge can be daunting, given the diffusion of power on local governing boards.

THE MANAGER'S FACILITATING ROLE

Although a municipal or county manager has no formal authority over the governing body, there are a number of basic steps he or she can take to help improve its deliberations. ICMA's State of the Profession Survey found that "when top administrators always work to promote interaction among council members, 7 of 10 governing boards are highly effective at decision making, compared to 4 in 10 when interaction is never or only occasionally supported" (Nelson & Svara, 2014, p. 3). Many of these best practices could also apply to a mayor in the mayor–council form without a CAO.

A useful beginning point is for the manager to hold onboarding orientations for new members of the governing body, perhaps building on candidate briefing sessions during the election campaign. At the same time, the presiding officer could work with members to improve the conduct of the governing body's business and encourage adoption and adherence to protocols or rules of procedure. These could include encouraging colleagues to do their homework; asking pertinent questions; staying within time limits during deliberations; not making criticism or disagreement personal; and not embarrassing the staff with public comments that would be better made in private.

The manager is responsible for drafting the meeting agenda. To help elected officials prepare for meetings, the agenda should be distributed well in advance of meetings with background documentation attached. When appropriate, policy alternatives should be accompanied by cost estimates. The form of distribution—electronic or paper—is determined by the governing body.

Choices about how often to schedule meetings of elected officials and what types of meetings are most appropriate are usually in the hands of the mayor or CAO. If a topic is more technical or requires more in-depth discussion, a work session may be more appropriate than a normal board meeting. Managers need to be sensitive to the time commitment that is being asked of elected officials and be sure that the meeting time is being used judiciously.

The manager should be cautious about overwhelming elected officials with highly detailed, lengthy technical reports. Ideally, an annual policy calendar will be developed to identify and address long-range issues.

The presiding officer also should let the manager know if elected officials want other professional staff members to be present and contribute to the meeting and whether the agenda and related materials satisfy the governing body's expectations in terms of timeliness, priority, and quantity and quality of the information. In these respects, both the manager and the presiding officer can play the important role of informal coach to the governing body and smooth the members' transition from campaigning to governing as well as to help them develop high-performance habits.

MUTUAL EXPECTATIONS

Specific expectations regarding effectiveness and related practices among the governing body, the mayor or chair serving as presiding officer, and the manager vary greatly from state to state and community to community, depending on social and political norms, traditions, and laws. They can also vary with changes in the personalities involved as elected officials turn over and managers move on. However, research and experience have shown that in some critical aspects of these partnerships, there are fairly consistent expectations across jurisdictions and over time. For the most part, the following eight expectations may be regarded as basic and necessary to defining roles and maintaining healthy relationships among the elected members of the governing body, the presiding officer, and the manager and professional staff. Fulfilling them is critical to becoming a high-performing organization. These expectations have been developed and are used by the University of North Carolina School of Government Faculty in retreat facilitations with governing bodies and management teams.[1]

Expectation 1: The Manager Is an Organization Capacity Builder

From the inception of the council–manager form, governing bodies have expected their professional managers to see to it that local operations run smoothly, services are provided efficiently and effectively, and prudent fiscal practices are followed. The focus here is on the technical expertise of the manager and on his or her ability to adapt modern management techniques into the organization.

In order to meet governing body and citizen expectations, the manager must build an organization that has both capacity and competence. This entails implementing and updating business practices and processes for personnel administration, finance, purchasing, payroll, contracting, and other basic local systems. More recently, it involves adept use of management techniques in his or her toolbox, such as strategic planning, performance measurement, benchmarking, and program evaluation, to ensure continuous improvement of operations and to base advice, recommendations, and decisions on evidence. Technologies such as websites and social media are being used to increase public outreach and access and to reduce costs. And increasingly, managers seek to build organizations that promote innovation.

A critical component of this organization capacity building is professional staff. Given the substantial number of employees who will be eligible for retirement in the next decade, the manager must attract and retain talented and motivated personnel in order for the government to work well. Workforce and succession planning and investments in training and professional development are essential. Increasingly, as local government workforces become more diverse and multigenerational, strategies will be needed to recruit and respond to the changing faces of the administrative staff, such as bilingual education, job rotation, job sharing, and flexible work hours. Also important are redesigning position vacancy announcements and revamping human relations management processes. A 2016 report published by the Alliance for Innovation observed that "transforming local government human resources policies and practices is at the heart of building the workforce of tomorrow" (2016, p. 2).

The stakes are high. When the processes and personnel perform as expected, local operations run smoothly and routinely. Their workings might be almost invisible to citizens and elected officials. If there is a breakdown in organizational capacity, however, both managers and elected officials can be placed under a harsh public spotlight and confidence in local government quickly diminishes.

Expectation 2: The Manager Is a Valued, Unbiased Advisor to the Governing Body

While the ICMA Code of Ethics and some state statutes require the manager to give policy advice to the governing body and faithfully carry out its policy decisions, neither deals specifically with some subtle but important aspects of the advice-giving and implementation processes. Illinois Compiled Statutes, for example, require the manager "to attend all meetings of the council or board of trustees with the right to take part in the discussions, but with no right to vote," and "to recommend to the council or board of trustees for adoption such measures as he may deem necessary or expedient (Illinois General Assembly, n.d., 65 ILCS 5/5-3-7). Alternatively, through the ICMA Code of Ethics, managers are directed to submit policy proposals and provide facts and advice to help the governing body make policy decisions and set goals.

Governing bodies expect the manager to offer balanced and impartial advice. This involves presenting alternatives and providing all relevant information that is reasonably available on the different options, assessing the advantages and disadvantages of each option, explaining the professional reasoning and analysis that led him or her to a recommendation, and basing that reasoning on established professional, technical, ethical, or legal principles and not on personal beliefs, unless the governing body specifically solicits them. Even the appearance or the suspicion that the manager is being selective in the information provided, personally biased in the judgment rendered, or unduly influencing of the governing body's decision by the way material is presented can severely damage the manager's credibility, erode trust, undermine effectiveness, and threaten longevity. This does not mean that the manager should act with no consideration for political reality. Some policy proposals will not be politically acceptable, regardless of the quality of the option in the manager's opinion or recommendation.

Early in the development of the profession, Leonard D. White called attention to one of the hazards found in the "adventuresome spirit" of many managers, particularly those new to the profession:

> This course (community or civic leadership) is one which, if persisted in, will sound the death knell of the manager plan as now conceived, for a manager who undertakes civic leadership stakes his position on the acceptance of his program by the voters. If his program is rejected . . . he sacrifices his position as manager. Moreover by entering the arena of public opinion and identifying himself with a policy or program, he allies himself with one group of citizens and against another and incurs ill will which is bound to be transferred to the purely administrative phases of his work. (White, 1927, p. 300)

Despite White's admonitions, most managers will express support and sometimes advocate for a course of action they believe in, even though it might be unpopular with the public or the governing body and might not have very good prospects of being accepted. Elected officials or citizens who are upset or disagree over the facts, options, or advice that are presented by the manager might attack the validity of the manager's advice or challenge his or her competence, motives, judgment, or character. One of the most difficult tests for a manager acting as policy advisor is to remain nondefensive and under control during heated debates over the information and the recommendations that he or she has brought to the governing body.

Managers must develop a sense of when to lead and when to follow, when to advocate and when to remain passive. Even as they look to the manager for leadership, elected officials might push back when their "employee" makes a strong case that some members do not want to hear. But, as a former city manager points out from his 29 years of experience, strong managers add value:

> Politicians clearly think, feel, and believe that granting authority to management diminishes, or would diminish, their own. In fact the opposite is true.

Strong and capable politicians need strong and capable managers if they want long-term achievement. Strong managers would make strong politicians look good, not weak. Strong managers have no desire to intrude into the political arena; they are quite happy to work behind the scenes. They pose no challenge whatsoever to elected officials. (White, 1927, pp. 85–86)

Once the governing body has made a decision, the manager must get behind it fully and ensure that the staff does the same. Many state statutes and local charters require the manager to see that all actions of the council are faithfully executed, and the ICMA Code of Ethics requires him or her to uphold and implement all policies adopted by elected officials. This sometimes requires the manager to implement what he or she thinks is a bad idea. If the manager believes that the directive the governing body has given is illegal or unethical and if he or she cannot convince the governing body to change its action, resignation may be an option to consider. Two veteran former managers observed:

One of the toughest challenges for professional staff is to be fully accepting of the right in a democratic system for the governing board to make the final decision when staff think, from their professional perspectives, it is the "wrong" decision. Governing boards have the right to make decisions within their authority, even if managers and staff don't agree with them. (Duggan & Conduff, 2016, p. 82)

Sometimes the manager will be put in the awkward position of arguing strenuously for a course of action that the governing body subsequently rejects and then having the media ask what he or she thinks of the decision. Unless discussion and debate have changed the manager's mind, to agree completely with the governing body will make the manager look weak, even though he or she is their employee. On the other hand, to criticize the governing body for its decision will violate the ICMA Code of Ethics and invite censure. Most professional managers who find themselves in this situation will acknowledge the differences in judgment that were exhibited in the deliberations and try to explain the reasoning that brought the governing body to the decision it made. In other words, they will help elected officials explain their decision to the public to promote understanding of the governing body's point of view. Carrying out this important responsibility often takes great emotional intelligence, diplomatic, and communications skills.

It is also important to recognize that elected officials and professional staff interpret situations differently. Staff members are expected to produce plans and reports, analyze data, and provide other information relevant to the policy issue under consideration by the governing body. Elected officials are often moved in a direction different from that suggested by data and analysis by anecdotes and powerful stories. As Nalbandian's (2016) table in the previous chapter shows, staff focus on "What do you know?" while elected officials focus on "What do you hear?" Both approaches are key to making good decisions.

Expectation 3: The Governing Body and the Manager Jointly Strive for Good Service to Citizens

Service to all citizens is the litmus test of local operations. Regardless of what the governing body accomplishes or the capacity, competence, and commitment of the administration, if the municipality or county does not satisfactorily deliver basic services, citizens will be dissatisfied with the elected officials and the governing body will be dissatisfied with the manager and the staff. Therefore, ensuring that local employees provide the very best service possible to the community is one of the key responsibilities of a manager.

Careful planning, budgeting, and management are helpful, but the manager cannot supervise all day-to-day execution. Thus, he or she has to create a culture of responsiveness and performance within the organization, both by providing routine service to citizens and by handling special requests and complaints. A key aspect of creating this culture is equipping staff to provide high quality, customer-oriented service. To do this, a manager or assistant manager should not micromanage. Line employees and staff need to be delegated the responsibility and authority to make decisions and take action. Employees also must be provided with the training, technology, and equipment necessary to efficiently and effectively carry out their responsibilities.

To promote the development of new and innovative ways to provide services, staff should be encouraged by managers to take initiative and risks, which also means supporting staff when they take a risk in good faith and fail. Failure should be used as a learning opportunity rather than a call for discipline or punishment. If managers encourage employees to take risks, they should be prepared to accept responsibility with the governing body when things go wrong.

Expectation 4: Elected Officials' Relationships with Employees Are Carefully Managed

Citizens often ask their elected officials for help in getting their problems or needs addressed, and governing body members may identify a problem requiring immediate attention. Observing a chain of command in these situations is essential. Problems can arise when elected officials intervene directly in service operations. These include confusing employees with conflicting directives or priorities from supervisors and elected officials, weakening accountability for results, disrupting workflow, wasting staff time and resources, and short-circuiting coordinated plans developed by the supervisor responsible for day-to-day operations. This does not mean that elected officials should not have regular or even periodic contact with city or county employees to gain information or report problems.

Statutes and charter language defining the responsibilities of the manager in council–manager form commonly state that the municipal manager shall direct and supervise the administration of all departments, offices, and agencies of the city, subject to the general direction and control of the council, except as otherwise provided by law. This language reflects the long-standing prohibition in the *Model City Charter* (National Civic League, 2014) on interference with administration, which provides that council members should deal with employees through the manager. To make sure that the noninterference tenet is honored, some managers have insisted that there be no contact between employees and council members without their permission. However, as a practical matter, this can prove frustrating for everyone involved: Employees may feel as if they are being treated as second-class citizens, the manager might find that he or she has to devote too much time to managing communications traffic, and council members could come to regard the "contact only with permission" rule as unduly restrictive of their ability to keep track of the pulse of government, express constituent concerns, alert staff to problems, or get basic information. Most managers have an understanding that prevents the council or board from issuing directives to employees but allows members to freely seek information. Managers also expect that employees will keep them informed of contacts with elected officials.

Research conducted in 2005 found that the charters of nine of the 28 largest municipalities in North Carolina contained "work through the manager" language, while the remaining charters were silent on the matter of council–staff relations. In the latter municipalities, there was either an informal unwritten policy or no policy at all. The majority of managers interviewed in 2005 agreed that the norm applicable to their city could be best described as "direct communication between council members/mayor and city employees is neither strongly discouraged nor prohibited, but city employees are advised to inform a supervisor when contacted by council members/mayor." They also stated that violations of the council member/staff contact policy or norm seldom occurred. More than three fourths of the managers indicated that their councils were respectful of the manager's role as chief executive officer and that their city's policy on council member/staff contact was about right.

Reflecting the changing times, one manager stated, "Twenty-five years ago managers wanted everything to go through the manager's office, and that's just not practical today" (Wiseman, 2005, p. 5).

A common arrangement designed to protect planned workflow and promote regular interaction is to encourage direct contact between elected officials and employees for routine inquiries or requests that do not affect administrative workloads and to route more significant requests through the manager. This lets elected officials get the information they need quickly and accurately from the persons who are closest to the action and most informed about details. This arrangement also provides the opportunity for informal communication between elected officials and employees, helping each party become more familiar, comfortable, and trusting of the other over time. Requests from an elected official that will involve significant and unplanned expenditures of time or money or that will disrupt work schedules are taken up with the manager.

Any elected official concerns regarding personnel issues should be discussed with the manager directly. For example, if a council member receives complaints from staff who believe they are being unfairly treated by their department supervisor, the elected official should bring that complaint directly to the manager's attention for investigation and appropriate action. If the elected official becomes involved and a lawsuit is filed subsequently, he or she could be pulled into the suit.

Depending on the nature of an elected official's request, the manager can decide whether it should take precedence over existing commitments, whether something could be done that would meet the official's needs but not be disruptive, or whether nothing should be done at all, given other priorities or legal concerns. The request of a single elected official may be of interest to the entire governing body, in which case, the manager should consider whether a written report should be prepared for all of the elected officials.

Expectation 5: The Governing Body Acts as a Body and Is Dealt with as a Body

By law, the governing body takes official action as a body, yet it is made up of individual politicians with various constituencies, personal interests, public values, political philosophies, agendas, and personalities. "Elected officials are sole practitioners. They do not join teams, partnerships, firms, or companies. There are no organizational support systems they can turn to. Politicians succeed or fail one at a time" (Wilson, 2013, p. 17). Despite the individual nature of the politician's world, when serving on a local government board or council, individual members have no autonomous authority.

Ricky Carioti/*The Washington Post* via Getty Images

Chairman Phil Mendelson listens during a meeting of the Washington, D.C., City Council.

This situation can sometimes make dealing with the governing body a delicate proposition. Without benefit of consensus or at least formal support of a majority of the council or board, individual elected officials may seek to make their views known and impose their own personal agendas on the administration. Most managers will welcome, discuss, and frequently respond at any time to suggestions from individual members, as long as they do not conflict with the will of the governing body as a whole. However, if a request sets new directions or requires allocation of funds or staff time not anticipated by the governing body, the manager will usually ask the member making the proposal to put it to the entire body for consideration.

Contemporary local elected officials often run for office due to a desire to resolve a single issue. The issue may be as simple as a concern that potholes are not being filled quickly enough. But the single-issue-candidate-turned-elected-official is unlikely to take an interest in other policy areas until his or her issue is resolved. These officials may focus their attention on the department that aligns with their issue and make special requests of staff.

It is critical for the manager to treat all members alike. Unless he or she is scrupulous in avoiding even the appearance of favoritism, the manager can seriously undermine his or her effectiveness by alienating members who feel slighted or barred from some inner circle, real or perceived. Even in the case of routine requests for information, most managers will keep all members informed of transactions with individuals by sending copies of written responses or summaries of opinions rendered or actions agreed to in conversations.

One area in which managers must be especially ardent is keeping members up to date on day-to-day events. Elected officials do not like surprises. It is embarrassing for an official to be asked about some local newsworthy item and have to admit that he or she does not know much about it. Governing bodies expect their managers to be sensitive, alert, and responsive to their needs for current information and to be barometers of changing community sentiments and emerging issues. This expectation includes the manager making occasional extraordinary efforts necessary to ensure that every member has the same level of information and understanding. A common practice is a weekly e-mail from the manager to all governing body members. Social media is increasingly being used by managers to provide information to and get reactions from elected officials.

Expectation 6: The Manager and Members of the Governing Body Give One Another a Chance to Prove Themselves

One of the implicit foundations of the council–manager form of government is that a professional manager who is dedicated to serving whatever governing body is elected by the people will ensure smooth transitions and institutional stability and memory and will make substantive and stylistic changes as different individuals transition on and off the governing body. New members may find it hard to trust the loyalty of the manager and to have confidence in him or her to help bring about the changes they campaigned on and want to be made. Even in communities where the manager routinely makes information available to all candidates about local operations and finances to help inform discussion and debate during the election campaign, this behavior could be viewed as defense of the status quo. In short, members sometimes view the manager as inextricably tied to the old way of doing things and an impediment to progress and new ideas.

After an election, the manager may find himself or herself working for one or more board or council members who, as candidates, criticized the way in which the community was governed and managed. During their campaigns, some of these members may have called for the manager's dismissal and they might try to convince a majority of their new colleagues that this step needs to be taken. Few elected officials would dispute that even if they had prior municipal or county service on volunteer boards or commissions, the view of government from the inside is very different than the view from the outside.

Candidates, upon taking office, usually learn that the simplicity of campaign rhetoric seldom stands up to the complexity of governing, leading, or managing. Realizing this, experienced managers will withhold judgment on members whose campaigning seems threatening and will set about to prove that they can serve the new governing body as well as they served the previous one. Managers should consider holding a governing body retreat after new members are elected. In addition to educating new officials about current policies, practices, and finances, the retreat can be an important opportunity to discuss appropriate roles for elected officials, the manager, and staff. Most managers anticipate that, given a chance, they will eventually earn the trust and confidence of new members as those members learn the realities of governing, gain skill as legislators, and observe the manager's performance.

Expectation 7: The Manager and the Governing Body Give and Seek Feedback

The nature of the job of both elected officials and managers can make the persons holding them feel very isolated. One of the main ingredients for curing these feelings and for building and maintaining a relationship of trust and confidence is open communication and candid feedback. While managers must provide all governing body members with accurate, relevant, and timely information, the members must take initiative to ask questions and make their interests, positions, and feelings known to the manager. When an elected official openly directs constructive criticism toward the manager and gets issues out on the table, the manager can ask questions, provide information the member might not have, and respond to his or her concerns.

High-quality feedback can be provided to the manager through the annual evaluation process. As will be discussed in greater detail in the next section, annual evaluations can be very helpful for both managers and elected officials. They provide the manager with constructive criticism about areas for improvement and give the elected officials an opportunity to raise concerns in a professional manner.

Such feedback gives members the opportunity to clarify their expectations of the manager by means of concrete examples as they arise, and it gives the manager more certainty about what needs to be done to satisfy the elected officials and how well he or she is succeeding. Many elected officials appreciate the same sort of candor from the manager when they are behaving in a way that impedes effective management and frustrates the staff.

Expectation 8: The Manager and Governing Body Work Together to Promote Civility and Transparency

The dynamics of contemporary local government presented previously underscore why civility and transparency have increasingly become important dimensions of the relationship between elected officials and managers. A key concern is that the political and philosophical polarization that has characterized Congress for several years (and, recently, the deliberations of several state legislatures) is beginning to filter down to city councils and county boards. Of the respondents to ICMA's 2012 State of the Profession Survey, 33% reported that political discourse in their community in the past year had been "somewhat polarized and strident, occasionally rude," 6% indicated it had been "very polarized and strident, often rude," and 52% stated that discourse had been "generally polite and tolerant of different opinions" (Nelson & Svara, 2014, p. 13). If polarization spreads, citizen trust and confidence in their local governments will likely further erode. This decline could be reflected in low turnout at the polls for general and special elections, lack of public support for bond issues, negative comments in the media and blogger world about the competence of local officials and the appropriateness of their actions, unwillingness of citizens to serve on boards and commissions or to volunteer for community service, and reluctance of millennials to pursue local government careers.

Becoming a more high-performing council or board can pay important dividends beyond just the efficient and effective conduct of the public's business. Many governing bodies routinely televise their hearings and deliberations, and increasingly, bloggers use social media to comment on public meetings. The image of governing body members behaving civilly, asking thoughtful questions of one another and the professional staff, listening carefully to the views expressed by citizens, treating all who are present with courtesy and respect, and making decisions after assessing options and alternatives presented by the manager goes a long way toward building citizen confidence in local government and conveying a sense of genuine partnership between the governing body and administration in the governance process.

Similar to other high-performing qualities, there is no set formula for establishing and maintaining civility. Soon after an election and before the governing body begins complex and sometimes contentious budget deliberations, it will be important for the members to revisit their protocols and rules of procedure for their deliberations to determine how well these have worked and what changes need to be made in order to promote greater civility in their dealings with one another and with the manager and staff. These conversations could be part of the agenda for a retreat or work session of the council or board.

Turning to transparency, technology has opened up the world of local government for all to see. Advances in computer and communications technology have made local government operations more transparent and accessible. Although the digital divide still exists in some places, most local governments have websites that provide wide-ranging information, such as about community events or activities, council agendas, elected official and staff contacts, financial conditions, strategic plans, and departmental performance indicators. These websites enable citizens to pay bills, register for activities, ask questions, and provide commentary from their home or office without having to make the journey to city hall or county courthouse. Governing body members and staff have also benefitted from technology. Instead of thick paper agendas, many jurisdictions provide laptops to elected officials to facilitate their review of agenda materials and allow them to check other sources of information and insight during council or board deliberations. Council members routinely communicate with staff, constituents, and one another via e-mail or social media sites, such as Facebook or LinkedIn. Also, the manager's weekly e-mail to all governing body members summarizing key actions and upcoming matters has become an important tool for promoting communications and avoiding surprises.

The fact that most of the above technology that we take for granted today did not exist or was not widely used until the early 2000s means the road ahead could be exciting. At the same time, closing the digital divide will remain a priority for many jurisdictions. While what lies ahead in the next wave of technological innovation is not fully clear, it is unquestionable that citizens will expect local governments to use these tools to become more transparent and to promote citizen engagement.

RECOGNIZING AND DEALING WITH PROBLEMS IN THE GOVERNING BODY

The relationship between a governing body and a manager can greatly enhance or impede the processes of governing, leading, and managing, so it is important that the parties devote time to properly establishing and maintaining it. The eight preceding expectations are good points of departure. In addition, ICMA has published several books and reports offering advice and showcasing best practices for managers to use to strengthen their relationships with elected officials (Duggan & Conduff, 2016). But how can a manager know when problems noted in the opening of this chapter arise in the relationship with the governing board in time to take corrective action before dismissal?

As soon as possible, the elected officials and manager should decide what they expect of one another beyond the general tenets of statutory and professional responsibilities. No matter how much previous experience a new manager has had or how many managers have served a particular community, the relationship between a council or board and a manager is certain to be different in some ways from any other relationship previously experienced by either party. Problems will arise if there is uncertainty and disagreement concerning priorities, process, and performance. Each governing body and its manager must work out how they are willing to identify and deal with problems in their relationship.

Shortly after a new manager is hired, or if a significant turnover in governing body membership occurs or if a new presiding officer is elected, it will be essential to discuss their specific mutual expectations and what is needed from the others to effectively carry out major responsibilities. The presiding officer's and governing body's expectations of the manager inform their ability to both formally evaluate the manager and give him or her informal feedback about specific behaviors and general performance.

Once the governing body and manager have reached agreement on performance expectations in the context of the vision, goals, and objectives for the community, they should agree on the purpose, procedure, and timing of the manager's evaluation. Evaluating the city or county manager is a task that governing bodies often find difficult and uncomfortable. Sometimes a manager's evaluation is done in the context of decisions on an annual salary increase and the feedback is general or even perfunctory. In other cases, the presiding officer, outside of the yearly salary review, simply gives the manager feedback on how he or she is doing on behalf of the governing body. In still other communities, the fact that the manager continues to hold his or her job is a clear indication that performance is satisfactory to the majority of the governing body and amounts to a positive evaluation. Why, then, should a governing body take valuable time to more formally evaluate the manager, especially if things are going okay (Upshaw, 2014)?

Evaluations are important tools for giving the manager feedback on strong and weak points that can be useful in strengthening his or her competencies and approaches. This regular dialogue can go a long way in avoiding surprises and in building trust between the manager and governing body. The ICMA model employment agreement establishes the following minimum requirements for both the manager and the governing body: (1) a written evaluation, (2) a meeting to discuss the evaluation, (3) a written summary, and (4) delivery of the final written evaluation to the manager within thirty days of the evaluation meeting (ICMA, 2003).

There are a variety of evaluation approaches—from one-on-one reviews with the mayor or board chair to a complete 360-degree assessment of the manager by the governing body, professional staff, and community stakeholders. In accordance with the ICMA model employment agreement, elected officials are asked to complete a written form prior to the evaluation session with the manager, rating the manager on how well he or she exercises general organization management responsibilities; works with the governing body; carries out goals and objectives set by the council or board; develops and executes the budget; provides leadership; relates to the community; deals with the media and external audiences; communicates, delegates, and supervises; and performs in other key areas. Usually the manager is also rated on personal characteristics, such as objectivity, integrity, productivity, judgment, initiative and risk taking, ethics and morals, imagination, drive, self-assurance, stress management, and positive image. The manager normally does a self-assessment, which is shared with governing body members. These materials become the basis for a two-way conversation about the manager's performance and strong/weak points led by the mayor or chair or by an outside facilitator in a closed session. In addition to decisions on compensation and continuity, managers use evaluation results in their plan for personal and professional development prior to the next evaluation cycle.

Governing bodies are using retreats to set out these initial expectations between themselves and the manager and to address other issues that contribute to effective governance. The idea behind a retreat is that the governing body and other invitees can convene at a time and a place different from regular meetings to deliberate about matters that are difficult to fit into the routine formal business that fills their regular meeting agendas. Retreats are valuable ways to develop strategic goals, objectives, and priorities to advance the governing body's vision for the community; identify agreements and differences among members in their values, beliefs about, and goals for the community; plan how to achieve common goals and accommodate differences; understand one another's expectations about working together and learn individual leadership styles and behaviors; build teamwork; and review progress in achieving previously agreed-upon goals. Facilitators from outside the local government are often used to bring neutrality into the retreat proceedings and to enhance listening and communications among the participants. Annual retreats are an effective way to build and sustain a unity of effort that is difficult to develop in the course of a governing body's regular meetings and to help keep elected officials and the manager focused on the big picture for the community (Duggan & Conduff, 2016, pp. 87–96).

Increasingly, managers are giving feedback regarding the governing body's performance as councils and boards evaluate themselves as decision-making bodies and representatives of the citizens. As discussed previously, managing, leading, and governing in council–manager communities are shared responsibilities. Just as the governing body expects the manager to conduct himself or herself in accordance with state statutes, local ordinances, and the ICMA Code of Ethics, the manager has expectations of the governing body that impact upon his or her performance. These might include looking to the council or board to take ownership of its decisions, to recognize and uphold its role as policy maker (not micromanager), to defend staff members when they are criticized for carrying out council or board policy, to be decisive and consistent, and to show respect and support for professional staff. One useful approach involves elected officials filling out questionnaires assessing how the governing body as a unit sets goals, makes policy decisions, establishes priorities, understands the budget, engages the public, operates in a businesslike manner, handles information provided by the professional staff, and relates to the manager.

For some governing bodies, annually evaluating the manager might seem to be a big step, and evaluating their own effectiveness could be viewed as potentially disruptive and dysfunctional. However, just as regular feedback can enhance the manager's performance, introspection by the governing body as to how it conducts its work and relates to professional staff can lead to improvements in its decision-making effectiveness and ability to represent the community.

There is no set formula for closing the gaps between elected officials and managers and for developing a high-performing governing body, but meeting the above expectations are important steps in this direction. While the lines between policy and administration will always be blurred, the desired outcome is for governing body members and managers to be able and willing to successfully balance a number of competing interests—to focus on the vision and big picture for the community while dealing with concrete projects and programs, to think and act long-term and strategically while dealing with pressing immediate problems and needs, and to decide on the collective best interest while satisfying constituent expectations.

NOTE

1. Portions of this section have been excerpted from Stenberg (2014, pp. 66–70).

REFERENCES

Alliance for Innovation. (2016). *Workforce of tomorrow*. Phoenix, AZ: Author.

Duggan, K., & Conduff, M. (2016). *Making it work: The essentials of council–manager relations*. Washington, DC: International City/County Management Association.

Illinois General Assembly. (n.d.). Retrieved April 2, 2017, from http://www.ilga.gov/legislation/ilcs/ilcs.asp

International City/County Management Association. (2003). *ICMA model employment agreement*. Retrieved March 19, 2017, from http://icma.org/en/icma/career_network/career_resources/model_employment_agreement

Nalbandian, J. (2016). High-performance local government. *Public Management, 98*(1), 22–23.

Nalbandian, J., & Nalbandian, C. (2002, December). Contemporary challenges in local government. *Public Management, 84,* 6–11.

National Civic League. (2014). *Model city charter* (8th ed.). Philadelphia, PA: Author.

Nelson, K. L., & Svara, J. H. (2014). Upholding and expanding the roles of local government managers: State of the profession 2012. In *The municipal year book 2014* (pp. 3–20). Washington, DC: International City/County Management Association.

Neu, C. H., Jr. (2003, October). The manager as coach: Increasing the effectiveness of elected officials. *ICMA IQ Report,* 10.

Stenberg, C. W. (2014). City and county managers. In F. S. Bluestein (Ed.), *County and municipal government in North Carolina.* Chapel Hill: University of North Carolina at Chapel Hill School of Government.

Svara, J. H. (1985). Dichotomy and duality: Reconceptualizing the relationship between policy and administration in council–manager cities. *Public Administration Review, 45*(1), 221–232.

Upshaw, V. M. (2014). *How are we doing? Evaluating manager and board performance.* Chapel Hill: University of North Carolina at Chapel Hill School of Government.

White, L. D. (1927). *The city manager.* Chicago, IL: University of Chicago Press.

Wilson, R. C., Jr. (2013). *Rethinking public administration: The case for management* (2nd ed.). Irvine, CA: Melvin & Leigh, Publishers.

Wiseman, P. (2005). *Examining Council Contact with Subordinate Staff in Large and Mid-Size North Carolina Municipalities.* Paper submitted to the faculty of The University of North Carolina at Chapel Hill in partial fulfillment of the requirements for the degree of master of public administration.

RESOURCE LIST/TO EXPLORE FURTHER

Books/Articles

Upshaw, V. M. (2014). *How are we doing? Evaluating manager and board performance.* Chapel Hill: University of North Carolina School of Government.

CITIZEN ENGAGEMENT

Never doubt that a small group of thoughtful, concerned citizens
can change the world. Indeed, it is the only thing that ever has.

—Margaret Mead

The participative model of decision making has many motives, takes many forms, and involves many different community stakeholders. Collaborative governance arrangements call upon public administrators to engage in and sometimes share authority with intergovernmental organizations in order to successfully tackle problems that often do not respect jurisdictional boundaries. In addition to other governments, those who typically have a vested interest, or *stake*, in the work of a city or county include employees and clientele of the governmental agency as well as representatives of nonprofit and community organizations, the private for-profit sector, volunteers, and faith-based groups.

The largest group of stakeholders is the citizens who are the owners of government in their roles as voters and taxpayers. Today, engaging citizens in the work of governance is not only mandated by many federal and state programs, it is also recognized by practitioners and scholars as an effective approach for improving decision making and execution. "The idea of citizen participation is a little like eating spinach: No one is against it in principle because it is good for you" (Arnstein, 1969, p. 216). Yet, managers and elected officials sometimes complain that participating citizens are not representative of the broader community, that the participatory process does not add significant value to the outcomes, and that too much staff time is required to get citizens more engaged in governmental affairs. A former city manager reported:

Overwhelmingly, managers consistently describe the public with negative adjectives about 80 percent of the time, and elected officials describe the public with negative adjectives 70 percent of the time. Some of the common negative adjectives I hear about the public are: uninformed, not interested, entitled, rude, NIMBY (Not-In-My-Back-Yard) driven, and blames others. (Everett, 2015, p. 22)

At the same time, citizens often complain that their views are not being heard or acted upon and that local officials manipulate the engagement process to achieve predetermined outcomes. This chapter reviews the rationale for and record of citizen engagement, the types of tools that are available, and how these tools can be used to add value to local policy-making and implementation processes.

WHY ENGAGE CITIZENS?

Citizen participation in government is neither new nor unique. The term has evolved since the 1930s without much agreement on who the "citizens" are, how they should be engaged, which approaches are most effective, and what outcomes should be expected. Participating citizens have included middle- and upper-income white suburbanites as well as low-income minority inner-city residents. The form of involvement has ranged from merely being informed of decisions or actions to providing information and feedback (such as in public hearings) to advising on planned programs to influencing or controlling implementation.

The literature indicates a subtle but significant change in the terminology over this time period from citizen *involvement* to citizen *participation* to the current reference of citizen *engagement*. According to Ben Berger (2009), "Engagement connotes activity and attention, an investment of energy and a consciousness of purpose" (p. 340).

During the 1960s and 1970s, the term *citizen control* was often used with respect to programs impacting central cities, minority neighborhoods, and poor citizens, reflecting the community power movement at that time. In 1969, Sherry Arnstein observed:

Citizen participation is a categorical term for citizen power. It is the redistribution of power that enables the have-not citizens, presently excluded from the political and economic processes, to be deliberately included in the future. . . . It is the means by which they can induce significant social reform which enables them to share in the benefits of the affluent society. (p. 216)

However, as will be seen, "control" was more rhetoric than reality. By contrast, 37 years later, the citizen engagement process was defined as the "ability and incentive for ordinary people to come together, deliberate, and take action on problems or issues that they themselves have defined as 'important'" (Gibson, 2006, p. 2).

There are two general rationales for including those affected by a program in the planning, priority-setting, decision-making, and implementation stages. First, normatively, as stated by Janet and Robert Denhardt, engagement is key to building citizenship:

We should facilitate citizen engagement because it is the right thing to do according to democratic ideals and our desire to build a sense of community identity and responsibility. Rather than being a means to an end, engagement *is* the end. (Denhardt & Denhardt, 2011, p. 172)

Second, pragmatically, engagement produces better outcomes in terms of identifying and responding to needs of the targeted populations or areas and achieves more buy-in from both funding agencies and affected citizens. As the Denhardts put it,

From an instrumental or "smart" perspective, we should work to increase citizen involvement because government cannot solve public problems alone. Effective governance increasingly requires active and ongoing citizen participation in planning, policymaking, implementation, and service delivery. The complexity of the problems facing government demands citizen involvement and acceptance, if not active cooperation. (2011, p. 172)

However, empirical evidence of the value added to both public agencies and citizens resulting from engagement is sparse.

HISTORY OF U.S. CITIZEN ENGAGEMENT

Early in the history of the United States, citizen involvement in government was limited to voting. Given the legal restrictions that determined who was eligible to vote at the time, this meant that a large proportion of the public was not engaged in government at all. Although Progressivists began arguing for a greater role for citizens and more government transparency to facilitate citizen oversight in the early 1900s, it was not until many years later that citizen participation was widely considered a necessary part of the governing process.

The Federal Government and Citizen Engagement

The federal government has been a leader in the citizen participation movement. Many different agencies have been involved. Early examples include the role of tribal organizations in dealings with the Bureau of Indian Affairs and the Indian Division of the Public Health Service, use of advisory committees of private citizens in the decision-making process for research grant awards by the National Science Foundation, farmers serving on county-based committees established by the Department of Agriculture, and the activities of tenant associations in low-income public housing projects and "blue ribbon" nonresident citizens serving on urban renewal project advisory committees funded by the U.S. Department of Housing and Urban Development (HUD).

Major changes in the types of engaged citizens and goals for involvement accompanied the establishment in the 1960s of Community Action Agencies under the Economic Opportunity Act and City Demonstration Agencies under the Model Cities Act. The former was the cornerstone of the Johnson administration's War on Poverty, while the latter spearheaded the administration's efforts to revitalize urban neighborhoods. "Citizens" were predominantly poor minority group members, not affluent whites, who were more neighborhood- than citywide-oriented. Federal legislation called for their maximum feasible or widespread involvement. In some programs, the forms of engagement were not specified; others required that the majority of members of advisory committees be residents of affected areas. Some citizens were elected in community forums, others were appointed by the mayor or city council, and still others were self-designated. In some cities, residents were hired and paid for with grant funds, leading to charges of manipulation and co-optation by the powerful elites (Arnstein, 1969). Nevertheless, the overall goal was a partnership between the local agency and neighborhood organizations and their representatives to alleviate poverty and rebuild communities. Citizen representatives were involved to varying degrees in policy making, funding priority setting, and hiring staff (Stenberg, 1972, pp. 191–192).

Although some of the pioneering citizen engagement programs are no longer in existence, the federal government's leadership role has continued and has spurred efforts at the local level. The chief vehicle for the spread of citizen participation has been the grant-in-aid program. A study by the U.S. Advisory Commission on Intergovernmental Relations (ACIR) found that as of December 1978, requirements for various types of citizen participation were attached to 155 federal grant programs, at that time about one third of the total number of programs and accounting for 80% of the grant funds. Most of these programs had been established since 1970, and about half were found in the health, education, and welfare areas. The ACIR identified 31 different forms of participation, ranging from speaking at public hearings to serving on a committee that has some control over decisions. The most common forms of engagement were advisory committees and public hearings (ACIR, 1979, pp. 4–5).

State and Local Government Citizen Engagement

Citizen participation requirements are not confined to federal grant-in-aid programs. At the state and local levels, for example, public hearings in advance of budget approval are mandated by state statute or local ordinance. City and county governing bodies allocate public comment time on their meeting agendas. States have sought to promote greater transparency and access by enacting open-meeting and open-record laws and providing for citizen comments in agency rulemaking under administrative procedure acts. Local voters must often approve proposed bond issuances or other policy changes through referenda. And across the country, there are thousands of citizen advisory boards and local planning committees.

Citizens also participate as coproducers with government agencies in neighborhood watch programs, Adopt a Highway programs, Friends of the Library, recycling, and Crime Stoppers programs as well as serve as volunteers in libraries, recreation program coaching, park maintenance crews, and museums. They provide feedback on local government performance via citizen surveys, citizen academies, and social media. Homeowners associations and other neighborhood organizations provide services in many localities and serve as vehicles for self-governance. Perhaps the best example of the coproducer role is the venerable volunteer fire departments that are found in many small and medium-sized communities across the country. According to the National Fire Protection Association, 31% of the 1,134,400 firefighters in 2014 were careerists, while 69% were volunteers. Ninety-five percent of the volunteers served jurisdictions under 25,000 in population (National Fire Protection Association website, www.NFPA.org).

As noted in Chapter 2, the Progressive movement introduced the initiative and referendum to some states and localities. These instruments of direct democracy, which bypass representative democracy and the legislative process, are found in 27 states and enable citizens to place policy proposals on the general election ballot or vote to confirm legislative actions and make public policy. Typically, such state ballot measures include proposals for tax increases, such as on general sales and cigarettes, and for bond issuances for transportation and other infrastructure purposes. In addition to fiscal matters, voters in several states were asked recently to decide on medical and recreational marijuana, the death penalty, minimum wage, and campaign finance reforms (Underhill, 2016, p. 13). Eighteen states also permit citizens to recall a public official by direct vote before his or her term of office expires.

This overview of the wide range of governmental programs and activities in which citizen engagement is encouraged or mandated leads us to return to the question: Why engage citizens? Similar to the participatory instruments, the motives, expectations, and results have varied. What are some of the challenges associated with engagement?

OBJECTIVES OF CITIZEN PARTICIPATION

This chapter began by asking why we should engage citizens. Combining normative and pragmatic arguments, the rationale underlying citizen engagement rests on several anticipated positive outcomes. Involving citizens in the governmental process involves costs—staff time, expense, opening the government up to criticism—but today, the benefits of citizen engagement are considered well worth the costs.

Benefits of Citizen Engagement

The first set of benefits are related to the quality of the public policy solution or decisions that result from involving citizens:

- Both citizens and staff will have a better understanding of problems and needs, options, and priorities.

- Decisions will be improved in terms of their administrative feasibility and political acceptance.

The second set of potential goals from engaging the public relates to the outcomes from the resulting policies or decisions:

- There will be greater buy-in of outcomes by both affected citizens and agency representatives.

- Citizen representatives will facilitate getting the word out to the community as to what action the local government is taking and why.

Finally, welcoming the public to be active participants in the governance process helps to make better citizens and better communities:

- Community representation in decision making will promote community building and reduce antigovernment sentiments.

- Citizen engagement efforts serve as an introduction to the ways citizens can get involved and may lead to more extensive types of government participation.

- Decision making will be open and more transparent, which will help build citizen trust in government.

When Is Citizen Engagement Appropriate?

Although the engagement model rests on these important assumptions about benefits, as a practical matter, citizens do not always want to be engaged nor are they always able to do so. They might not desire to collaborate with local officials or to have control over decentralized local service operations. And public administrators may not welcome their voice or vote. The following observation by George Frederickson (2005) in an assessment of the state of social equity in America is relevant to citizen engagement: "Like it or not, senior public administrators and those of us who study public administration are part of the elite, the privileged. In much of the literature and ideology there is a distinctly patronizing tone" (p. 36).

Citizen engagement is not appropriate across the board. In fact, most local issues may not call for engagement, as they involve the routine performance of basic functions. Types of situations where engagement can add value are where (1) strong, conflicting values or emotions are involved; (2) a controversial or gridlock situation exists and community support is needed for taking action; (3) citizens recognize that a situation has moved from a condition to an issue or problem and will turn into a crisis if actions are not taken; (4) there is more than one right answer or approach; (5) the subject matter does not require citizens to quickly master complex technical information or data; and (6) hostility to government action and distrust of local officials are high (Everett, 2015, p. 24; Irvin & Stansbury, 2004, p. 62). So, citizen engagement is especially useful for diffusing highly emotional policy deliberation and for finding the most satisfactory policy solution for a community when there is disagreement about the direction.

ENGAGEMENT CHALLENGES

Proponents of engagement confront challenges on both the citizen and public official fronts. Consider a hypothetical case in this chapter: While city leaders had good intentions about creating a citizens' committee to help with the budget formulation, there were a number of potential concerns that were not discussed or addressed prior to moving forward with the creation of the committee.

CHAPTER CASE

BACKGROUND

It is February and the local budget process is about to get underway in the city of Harmony. Located in the Midwest, Harmony has just over 40,000 residents. The population is diverse and most of the residents are middle income. The mayor and members of council in Harmony have decided to reach out to citizens to get a fresh look at the city's finances and identify ways to save money to avoid tax and fee increases while maintaining current service levels. They have voted to establish a citizen's advisory committee on government economy and efficiency. The city manager supports this decision and, at the council's direction, submits the names of prospective appointees, most of whom are graduates of the city-sponsored Citizen's Leadership Academy. The mayor, with council concurrence, appoints the committee members and chair and gives them their charge with a deadline for submitting their report and recommendations one month before the close of the fiscal year on June 30. But the budget director and senior staff members are ambivalent. There are several reasons why all parties might have reservations about participating.

POTENTIAL CITIZEN CONCERNS

- Some citizens may not trust "privileged" public administrators and feel that they are being manipulated to produce outcomes incorporating the values and policies the government wants, not what the community wants. This is especially the case in cities similar to Harmony, where the demographics of the local bureaucracy do not reflect the diversity of the community.

- Citizens might suspect that they are being provided with incomplete or biased information by the staff.

- Citizens might believe that the main reason they have been asked to participate is to give their stamp of approval to otherwise unpopular decisions, such as increasing property tax rates, raising utility or parking fees, installing traffic calming sites, laying off personnel, or closing some branch libraries or fire stations.

- Citizens may be concerned that staff and elected officials will use the commission to buffer criticism from the community or to blame them for recommending tough budget-balancing steps.

STAFF CONCERNS

- The committee was given only a four-month timetable for its work. Even in smaller localities, budgets are lengthy and complex documents. Budgets encompass the entire scope of local operating and capital programs and human capital commitments and are used to articulate strategic priorities. This comprehensive picture takes time to understand.

- The budget process is also driven by the financial history of the jurisdiction as well as by fiscal projections involving a combination of revenue estimates, such as from local property tax collections, state aid, and federal grants. It will likely take several meetings for the committee members to begin to absorb the detailed information on city operations and work through the budget document, so four months is an ambitious deadline if the council is serious about achieving economy and efficiency savings.

- As well-informed, trained, and experienced professionals, the staff knows best about the city's financial condition, budget history, priorities, and fiscal projections.

- The resources required to help ensure successful engagement could drain the staff's capacity to address other, more important needs.

- Citizen activists could use the advisory committee as a bully pulpit and be disruptive if they do not get their way, attracting bad publicity to the city, which elected officials will not appreciate.

- Too much staff time would be required to bring the citizens up to speed on the budget and service delivery responsibilities so they can give informed advice.

- Administrators could lose control of the budget process timelines, and delays could jeopardize completion and adoption by the end of the fiscal year.

- Media stories about fraud, waste, and abuse and citizen distrust and dissatisfaction with government could bias or skew the objectivity of the committee and its receptivity to staff input.

- High and unrealistic expectations could be established about the levels of economy and efficiency that are to be attained through the advisory committee's work, and elected officials will likely blame the staff for any shortfalls.

(Continued)

(Continued)

LOGISTICAL CONCERNS

- Citizens may not have the time to attend committee meetings, especially if they are held during regular working hours.

- There may be other barriers to attending meetings. For example, if the participants have to pay for child care and parking expenses while engaged with the committee, this could be a disincentive to participation.

- Due to these barriers, There is no assurance that members of the committee are representative of and respected by the community, especially since they were selected by city officials from a pool of Citizen Academy graduates.

DISCONNECT BETWEEN CITIZENS AND GOVERNMENT OFFICIALS

- Although a priority for elected officials and staff, the search for economy and efficiency in governmental operations might not be as urgent, compelling, or critical to the community as it is to public officials. After all, citizens care most about the level, quality, and timeliness of services and not as much about what these cost or who provides them.

- Unlike staff and management who are faced on a daily basis with considering the tough value trade-offs among liberty, community, prosperity, and equality that often arise in decision making (Boyle, 2001), citizens may not be aware of these tensions. Elected officials are experienced in making these judgments, while citizen volunteers might not recognize the underlying values or might be uncomfortable balancing them. For example, initiatives to increase service efficiency and productivity, such as reductions in trash collection and neighborhood policing patrols, could have negative impacts on equity. Economic development plans to create jobs and bolster tax revenues by focusing on recruiting technology companies would likely not benefit low-skilled workers formerly employed in manufacturing.

- Staff are able to take a community-wide perspective, while community members may be more concerned about their own neighborhood.

DISCUSSION QUESTION

If you were the city manager, what steps could you take to try to preempt these concerns?

Engaging citizens in ways that are more meaningful than a traditional public hearing is complicated and involves a great deal of planning and foresight. As the case above points out, the perspective of citizens can be very different from that of those working inside of government. Those differing perspectives can influence the attitudes of potential participants and staff, thereby affecting the overall process and outcomes of the engagement effort.

Despite these mutual concerns and reservations, the citizen participation literature cautions that failure to engage citizens creates more serious problems. There could be a mismatch between the assessment of needs and priorities by citizens and by public administrators. For example, let us say that the new Harmony police chief is a champion of community-oriented policing while residents of poorer and minority neighborhoods are skeptical of the intentions underlying the increased police presence and are uncomfortable having armed personnel in uniform patrolling their streets. As this example demonstrates, local staff may be considered out of touch with community sentiments and concerns. Top-down, us-versus-them staff attitudes fuel alienation, not collaboration. And distrust of government could grow, not diminish. Janet and Robert Denhardt (2011) observe:

> What appears to be most important from a citizen's perspective and from the standpoint of attaining ongoing engagement is not the strategy employed, but the government's response when citizens voice their preferences. For citizens, two questions are paramount: Did the government listen and take action based on what it heard? Was the response worth the citizen's time and effort? (p. 181)

Valerie Lemmie, former city manager of Petersburg, Virginia, and Dayton and Cincinnati, Ohio, provides a community safety example of working together:

> In one neighborhood, drug dealers congregated on a dimly lit pedestrian bridge, making it unsafe for neighborhood residents and [providing] a quick, undetected "in and out" for those buying drugs. For the police, this was a minor concern given other, more flagrant violations in the neighborhood and they agreed only to add temporary patrols. It was citizens who came up with the best solution to "take back" convenient access to their neighborhood. With the city's endorsement, they glued plastic eggs to the railings, making it an uncomfortable place to sit. That was the end of drug dealing. Better lighting,

more police patrols, and improved landscaping helped ensure that the dealers did not return. (Lemmie, 2008, p. 37)

Engagement is challenging because citizen participation in local government has historically been low, both at the ballot box or in other venues. According to Kevin Desouza (2015), "In 2014, the National Research Center conducted a survey on resident activity and found that only 19 percent of Americans contacted their local elected officials over a 12-month period, and about 25 percent attended a public meeting" (p. 14). Noting that many previous citizen participation attempts have not produced fruitful results despite investments of time and resources, he concluded:

The strong temptation to engage people more because it's popular can be detrimental to a local government. While I would never go as far as to say stop seeking citizen engagement, I would implore that you find the right balance of engagement. (p. 16)

At the same time, it is noteworthy that public opinion polls since the early 1970s have shown that citizens have more positive views of local government compared with state and federal governments, which could facilitate engagement. A 2009 survey conducted by John Kincaid and Richard Cole found that 62% of the respondents believed that local governments were trustworthy, compared to 55% for states and 50% for the federal government. Thirty-one percent reported that localities delivered the "most for the money," compared to 29% for the federal government and 26% for states (Kincaid & Cole, 2011). While these percentages were lower than the 2002 figures, the trend did not change. Nevertheless, "the comparisons provide little solace because none of the trust levels is very high" and, therefore, local officials may be concerned about a lack of "legitimacy for action" on problems or issues confronting their community (Barnes, 2016, p. 3).

Citizen engagement advocates take some credit for these survey results, pointing out that the amount of openness of local governments and availability of officials are important factors. Even though functional responsibilities have become highly intergovernmentalized, citizens see their cities and counties as being on the front lines in providing basic services such as schools, water and sewer services, police and fire protection, parks and recreation, road maintenance, trash collection, and libraries. Many communities televise meetings of their governing bodies, have websites, and use blogs and social media to communicate

Citizens participate in a public hearing for rent control proposals in Portland, Oregon.

information to citizens. Citizens can also participate in local affairs via public hearings and service on advisory boards. And they can meet with elected officials and public administrators in the city hall or county courthouse as well as at the grocery store, church, or athletic field. While these are positive features, elected officials and public administrators sometimes complain that being so close to the citizens has a price tag: They live in a fishbowl-like environment and find it difficult to have privacy.

To sum up, even though engagement may be both the right and smart thing to do, administrators should be aware that there are both advantages and disadvantages for the citizens and for local governments. These are summarized by Renee Irvin and John Stansbury in Table 8.1. The next section reviews different types of participation and considers the expectations associated with engagement.

FROM PARTICIPATION TO POWER

As indicated previously, the 1960s witnessed an upsurge of federally mandated or promoted citizen participation initiatives, mostly as crosscutting requirements

TABLE 8.1 ■ Advantages and Disadvantages of Citizen Participation in Governmental Decision Making

	Advantages of Citizen Participation		Disadvantages of Citizen Participation	
	Advantages to citizens	Advantages to government	Disadvantages to citizens	Disadvantages to government
Decision Process	• Education (learn from and inform government representatives) • Persuade and enlighten government • Gain skills for activist citizenship	• Educating (learn from and inform citizens) • Persuade citizens; build trust and allay anxiety or hostility • Build strategic alliances • Gain legitimacy of decisions	• Time consuming (even dull) • Pointless if decision is ignored	• Time consuming • Costly • May backfire, creating more hostility toward government
Outcomes	• Break gridlock; achieve outcomes • Gain some control over policy process • Better policy and implementation decisions	• Break gridlock; achieve outcomes • Avoid litigation costs • Better policy and implementation decisions	• Worse policy decision may be selected if heavily influenced by opposing interest groups	• Loss of decision-making control • Possibility of bad decision that is politically impossible to ignore • Less budget for implementation of actual projects

Source: Irvin & Stansbury, 2004.

accompanying grant-in-aid programs. These initiatives were greeted with controversy in some communities, as sometimes there was a mismatch between the expectations of federal and local officials and engaged citizens regarding the outcomes of engagement. One of the most influential examinations of the range and results of participation at that time was conducted by Sherry Arnstein.

Arnstein's Ladder of Citizen Participation

Drawing on examples from the federal urban renewal, antipoverty, and model cities programs, Arnstein developed a typology of participation depicting the interplay between the powerless and powerholders. Figure 8.1 shows her ladder of participation, with each of the eight rungs indicating the "extent of citizens' power in determining the end product" (Arnstein, 1969, p. 217).

At the lowest rungs, manipulation and therapy, the privileged dimension of public administrators and elected officials is apparent, as these officials (powerholders) seek to educate or remediate citizens through service on rubber stamp advisory committees or neighborhood councils. To Arnstein, these steps are nonparticipatory for the citizens and are chiefly public relations vehicles for the powerholders.

The next three steps—informing, consultation, and placation—involve officials providing information and seeking advice. Citizen surveys, neighborhood meetings, and public hearings are common approaches in this category. However, these steps are mainly one-dimensional and there is no assurance that citizen voices will be heard, advice will be heeded, and the status quo changed. After reviewing program evaluations conducted for HUD and Office of Economic Opportunity (OEO), Arnstein concluded that the level of participation in most of the Model Cities Act's city demonstration agencies and the OEO's community action agencies was at the placation rung or below. As in previous federal programs, citizens were being planned for by those in city hall. Boards tended to rubber stamp staff decisions instead of taking the initiative to identify and prioritize citizen or community needs and develop ways to address them.

At the highest rungs of the ladder are three degrees of power redistribution—partnership, delegated power, and citizen control. Partnership involves negotiations and trade-offs between citizens and officials, sometimes because of citizen anger and protests that attract media and federal attention. At the top are actions that give citizens a voting majority on decision-making bodies or control of policy and management, such as through establishment of a neighborhood corporation or decentralization of public services such as police, schools, and health to neighborhood governing bodies (Arnstein, 1969, p. 217). Not surprisingly, Arnstein's review

FIGURE 8.1 ■ Eight Rungs on a Ladder of Citizen Participation

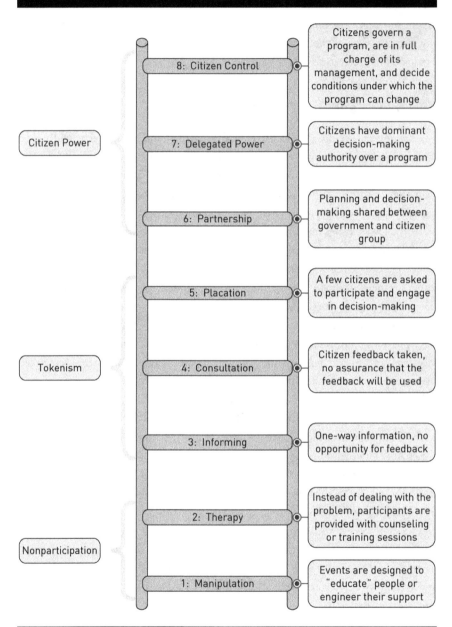

	8: Citizen Control	Citizens govern a program, are in full charge of its management, and decide conditions under which the program can change
Citizen Power	7: Delegated Power	Citizens have dominant decision-making authority over a program
	6: Partnership	Planning and decision-making shared between government and citizen group
	5: Placation	A few citizens are asked to participate and engage in decision-making
Tokenism	4: Consultation	Citizen feedback taken, no assurance that the feedback will be used
	3: Informing	One-way information, no opportunity for feedback
	2: Therapy	Instead of dealing with the problem, participants are provided with counseling or training sessions
Nonparticipation	1: Manipulation	Events are designed to "educate" people or engineer their support

Source: Arnstein, 1969, p. 217.

did not reveal a significant number of examples of power sharing and community control. She did cite a number of arguments made by opponents:

> It [community control] supports separatism; it creates balkanization of public services; it is more costly and less efficient; it enables minority group "hustlers" to be just as opportunistic and disdainful of the have-nots as their white predecessors; it is incompatible with merit systems and professionalism; and ironically enough, it can turn out to be a new Mickey Mouse game for the have-nots by allowing them to gain control but not allowing them sufficient dollar resources to succeed. (p. 224)

At the same time, there are some instructive examples of localities sharing power. Beginning in 1971, the Dayton city council awarded grants to seven neighborhood priority boards that served as the voice for the city's 65 neighborhoods and were recognized as Dayton's citizen participation structure. The boards made investments in priority projects within their respective boundaries, such as festivals, beautification efforts, and other neighborhood improvements. Members and officers were elected and each board had a city staff liaison assigned. According to the Dayton Priority Board's website (City of Dayton, 2017):

> They [priority boards] have been instrumental at both the City and grassroots level in their support of the legislative changes, new program implementation, and leadership development. The City of Dayton and the Priority Boards have worked together to improve Dayton by supporting income tax increase and renewals, the passage of local school levies, and support of innovative City ordinances.

In 2014, the city changed its community engagement strategy and stopped funding the priority boards due to concerns about insufficient neighborhood organizational volunteer leadership and domination of some boards by longtime members. Under the revamped system, instead of the boards acting as intermediaries and distributing money to neighborhood groups and business associations, all three organizations were considered as equals by the city in the competition for funding. In 2015, the city awarded mini-grants totaling nearly $100,000 for neighborhood projects (Frolik, 2015).

In Reno, Nevada, eight neighborhood advisory boards are allocated a total of $380,000 annually divided on a per capita basis to meet needs such as swimming pools, litter control, neighborhood watches, and festivals. According to the city manager:

> Having real resources to dedicate to neighborhood priorities has raised the profile of these boards, and the sense of local participation has caught on. . . . The NABs [neighborhood advisory boards] have become influential bodies and consistently communicate with their respective city councilmembers as well as with city staff. (McNeely, 2007, p. 17)

These examples demonstrate that the stridency and tone of the community power movement have changed since the 1960s. But Arnstein's ladder remains a useful way to differentiate approaches to citizen engagement.

International Association of Public Participation Spectrum

A second useful model, shown in Figure 8.2, was developed by the International Association of Public Participation (IAP2). The IAP2 model features a continuum of participation moving from inform to consult to involve to collaborate to empower. Particularly helpful to both citizens and public officials are the promises made to the public by the latter at each stage together with the tools or techniques that are appropriate, given the level of public input being sought.

E-GOVERNMENT ENGAGEMENT

Today, engaging the public in the governance process can be facilitated with technology. The e-government movement and growth of social media applications have provided additional opportunities for localities to move beyond the traditional tools to engage citizens. While technology can make it easier for governments to reach larger proportions of their populations, due to some drawbacks, these methods should not wholly replace more traditional ways of involving the public.

Examples of E-Engagement

Among the examples of approaches that are being used by local government are the following, taken from the website of the Alliance for Innovation (2014):

- conducting electronic surveys, which can be quantified to solicit information and views from citizens on subjects such as spending priorities, neighborhood service adequacy, and planned development;

FIGURE 8.2 ■ IAP2 Spectrum of Public Participation

	Inform	Consult	Involve	Collaborate	Empower
Public participation goal	To provide the public with balanced and objective information to assist them in understanding the problem, alternatives, opportunities, and/or solutions.	To obtain public feedback on analysis, alternatives, and/or decisions.	To work directly with the public throughout the process to ensure that public concerns and aspirations are consistently understood and considered.	To partner with the public in each aspect of the decision, including the development of alternatives and the identification of the preferred solution.	To place final decision-making power in the hands of the public.
Promise to the public	We will keep you informed.	We will keep you informed, listen and acknowledge concerns and aspirations, and provide feedback on how public input influenced the decision.	We will work with you to ensure that your concerns and aspirations are directly reflected in the alternatives developed and provide feedback on how public input influenced the decision.	We will look to you for advice and innovation in formulating solutions and incorporate your advice and recommendations into the decisions to the maximum extent possible.	We will implement what you decide.
Example techniques	• Fact sheets • Websites • Open houses	• Public comments • Focus groups • Surveys • Public meetings	• Workshops • Deliberative polling	• Citizen advisory committees • Consensus building • Participatory decision making	• Citizen juries • Ballots • Delegated decision

Source: International Association for Public Participation, 2007.

- using social media such as Twitter and Facebook, blogs, online forums, and open city halls to enable citizens to receive real-time information such as street closings and traffic jams, communicate with one another and with public officials, and comment on local issues and personalities;

- changing the format of town hall meetings to become call-in shows or "telephone town halls," enabling citizens to participate in discussions by telephone or e-mail as well as in person, and recording sessions for YouTube and local website access;

- providing a website for citizens to use to speak up on local services and interact with administrators and elected officials;

- scheduling "hangout at city hall" opportunities during which citizens can interact virtually with the mayor, council members, and city manager;

- relying on government-access cable to showcase local projects such as arts festivals, entertainer performances, and live conversations with the mayor, other elected officials, and the city manager;

- using 311 call centers or other one-stop shops for handling citizen nonemergency requests and complaints—such as missed trash collections, potholes, and nonfunctioning traffic signals—together with tracking, referral, and responding capacities;

- developing civic applications of high-speed Internet access and webinars to spur citizen engagement in budgeting, visioning, planning, and transportation;

- giving citizens access to local data using dashboards, websites, and apps to facilitate comparisons of their community's cost of doing business and performance with peer jurisdictions; and

- offering online engagement games and simulations that allow citizens to participate and compete in comprehensive and land use planning or budgeting development exercises to give them greater appreciation of the difficulties of local decision making.

Concerns about E-Engagement

Using technology to involve the public is not without its drawbacks. There are two concerns to be had about e-engagement. First, it may be too customer-service oriented and one dimensional. While citizens may be viewed as customers of public agencies and should be informed about the activities of their local government, this is not sufficient. As Arnstein's ladder and the IAP2 spectrum indicate, authentic citizen engagement involves using citizen input to inform government decisions or policies.

Second, there are also social equity concerns related to e-governance tools. E-government is available to those who have access to technology but it could adversely affect disadvantaged citizens (Durant & Ali, 2013, p. 280). While public programs exist to make computers available in libraries and provide high-speed Internet access to rural communities and low-income areas, there still exists a digital divide. Even in cases where citizens have the means to purchase computer equipment and Internet service, there exist issues with computer literacy, particularly with senior citizens. As Reno, Nevada's city manager cautioned: "When turning to technology to improve on these traditional methods of citizen participation, we must remember that the heart of the matter is the residents' experience, not the tools used to improve it" (McNeely, 2007, p. 17).

As local governments implement new technologies to reach their residents, they must consider whether access disparities exist. Where disparities do exist, caution should be taken not to rely too extensively for social media to determine how to provide or prioritize services. For example, during Hurricane Sandy in Newark, New Jersey, Mayor Cory Booker rose to national prominence by quickly responding to Tweets from residents seeking assistance (O'Connor, 2012). While Mayor Booker demonstrated concern and responsiveness for his constituents during the storm, he may have also diverted city resources based on who had access to technology rather than who had the greatest need.

In addition to modifying responsiveness based on social media requests, there is the question of how uniform the use of social media is among different communities. A review of research on the use of social media by local governments concluded that social media use is not dependent on form of government or population size, although the literature hypothesizes that council–manager localities and larger units are more likely to use social media. The former jurisdictions might be expected to have an environment that is more conducive to citizen engagement due to the tenets of the ICMA Code of Ethics and professional training of the manager and management team. The latter type of community has more resources to invest in technology. Bryer and Nelson (2013) also concluded that local governments "are not using the technologies in much more than a unidirectional manner; this has potential implications for citizen engagement both in process (what do we expect of our citizens) and outcome (such as trust in government and efficacy)" (pp. 241–242). Other research found that the most common use of e-government has involved sharing information about local meetings and events and transacting services such as paying taxes, fees, or fines; registering for local athletic teams; or renewing library books and DVDs.

MAKING ENGAGEMENT WORK

Research has shown widely varying results from local application of the citizen engagement approaches across jurisdictions of all sizes and forms of government. There are many examples of successful and unsuccessful engagement efforts by municipalities and counties (Beierle, 2002). Even though there is more anecdotal than empirical evidence, what is clear from the literature is that there is tension between professionalism and participation and that administrative systems that emphasize the former can marginalize engagement.

Nevertheless, it is argued that the likely benefits of engagement outweigh the costs—that engagement is both the right thing to do and the smart thing to do (Denhardt & Denhardt, 2011, p. 183). What is also clear is that despite a checkered history and mixed results, leadership in promoting citizen engagement has shifted from the federal government to municipalities and counties. While federal crosscutting grant program requirements in this area continue to be influential, a review of the literature reveals a strong commitment, particularly from the local management profession, to reach out to citizens. For example, included among the competencies and skills expected of managers in ICMA's Practices for Effective Local Government Management (Appendix 2) is "recognizing the right of citizens to influence local decisions and promoting active citizen involvement in local governance."

John Nalbandian (2008) argues that citizen engagement is no longer optional; it is imperative as an anchor for managers to use in bridging the growing gap between political acceptability and administrative feasibility (p. 37). And Valerie Lemmie (2008) contends that engagement needs to join economy, efficiency, effectiveness, and equity as the fifth core component of the manager's value proposition because "never before has the gulf between citizens and their government been so wide, frustrations and anger so high, and the solutions so seemingly elusive" (p. 34).

Robust citizen engagement in local performance management is a recent example of how managers and citizens can work together in the ways indicated by Nalbandian and Lemmie. These engagement efforts are multidimensional and entail citizens playing some or all of five roles that are key to aligning performance information with programs and services that citizens value. These involve treating citizens as more than just customers and seeking to engage citizens and exchange ideas about community activities that they really care about as (1) stakeholders who have expectations about local services and views on how well they are performed; (2) advocates on behalf of community interests, needs, and priorities; (3) issue framers for community visions, goals, strategies, alternatives, and outcomes; (4) evaluators of service quality and costs; and (5) collaborators and coproducers to help achieve community goals. As local governments embark on the challenging journey from performance measurement to performance management, the most crucial of these five roles is issue framing (Epstein, Wray, & Harding, 2006, p. 19).

The effectiveness of citizen engagement depends on having the appropriate structure and process. Nalbandian (2008) stresses the importance of *planned* engagement, which "comes in many shapes and sizes but, generally speaking, brings diverse groups together either as individuals or as representatives in semiformal, facilitated settings to plan and problem solve" (p. 36). While there is no formula that guarantees positive results, there are at least twelve steps that local managers could take to increase prospects that the engagement experience will add value to both the government and citizens. These are (1) identifying important tasks for the citizens to perform in addressing a well-recognized problem; (2) selecting the appropriate engagement approach or technique in light of the goal of engagement (see Figure 8.2); (3) encouraging the community to volunteer for service, consulting with community leaders on possible representatives and chair candidates, and ensuring membership diversity; (4) clarifying the charge of the group and expectations of the members, elected officials, and staff; (5) determining roles, duties, and authorities; (6) establishing a transparent decision-making process; (7) giving realistic time limits and reasonable deliverables; (8) scheduling regular meetings at convenient times and in neutral, comfortable locations, preferably other than city hall or a county courthouse; (9) making staff available to provide information and historical perspective as well as arranging for neutral facilitation of meetings; (10) reimbursing citizen representatives for their transportation and child care expenses and providing food at meetings; (11) determining specific, realistic, and measurable outputs; and (12) developing an action plan for implementation, including communications and evaluations strategies (Stephens, Morse, & O'Brien, 2011).

Beyond these steps, success will depend on the readiness of elected officials, professional staff, and citizens to work together as well as on the community's capacity to encourage and sustain engagement. The Davenport Institute for Public Engagement and Civic Leadership at Pepperdine University has developed a self-evaluation scorecard that enables local officials to ask themselves, "How are we doing?" The scorecard lists 20 practices shared by agencies that take engagement seriously under three categories: culture of engagement, engagement practices, and community capacity and partnerships. The Institute also recognizes communities that embrace these best practices. In July 2016, it gave its highest award to San Rafael, California, for its use of

advanced technologies for involving its residents in a variety of thorny issues, including the development of a homeless action plan, quiet zones for a new commuter train, business issues, negotiations with unionized municipal employees, climate-change activities, safety facilities, sidewalk maintenance and downtown parking. (Gould, 2016)

In some cases, managers might conclude that the costs of engagement outweigh the benefits and choose to use traditional top-down decision making. In other circumstances, the reverse may be true. The message to managers is that "it behooves the administrator to consider the advantages and disadvantages of the decision-making process when determining the most effective implementation strategy, bearing in mind that talk is not cheap—and may not even be effective" (Irvin & Stansbury, 2004, p. 63).

REFERENCES

Advisory Commission on Intergovernmental Relations. (1979). *Citizen participation in the American federal system.* Washington, DC: U.S. Government Printing Office.

Alliance for Innovation. (2014). [Website]. Retrieved April 1, 2017, from http://www.transformgov.org

Arnstein, S. R. (1969). A ladder of citizen participation. *Journal of the American Institute of Planners, 34*(4), 216–224.

Barnes, W. R. (2016). *Developing legitimacy for action by connecting citizens and government: Lessons for U.S. local government leaders from a citizen engagement process in Australia.* Phoenix, AZ: Alliance for Innovation.

Beierle, T. C. (2002). The quality of stakeholder-based decisions. *Risk Analysis, 22*(4), 739–749.

Berger, B. (2009). Political theory, political science, and the end of civic engagement. *Perspectives on Politics, 7*(2), 335–350.

Boyle, P. (2001, Fall). Public problems, values, and choices. *Popular Government,* 18–23.

Bryer, T. A., & Nelson, K. L. (2013). Social media for civic engagement. In C. N. Silva (Ed.), *Citizen e-participation in urban governance: Crowdsourcing and collaborative creativity* (pp. 226–246). Hershey, PA: IGI Global.

City of Dayton. (2017). *Dayton priority board system.* Retrieved April 1, 2017, from http://daytonoriginals .org/2011/02/16/dayton-priority-board-system/

Denhardt, J. V., & Denhardt, R. B. (2011). *The new public service: Serving, not steering* (3rd ed.). Armonk, NY: M.E. Sharpe.

Desouza, K. (2015). Citizen disengagement: The minority opinion. *Public Management, 97*(2), 12–16.

Durant, R. F., & Ali, S. B. (2013). Repositioning American public administration? Citizen estrangement, administrative reform, and the disarticulated state. *Public Administration Review, 73*(2), 278–289.

Epstein, P., Wray, L., & Harding, C. (2006). Citizens as partners in performance management. *Public Management, 88*(10), 18–22.

Everett, E. (2015). Today's local government management model. *Public Management, 97*(7), 22–25.

Frederickson, H. G. (2005, Winter). The state of social equity in American public administration. *National Civic Review,* 31–38.

Frolik, C. (2015, December 12). *City touts success of new engagement strategy.* Retrieved March 20, 2017, from http://www.mydaytondailynews.com/news/local/city-touts-success-new-engagement-strategy/jHj5Gaz6jvKgQWBBUtWhIM/

Gibson, C. (2006). *Citizens at the center: A new approach to citizen engagement.* Washington, DC: The Case Foundation.

Gould, R. (2016). *A scorecard for public engagement.* Retrieved March 21, 2017, from http://www.governing.com/gov-institute/voices/col-scorecard-community-public-engagement-policymaking.html

International Association for Public Participation. (2007). *IAP2's public participation spectrum.* Retrieved March 20, 2017, from http://c.ymcdn.com/sites/www.iap2.org/resource/resmgr/foundations_course/IAP2_P2_Spectrum_FINAL.pdf

Irvin, R. A., & Stansbury, J. (2004). Citizen participation in decision-making: Is it worth the effort? *Public Administration Review, 64*(1), 55–65.

Kincaid, J., & Cole, R. L. (2011). Citizen attitudes toward issues of federalism in Canada, Mexico, and the United States. *Publius, 41*(1), 53–75.

Lemmie, V. A. (2008). *Democracy beyond the ballot box: A new role for elected officials, city managers, and citizens.* Washington, DC: National Academy of Public Administration.

McNeely, C. (2007). Communication and citizen participation: Blending old tools with new technology. *Public Management, 89*(10), 16–20.

Nalbandian, J. (2008). Predicting the future: Why citizen engagement no longer is optional. *Public Management, 90*(11), 35–37.

O'Connor, E. (2012, November 2). Cory Booker cements his reputation as Newark 'super mayor,' lets Sandy victims crash at his house. *Time.* Retrieved March 20, 2017, from http://newsfeed.time.com/2012/11/02/cory-booker-cements-his-reputation-as-newarks-super-mayor/

Stenberg, C. W. (1972). Citizens and the administrative state: From participation to power. *Public Administration Review, 32*(3), 190–198.

Stephens, J. B., Morse, R. S., & O'Brien, K. T. (2011). *Public outreach and participation.* Chapel Hill: University of North Carolina School of Government.

Underhill, W. (2016). What voters face. *State Legislatures, 42*(9), 13–15.

RESOURCE LIST/TO EXPLORE FURTHER

Books/Articles

Nabatchi, T., & Leighninger, M. (2015). *Public participation for 21st century democracy.* Hoboken, NJ: Jossey-Bass.

Stephens, J. B., Morse, R. S., & O'Brien, K. T. (2011). *Public outreach and participation.* Chapel Hill: University of North Carolina School of Government

Upshaw, V. M. (2010). *Creating and maintaining effective local government citizen advisory committees.* Chapel Hill: University of North Carolina School of Government.

Web Resources

Davenport Institute for Public Engagement and Civic Leadership, School of Public Policy, Pepperdine University. (2017). *How are we doing?* Available at https://publicpolicy.pepperdine.edu/davenport-institute/evaluating-engagement/

SERVICE DELIVERY STRATEGIES AND INNOVATION

The word government is from a Greek word, which means "to steer."
The job of government is to steer, not to row the boat. Delivering services
is rowing, and government is not very good at rowing.

—E. S. Savas (Osborne & Gaebler, 1992, p. 25)

Previous chapters have discussed the mismatch between the jurisdictional boundaries of local governments in the United States and the scope of the problems they confront. It is clear that many contemporary problems ignore municipal and county boundary lines and call for intergovernmental and intersectoral collaboration in order to be effectively addressed. The challenge for the local manager is to find ways to develop scale capacity to tackle service needs and challenges while demonstrating to citizens and elected officials that their community is still viable and continues to add value to residents' quality of life. This balancing act is difficult, but there are both traditional and nontraditional tools available to assist this effort.

Chapter 4 reviewed the traditional procedural or institutional approaches to cross-boundary service delivery, ranging from informal cooperation to functional transfers to new or renewed entities such as regional and multipurpose special districts and public authorities. This chapter builds on that discussion by focusing on the promising public and private collaborative alternatives to service delivery (ASD) that are being practiced by local governments. The advantages and disadvantages of a range of major alternatives will be considered. In addition, local governments are often considered laboratories for innovation, where successful initiatives taken by one jurisdiction can be diffused to other localities as well as to state and federal agencies. The chapter will provide guidance on how local managers can create and sustain an organizational culture that promotes and sustains innovation in service delivery.

WHO DOES WHAT? GOVERNMENT-TO-GOVERNMENT APPROACHES

There is no standard or set formula for dividing the job of service delivery among local governments and the local, regional, state, and national levels. Instead, the arrangement is messy. As noted in Chapter 3, there is wide variation from state to state in how local units are organized, their powers, and their scope of responsibilities. Strategies that work well in one city, county, region, or state may not be applicable elsewhere. This section examines common government-to-government strategies for delivering services.

Interlocal Contracts and Agreements

In terms of usage, formal and informal interlocal contracts and service agreements are the oldest and most popular ways to work across boundaries. Examples of this approach to pragmatic regionalism include mutual assistance pacts between police or fire departments, construction and provision of water and sewer infrastructure, and 911 call centers. Contracts are voluntary and usually involve two jurisdictions and a single service or activity. They often emerge from the informal conversations among managers about cooperative opportunities. Some 45 states authorize local governments to use this instrument, and even in Dillon's Rule states, the grant can be quite broad. Chapter 160A of Article 20 of North Carolina's General Statutes, for instance, states:

> Any unit of local government in this State and any one or more other units of local government in this State or any other state (to the extent permitted by the laws of the other state) may enter into contracts or agreements with each other in other to execute any undertaking. The contracts and agreements shall be of reasonable duration, as determined by the participating units, and shall

be ratified by resolution of the governing board of each unit spread upon its minutes. (North Carolina General Assembly, 2016)

Contracts and agreements are sometimes criticized on the grounds of their voluntary nature, single-function focus, and potentially limited duration. However, they make an important contribution to regional collaboration by enabling public officials from participating jurisdictions to get better acquainted and begin to build trust. This rapport is an essential foundation on which other regional initiatives could be built. According to David Warm (2011), executive director of the Mid-America Regional Council serving Greater Kansas City (Kansas/Missouri), "The most important aim of local government managers is not to run local government; rather the aim is to build trust—with one another, with citizens, and with community institutions" (p. 64). As such, contracts and agreements are the "low-hanging fruit" that could enable regional partners to eventually embark on more ambitious undertakings.

Service-sharing arrangements exemplify the key role the city or county manager plays in intergovernmental negotiations. As former Catawba County, North Carolina, manager Tom Lundy points out:

> Managers have to set the tone; set expectations. A lot of times managers see a much bigger picture. I remember contracting for capacity in a new sewer plant and we got stuck on how much the technical staff in the other jurisdiction wanted to charge; our staff didn't want to pay that, so we got stuck on a number. I finally just said, "What if we leave it the way it is and we agree that they will fund a water line sometime in the future?" The most important thing is that we were able to side step an issue that would have destroyed the agreement. Because technical staff is so good and so precise, sometimes the managers can see the bigger picture or set something for later to facilitate another agreement. Sometimes reaching agreement is as important as reaching total equity. (Perlman, 2015, pp. 119–120)

Reformed Urban County

County governments are readily available to address problems or needs that are of an areawide nature, and often, they are partners in interlocal contracting. As noted in Chapter 3, the county structure is in place in all but two states—Connecticut and Rhode Island—and can provide the geographic scope requisite to achieving scale economies. The chief limitation is the traditional role counties have played as arms of the state government responsible for performing a limited range of functions—law enforcement, tax assessment and collection, road maintenance, and elections—in unincorporated areas. Another impediment occurs when the governing body of many counties (such as part-time commissioners or supervisors) head departments and the chief administrator is weak or nonexistent. And in some metropolitan areas, boundaries of a single county may provide insufficient geographic coverage to deal effectively with regional issues and wicked problems (described in more detail in Chapter 11).

States such as California, Georgia, New York, Florida, Virginia, and Maryland have authorized their counties to perform municipal-type functions and, in some cases, given them home rule. Led by county executives who are separately elected or by chief administrative officers or county managers who are appointed by the governing board, these urban counties possess the structure, powers, and scope to serve as areawide or regional governments. But the urban county movement has not swept the country, due in part to concerns of municipal officials about usurpation of their authority and competition for public recognition and respect.

It was also noted in previous chapters that among the many prescriptions offered for improving local government and state–local relations, home rule for municipalities and counties usually ranks high on the list. Local empowerment is a crucial condition for achieving effective collaboration. Independent of the extent of jurisdictional or functional fragmentation, if local governments lack the authority to modernize and strengthen their form of government, manage their personnel, levy and adjust taxes and fees, and deliver a wide range of services—directly or collaboratively—they will be unable to meet the expectations of citizens and businesses. Empowerment also can produce strong local partners to regional collaborative arrangements that are key to competing successfully in a global marketplace.

Achieving this goal has been a stiff challenge for counties. Despite authorization given to counties in some states to modernize their form of government and assume a range of municipal-type responsibilities, many counties in the United States continue to play their traditional role as the arms of the state government for limited purposes. They were dubbed "the dark continent of American politics" in 1917 (Miller & Cox, 2014, p. 155), and for some, this characterization still applies. While municipalities deal with important functions such as police and fire protection, public transportation, and street and sidewalk repairs, "the image of county government as a sleepy, patronage-riddled organization resistant to change is frequently reinforced in the eyes of the public" (Miller & Cox, 2014, p. 155).

Especially where borders of the metropolitan area and a single county are coterminous or where a core county serves as the work destination of many residents of fringe counties, the county is a logical areawide performance unit. Reorganizing these counties to enable them to carry out functions that cross the boundaries of constituent units and that are amenable to achieving greater efficiency, effectiveness, and equity as a result of scale of delivery offers a number of advantages. Most urban counties usually require no local structural reorganization; they are derived from a unit of local government that is well-known to citizens and valued by state legislators and public administrators, and they have the capacity to facilitate interfunctional coordination and transfers among municipalities within their boundaries. They also promote a more systematic approach to sorting out local from areawide services and enable municipalities and other general-purpose units to contract with the county to deliver desired services while they continue to perform other local functions (Delabbio & Zeemering, 2013).

As an illustration of intrastate challenges to sorting out functions, counties were established under state constitutions or statutes as first-tier administrative subdivisions of the state. In North Carolina, counties provide state-supported public health, mental health, and social services as well as schools, roads, jails, deed registration, and law enforcement. Municipalities were created for regulatory and infrastructure maintenance purposes, especially in urban areas. These functions include streets and sidewalks, lighting, traffic control, and cemeteries. Over time, the list of services that both counties and municipalities are authorized or mandated to perform has grown, as shown in Table 9.1. Interestingly, the only state-mandated municipal function is building code enforcement; the others indicated in the table are discretionary.

Government-to-Government Contracting

The general trend in the past 50 years has been for counties to be authorized to perform more services traditionally provided by municipalities, and so one answer to the "Who does what?" question within the public sector is county governments. There are three practical reasons for this expansion: inefficiency of intracounty functional duplication, capacity to achieve economies of scale in some services, and personnel and capital cost increases. One of the pioneers in interlocal contracting was Lakewood, California, which when incorporated in 1954 chose to contract with Los Angeles county for most of its services. This arrangement has

TABLE 9.1 ■ Chief Services and Functions Authorized for City and County Governments in North Carolina

Services and Functions Authorized for Counties Only

Agricultural extension	Forest protection	Public schools
Community colleges	Juvenile detention homes	Register of deeds
County home	Medical examiner/ coroner	Social services
Court system support	Public health	Soil and water conservation
Drainage of land		

Services and Functions Authorized for Both Municipalities and Counties

Aging programs	Economic development	Parks
Air pollution control	Fire protection	Planning
Airports	Historic preservation	Ports and harbors
Alcoholic rehabilitation	Hospitals	Public housing
Ambulance services	Human relations	Railroad revitalization
Animal shelters	Industrial promotion	Recreation
Armories	Inspections	Rescue squads
Art galleries and museums	Jails	Senior citizens' programs
Auditoriums and coliseums	Law enforcement	Sewage treatment
Beach erosion	Libraries	Solid waste management
Public transportation	Manpower	Storm drainage
Emergency management	Mental health	Urban redevelopment
Community action	National Guard	Veterans' services
Community appearance	Off-street parking	Water

Community development	Open space	Watershed improvement
Drug abuse programs		

Services and Functions Authorized for Municipalities Only		
Cable TV/ communications	Gas systems	Streets
Cemeteries	Sidewalks	Traffic engineering
Electric systems	Street lighting	

Source: Author-created based on Lawrence, David M. 2014. An Overview of Local Government. In Frayda S. Bluestein, ed. *County and Municipal Government in North Carolina*, 2nd ed. Chapel Hill, NC: UNC School of Government.

been replicated elsewhere, with cities selecting from a cafeteria plan the services they would like the county to perform for them and agreeing to reimburse the county. This is a win–win arrangement in which the county achieves scale economies and efficiency is increased by the reduction of service duplication, while cities save money by not having to invest in their own personnel, equipment, technology, and space. An additional advantage of such government-to-government purchasing is public accountability, as the participating units must operate under established procurement, reporting, and other regulations.

Research has shown that "intergovernmental contracting yields similar efficiency gains as for-profit privatization but performs better in terms of equity and citizen responsiveness" (Warner & Hefetz, 2009, pp. 19–20). The extent to which counties are willing and able to engage in interlocal contracting varies from state-to-state, as does the number of so-called contract cities, but unquestionably, this tool will continue to be very popular.

While offering economies of scale and other advantages, public sector contracting and sharing involves other units than counties. A 2007 survey (called the ASD Survey) of 6,095 municipalities with populations over 10,000 and counties with populations over 25,000 and a random sample of smaller jurisdictions by the International City/County Management Association (ICMA) shows a wide range of services that local governments purchase from one another. The list in Table 9.2 indicates services that require specialized staff to deliver, incur high capital costs, or call upon government coercive powers.

TABLE 9.2 ■ Public Services Most Commonly Purchased from Other Local Governments in 2007		
Service	Number of Respondents Who Outsource Service	Percentage Purchased from Other Local Governments
Workforce development/job training	409	59%
Welfare intake/eligibility determination	388	59%
Mental health/retardation programs/facilities	369	58%
Child welfare programs	411	53%
Public health programs	512	52%
Drug and alcohol treatment programs	395	49%
Prisons/jails	648	44%
Bus/transit operations/maintenance	403	40%
Hazardous material disposal	615	38%
Paratransit operations/maintenance	366	37%
Homeless shelters	288	37%
Insect/rodent control	597	35%
Libraries	792	34%
Airports	422	34%

Source: Warner & Hefetz, 2010, Table 3/3, p. 22. Total number usable responses = 1,474.[1]

Many of the contracted-from-government services are clustered in the health and human services area. Therefore, it is likely that the purchasing jurisdiction can receive that service at a lower cost than if it provided it directly. Indeed, that is among the top expectations for intergovernmental contracting reported by survey respondents, who were chief administrative officers. The four top motivators were saving money (80%), achieving economies of scale (77%), strengthening collaborative intergovernmental relations (64%), and promoting regional service integration (59%). Among the top obstacles to intergovernmental contracting were loss of community control (64%), employee and elected official opposition (43%), and monitoring difficulties (32%) (Warner & Hefetz, 2009, p. 19). Other research has found that council–manager governments were more likely to engage in service contracting than municipalities operating under the mayor–council form (Carr, 2015, p. 681).

Reorganizing counties as full-service jurisdictions for planning, problem-solving, and functional performance requires adoption of home rule charters, broadening of functional and fiscal powers, and replacement of the commission form of government with elected county executives and/or appointed county managers or chief administrative officers. While philosophical, political, and cultural differences will be difficult to overcome, municipal officials will need to put aside historic concerns about competition from empowered counties and demonstrate a willingness to collaborate in order to avoid duplication and to promote coordination of efforts. At the same time, county officials will need to put aside parochial mindsets and overcome fears of the big city.

As indicated earlier, municipal and county managers are key players in efforts to identify ways their jurisdictions can work together. They serve as barometers of readiness to collaborate, as negotiators, and as monitors and evaluators. Their professional expertise is critical to ensuring win–win contractual arrangements, realistic and equitable contractual terms, and attainment of expected outcomes. The prevalence of part-time elected officials (albeit an important part of the citizen legislator tradition in the United States), the growing technical complexity of the problems confronting localities, the widespread intergovernmentalization and private-sector provision of services, and the explosion of networks and collaborative arrangements all underscore the critical need for professional local managers to be transcending leaders.

WHO DOES WHAT?
PUBLIC–PRIVATE PARTNERSHIPS

Although the most common method for delivering local services continues to be in-house provision, local governments are not confined to contracting with other governmental entities. Services provided through arrangements other than in-house are called *ASD methods*. These include the government-to-government arrangements discussed in the previous section and public–private arrangements.

Contracting versus Privatization

Many people confuse the terms *contracting* and *privatization*. Even those who work in government may erroneously say a service was privatized when it was, in fact, contracted out. The terms are not synonymous. When a government service is *privatized*, it is permanently transferred to the private sector. There is no contractual agreement for monitoring or an ongoing fee system that is established. The private sector agency takes over the service previously provided by government.

In the United States, there is not a great deal that can be transferred to the private sector because most industries were founded by private sector entities. So, while the UK and Australia privatized their coal industries in the 1990s, the U.S. coal industry has always been a private industry. Most of the privatization that occurs today in the United States involves the sale or long-term lease of government assets to the public sector. Local or state governments may sell the rights to tollway administration and maintenance or to parking meter provision (i.e., as in Chicago).

When a government service is *contracted* out, there is a contractual agreement that covers the arrangement. The private sector agency may be granted long-term control over the service. However, the public organization does not relinquish ownership or responsibility for provision of that service. For example, although there are a number of private prisons in the U.S., these prisons are run through a contractual arrangement with the state or federal government. Were it not for those contracts, the private prison would no longer be in business. The contracts govern many aspects of how the prisons are designed and run. Were these prisons truly privatized, it would be up to the private sector agency to decide how to provide the service.

Private Sector Contracts

Arrangements between governments and private organizations to provide services or run public facilities can be simple or complex, long term or short term. Government facilities that are now commonly administered by private sector corporations include prisons, public hospitals, sports facilities, and convention centers. Services that are commonly provided by the private sector include trash collection, utilities maintenance, and recreation services.

Since the 1980s, there has been considerable interest in using the private sector, including both nonprofit organizations and private firms, for services once provided by public employees in order to achieve efficiency (Warner & Hefetz, 2009). A local government that decides to purchase rather than produce a service still has a public obligation or responsibility regardless of the performing entity, which involves a trade-off between sovereignty and efficiency:

When state or local governments outsource services, they must be careful to safeguard . . . sovereignty. If a local government encounters a private vendor who is unable to, will not, or prefers not to comply with standards that governments must respect—whether for freedom of information, access, equity, record keeping, or process—then it cannot be allowed to win a contract. Compliance with basic standards for state and local government in the areas of ethical performance of public servants, open processes, and full exposure of public decisions must be a ground condition of actual contracting for the delivery of public services and not just something left to auditors or evaluators. (Perlman, 2013, p. 181)

Two contributors to the surge in interest in private sector contracting were the election of Ronald Reagan in 1980 and the Reinventing Government movement of the 1990s. Citizens have historically been averse to big government and expect more for less and quicker, better, cheaper in their service delivery. Politicians at all levels have campaigned in support of smaller, less expensive, and more efficient and businesslike government and against fraud, waste, and abuse—and bureaucrats. The election of Ronald Reagan put downsizing government high on the domestic agenda.

Thanks to contracting, more than 30 years later, the federal government's civilian workforce is about the same size as during the Kennedy administration, even as outlays have soared. Contractors have been called the "shadow of government" and are found across the spectrum of federal civilian and defense programs (Light, 1999). They conceal the true size of government and raise accountability and transparency concerns.

A second contributor to increases in government contracting was the Reinventing Government movement of the 1990s. The quote from privatization and public sector competition advocate E. S. Savas at the beginning of this chapter captures the spirit of reinvention. Savas served as an assistant secretary in the Department of Housing and Urban Development during part of the Reagan administration. A 2003 ICMA survey revealed "significant implementation" of the Reinventing Government principles relating to budgeting, including partnering to provide a program or service (68%) and contracting out a municipal service (68%) (Gaebler, Hilvert, & Holt, 2014, p. 37).

Contracting Out with For-Profit Organizations

As indicated in Tables 9.3 and 9.4, local governments purchase several services from private companies and nonprofit organizations. With respect to the former, vehicle towing and storage was reported as the most common service purchased from for-profit companies. Over 50% of the ICMA's ASD Survey respondents purchased gas utility operations and management, solid waste collection, and day care facilities from the for-profit sector. According to Gordon Whitaker (2007), some of the common features of these services are that they are also offered to private customers and they are "packagable" in the sense they can be purchased in measured units. Therefore, the marketplace should have a large number of providers, it should be competitive, and it should offer opportunities to benchmark or compare prices (p. 371). Another aspect of these services that facilitates contracting is that it is fairly easy to monitor performance. For example, when a resident's trash is not picked up, they are likely to call the local government and complain. These points are backed up by research that shows that the least contracted out services are those in which monitoring is difficult to perform (Warner & Hefetz, 2009).

A newer trend in contracting out for services involves hiring a private company to do most of the business of running the government. So far, this has only been implemented in municipalities, but county governments may adopt this model in the future. Unlike in Lakewood, California, where the county is the contract agent for provision of city services, in the private model, a for-profit company provides the services. For example, Sandy Springs, Georgia, incorporated in 2005, has only seven government employees. The others are employees of a set of private corporations contracted with the city to provide services such as building permitting, business licensing, and court operations. Cities that rely on contracts to run their governments may encounter problems, however, due to inadequate oversight. In 2016, three Beaumont, California, contract employees and several city employees were arrested for embezzling money

TABLE 9.3 ■ Public Services Most Commonly Purchased from For-Profit Companies in 2007		
Service	Number of Respondents Who Outsource Service	Percentage Purchased from For-Profit Entities
Vehicle towing and storage	422	65%
Gas utility operations/management	315	60%
Commercial solid waste collection	699	56%
Day care facilities	320	54%
Electric utility operations/management	387	48%
Residential solid waste collection	932	47%
Solid waste disposal	851	43%
Hospital operation/management	253	40%
Tree trimming/planting	1,066	33%
Disposal of hazardous materials	615	32%
Street repair	1,180	31%

Source: Warner & Hefetz, 2010, Table 3/3, p. 22. Total number of usable responses = 1,474.[1]

from the city to enrich their company, Urban Logic Consultants. The employees of the private company were hired to direct the planning, economic development, and public works departments (Keltman & Macy, 2016).

Contracting Out with Nonprofit Organizations

With respect to purchasing from nonprofit organizations, the percentages of participating respondents are far smaller than for private companies. The most commonly purchased services are homeless shelters, museum operations, operation and management of hospitals, drug and alcohol treatment programs, and cultural and arts programs. For these services, there is likely significantly less competition due to low profitability. Very few for-profit organizations are willing to provide these services. It might be necessary to supplement the local contract with private donations, federal or state grants, or volunteer time in order to meet the needs for some of these services.

Service	Number of Respondents Who Outsource Service	Percentage Purchased from Nonprofits
Homeless shelters	288	56%
Museum operations	433	38%
Operation/management of hospitals	253	38%
Drug and alcohol treatment programs	395	36%
Cultural and arts programs	567	35%
Day care facilities	320	33%
Mental health/retardation programs/facilities	369	32%
Programs for the elderly	799	29%
Job training programs	409	25%
Animal shelters	772	22%
Paratransit operations/maintenance	366	18%
Child welfare programs	411	15%

TABLE 9.4 ■ Public Services Most Commonly Purchased from Nonprofit Organizations in 2007

Source: Warner & Hefetz, 2010, Table 3/3, p. 22. Total number of usable responses = 1,474.[1]

Contracting out for a service, whether to another government or to a private firm, is one form of ASD that undoubtedly will continue to grow. However, there are a number of considerations that managers should take into account before moving forward with collaborative service sharing arrangements or outsourcing. These include (1) examining the rationale for collaboration, such as leveraging resources, better relationships, and improved processes and outcomes; (2) determining the most appropriate public–public or public–private arrangements in view of the goals to be achieved; (3) deciding on the correct number of partners; (4) analyzing whether the service should remain in-house based on financial considerations, service delivery models, and private partner profit expectations; (5) identifying and assessing the barriers to collaboration, including turf, political culture, trust, and management capacity; and (6) assessing the benefits to be gained through collaborative arrangements (Hilvert & Swindell, 2013, pp. 244–248).

Partnerships

Public–Private Partnerships (PPPs) have been in vogue for some time and have been defined as follows by the National Council for Public–Private Partnerships:

> A contractual agreement between a public agency . . . and a private sector entity. Through this agreement, the skills and assets of each sector (public and private) are shared in delivering a service or facility for the use of the general public. In addition to sharing resources, each party shares in the risks and rewards in the delivery of the service and/or facility. (Gabris, 2014, p. 118)

These expectations—sharing and risk—are not found in the other ASD approaches.

PPPs may be informal or formal and long term or short term and involve a variety of service planning, coordination, sharing, and/or execution relationships. Economic development initiatives (such as downtown revitalization) and real estate ventures (such as sports arenas) are popular areas for PPPs. Other interesting examples include a joint venture with a private company to burn trash that the city collects to produce steam, which is sold as heat; companies adopting a park or library and helping the locality to fund, staff, and maintain the property or facility; and holding public school classes on company sites for children of their employees (Osborne & Gaebler, 1992, pp. 335–336).

PPPs have management challenges and uncertainties associated with them. Restating these challenges positively, among the components of a successful partnership are (1) clarity of vision for the project; (2) a governing board that focuses on the long-term public good; (3) trust, teamwork, communications, and transparency among the staff, governing board, and partners; (4) two-way sharing of expertise between the local staff and private partners; (5) a flexible agreement that the partners can modify and fine-tune as they gain experience with the project and one another; and (6) a method for measuring outcomes and evaluating results (Gabris, 2014, pp. 131–135).

OTHER ALTERNATIVE SERVICE DELIVERY TOOLS

In addition to contracting, other forms of ASD are available to municipal and county managers. This section reviews three of the most common tools managers have available to use as nongovernmental alternatives to the in-house production: grants to subsidize services, franchises, and managed competition. The emphasis will be on the intersection between the local government and a private provider. Each tool will be highlighted, together with the advantages and cautions associated with it.

Most ASD methods discussed in this section involve the introduction of market competition into the provision of government services. Conceptually, the idea is to lower costs through competition. However, there must be adequate existing competition in the private market for this to work. Research has found that there is an inadequate supply of private sector firms offering many governmental-type services to sufficiently lead to lower costs and better quality than would be achieved through in-house service provision (Warner & Hefetz, 2009). This factor means that it is much easier to implement alternative service delivery in large urban areas than in small rural or suburban areas.

In addition to the needed awareness of competitive market conditions when considering ASD, it is also important to consider where opposition may arise. Since the most substantial portion of the costs of providing local government services comes from personnel, layoffs often accompany ASD arrangements. Elected officials may be concerned about the political ramifications of staff reductions. In states with collective bargaining, union opposition may also be an impediment to the introduction of outsourcing.

Grants to Subsidize Services

Another ASD tool local managers can use is grants to assist the provider in achieving the public purpose. This could be particularly helpful if a nonprofit organization is responsible for the service and it has a limited budget or staff expertise. The subsidies may take the form of an in-kind contribution from the local government, such as office space, staff support, and equipment or technology in addition to cash. Generally, grants are broader and less specific than purchasing transactions, so accountability problems could result.

Franchises

Franchise agreements allow companies to sell their services using public property or rights-of-way in exchange for fees to the local government. Franchises are popular in that they involve revenues instead of expenditures. The customers pay the private provider, not the locality, for the service. In some cases, the local government will franchise a sole provider or, in other cases, multiple companies will be allowed to compete with one another for customers. Usually, however, competition is restricted.

A common example is commercial and residential trash and solid waste collection. While some localities bundle trash and solid waste pickup with other services covered by property taxes or contract directly with private companies, others permit particular private companies such as Waste Industries and Waste Management to contract directly with citizens. The customers can choose among private providers based on cost, frequency of service, types of waste collected, and other factors. In addition to customer choice at the outset, if the provider fails to meet expectations, the citizen can select another vendor. With franchising, only customers who consume a service pay for it, such as recreation facilities. Other service areas where franchising is common include utilities, cable television, bus transportation, parking meters, and restaurants on turnpikes.

Managed Competition

The Reinventing Government movement encouraged public organizations to move from monopolistic to competitive practices. One such practice is managed competition, spearheaded by Phoenix, Arizona, in 1979, which required local departments to compete against private bidders for certain services. Competition could be citywide or could focus on certain districts or neighborhoods. Phoenix's Public Works Department divided the city into districts and started bidding them for five- to seven-year contracts on a one-district-per-year basis. Due to union concerns, the city adopted a no-layoff policy and required private contractors who were successful bidders to hire public works personnel who were displaced. Those who wanted to remain with the city were transferred to other departments. Initially, public works lost the first three bids, causing senior managers and employees to redesign routes and work schedules and purchase one-person trucks with mechanical arms instead of the traditional three-person vehicle. A suggestion program was established that gave employees 10% of the savings resulting from their idea, up to $2,000. Gradually, public works became more competitive and the city saved money—about $20 million during the first decade. Employee morale increased instead of declined, as was originally predicted. Based on its success with sanitation, Phoenix's managed competition spread to landfill operations, street repair, golf course management, printing, and security (Osborne & Gaebler, 1992, pp. 76–77).

Another bold effort was initiated by former Indianapolis Mayor Stephen Goldsmith, who used managed competition in some 80 services, such as street resurfacing and pothole filling. Public works staff worked with the mayor's office to apply activity-based costing methodology to determine delivery costs and establish a level playing field for all bidders, and strategies were employed to reduce expenditures. Between 1992 and 1995, the city saved about $100 million, thanks to managed competition (Nelson, 2014).

Managed competition can be an effective way to encourage or pressure public agencies to review and revamp their rules, procedures, and productivity. Not all services are amenable to the *"Yellow Pages* test" that Mayor Goldsmith used, whereby if an in-house provided service was also advertised in the *Yellow Pages* as a private service, managed competition was possible. While competing with private sector providers can threaten job security and undermine staff morale, it can also boost confidence if the public agency prevails.

At the same time, if the government constantly wins the competition, private companies might believe the bidding is tilted toward the local agency or that it is rigged in favor of public personnel. After all, public agencies do not need to make a profit or pay taxes, incur risk, or adhere to some regulations (Nelson, 2014, p. 56). If these concerns are valid, the number of potential private providers can dwindle, as was the case with the Charlotte–Mecklenburg Utility District (CMUD). During the early competition, CMUD invited private companies to compete with its staff for district waste treatment plant operation and in nearly all cases, staff won the bid, which had a chilling effect on the provider market (Gullet & Bean, 1997).

Adding to the complexity is whether the service requires a comprehensive or multifaceted provider network in order to be efficiently and effectively provided. For example, when the Indianapolis airport went through managed competition, consideration was given to whether requests for separate proposals (RFPs) should be sent to specialized providers for parking, concessions, and other airport operations or if a single source for managing all aspects of the airport's business should be hired:

After more careful analysis, the city determined that the real benefit would derive from a single organization managing all the pieces, thereby maximizing the experience for the passenger. From this model, BAA, the British company that manages Heathrow Airport and seven other U.K. airports, successfully competed for and won the contract. (Goldsmith & Eggers, 2004, p. 86)

KEY QUESTIONS

Before deciding on a service delivery alternative, local managers need to ask a number of important questions (Whitaker, 2007, pp. 377–380). First, what potential producers are available? It might be difficult to find many private companies who are experienced in comprehensive airport management, for example, compared to trash collectors. As with CMUD's experience, if the competition record weighs heavily in favor of the public agency, private firms might be reluctant to invest the time and staff to prepare bids. And managers in rural communities may find relatively few interested competitors. If the number of bidders is limited, the potential for driving down costs and improving quality through ASD is diminished.

A second question involves packageability, whether a service can be divided into distribution units for the citizens who use them. Water and sewer use can be readily measured, for example, compared with public parks. Packageable services enable managers to know how much of a service they are purchasing. If this is an important consideration, then franchises, managed competition, and some public–private partnerships work well. On the other hand, grants are less specific with respect to services to be produced and performance levels to be attained.

Accessibility and equity are the third considerations. If equal access to a service regardless of a customer's ability to pay is sought, then franchises are a less desirable option. The other alternatives can specify service availability as a condition of the agreement. Regarding equity, the local government can decide whether to subsidize the provision of a service by a company or nonprofit organization, such as covering a portion of bus or light-rail fares or water and sewer user fees.

A fourth factor to be considered is how much control over the production, delivery, quality, and cost of the service the local government desires. Some services, such as law enforcement, are considered inherently governmental due to their potential use of coercive power (such as deadly force) and are not amenable to delivery by nongovernmental agencies. The growth of prison contracting has also raised questions about the use of such power by private firms as well as the appropriateness of the ways in which company profits are made, such as reduced pay and benefits for corrections personnel and reduced quality of food and medical services for inmates.

But for the most part, the use of one or more of the alternative approaches covered in this chapter assumes that the local government is willing to relinquish direct control over service delivery, with franchises and grants allowing the greatest flexibility to providers. At the same time, managers are responsible for monitoring the provision of services, evaluating the performance of contractors and making needed contractual modifications, and ensuring transparency as well as for the sovereignty factor. These efforts can be challenging, as data might not be available to help determine service quality and managers might not be able to devote the time needed for effective oversight or possess negotiating skills required for successful contract bidding and renewal. A critical component of negotiations is determining mutual accountability obligations for the duration of the agreement, which entails a more collaborative relationship than a typical one-way buyer–seller arrangement.

At the 2013 ICMA National Conference, a special session was held in celebration of the 20th anniversary of the Reinventing Government movement. Managers on the panel indicated that while progress had been made on several fronts, including contracting out services, continuing work was needed in a number of areas. One of these is

> *letting go of programs and services that can be better supplied by others in order to focus on the things that really matter.* The important message for managers today is that government is not the sole solution provider, even though citizens often want it to be. With limited resources, managers must look to alternative methods for service delivery (and possibly shedding services altogether) so that they can direct those resources where they are most needed. (Gaebler et al., 2014, p. 39)

BUILDING CAPACITY FOR INNOVATION

Using the nontraditional approaches described above will be an important part of meeting the above challenge, but more creative approaches will likely be needed as well. In view of the disconcerting fiscal and intergovernmental trends that lie ahead for local governments, innovation will be critical to success and possibly survival. Moreover, while the future is difficult to predict, it is clear that technology has had a profound effect on how most local governments conduct business and will continue to have significant impacts. Many local governments now routinely use websites and social media to inform and engage their citizens. But consider other emerging technologies that could prove disruptive to local personnel and finances: For example, unmanned aerial vehicles (UAVs) or drones could be used in providing emergency services, surveilling high-crime neighborhoods, and delivering local products. Who should regulate drones and how should they be regulated? Automated vehicles are being tested in communities and will be mass manufactured in a few years. These vehicles obey speed limits, don't consume alcohol or text message while driving, and monitor parking meters. How will local governments absorb the significant loss of revenue from these sources even as citizen safety and health rates increase? The sharing economy that is now evident privately in Uber and in efforts by some local governments and universities to make bicycles and automobiles available for temporary rent call into question the long-term need for large municipal parking garages and public transit systems. And some local governments are experimenting with robots to carry out routine tasks such as building cleaning. In the not-too-distant future, humans may no longer be involved in routed traffic such as collecting trash or driving school buses. While these possibilities are speculative, they underscore the need for local governments to step up their innovation game and "rethink their design, strategy, operations, and processes in fundamental ways" because "the outlook for current governance models is exceedingly bleak" (DeSouza et al., 2015, pp. 1–2).

In light of these current developments and emerging trends, it is imperative for municipal and county managers to cultivate an environment that is conducive to "out of the box" thinking and acting and supportive of risk taking. This section reviews steps that could be taken to create and sustain an organizational culture that celebrates and embraces innovation.

Innovation has become a nearly ubiquitous term to describe high-performing organizations. However, the definition of innovation is not clear-cut. One definition of innovation is "the generation, acceptance, and implementation of new ideas, processes, products, or services" (Kanter, 1983, in Frost & Egri, 1991). Some scholars define *innovation* as the adoption of an existing idea by an organization or the improvement of such idea, while an *invention* is the creation of an original idea or breakthrough (Damanpour, 1991; Rogers, 2003). Generally accepted characteristics of innovation are that they are new to the organization and are intended to improve organizational performance. So an innovation does not have to be an invention, but it must be new to the organization and it must be intended to improve the organization in some way.

While everyone agrees that innovation is good for organizations, there is less likely to be consensus about how to build capacity for innovation into an organization. Challenges that are unique to the public sector make building innovation capacity even more difficult for local governments. Chief among these challenges is the fact that public organizations tend to be risk averse. Implementing new programs or ways of doing things often comes with some discomfort accompanying change. While private organizations take chances with the money of investors who have chosen to participate as shareholders in profits, governments use funds generated through taxes and fees paid by citizens. Some elected officials may be reluctant to take chances for fear of the political ramifications of failure.

Another challenge that is more likely to be experienced in public organizations than in the private sector is that there are fewer incentive opportunities for staff. Private companies can give bonuses and other types of cash awards. While financial rewards have been used to some degree in the public sector, there is less flexibility given revenue constraints, civil service rules, and public sensitivities.

Innovation requires creative thinking—thinking beyond what is done every day to develop new ways of doing things. Unfortunately, the rules and regulations that are in place in public sector organizations (intended to insulate the organization from political forces and biased actions) can also hinder creativity. Osborne and Gaebler (1992) argued that these industrial-age rules and regulations were similar to straightjackets that stifled entrepreneurship and innovation. Of course, bureaucracies were not originally designed to facilitate creativity and instead emphasized the importance of following rules and treating citizens fairly. Today, municipalities and counties are seeking ways to restructure human resources management and are changing their hiring practices and workplace policies and procedures to encourage creative thinkers to pursue careers in local management. Employee selection practices can be tailored to support greater innovation capacity. For example, testing assessments designed to evaluate creativity and risk acceptance may be used to determine which candidates may be more innovation ready.

The key question, then, is this: How does a municipality or county increase organizational capacity to innovate? Research has provided some answers to that question (Damanpour & Schneider, 2009; Franzel, 2008; Gabris, Golembiewski, & Ihrke, 2001; Jun & Weare, 2011; Nelson, Gabris, & Wood, 2011; Nelson & Svara, 2012). Some factors that have been linked to higher propensity to innovate are not those that government managers can influence. For example, larger communities and those with more higher-income residents are more likely to innovate. Also, municipalities with a council–manager government have also been found to adopt more innovations than those using other forms.

There are factors related to innovation capacity that the manager can help affect. First, the quality of leadership, both elected and administrative, is essential. The leadership of the organization must be able to handle some level of risk. In order to accept risk, there must be a positive working relationship among elected officials and a supportive and trusting relationship between elected officials and staff.

Evidence also supports the idea that managers who are innovation-oriented lead organizations that are more likely to innovate (Damanpour & Schneider, 2009). While this may seem to be obvious, even managers who embrace innovation may not know where to start. Organizations such as ICMA and the Alliance for Innovation provide support to managers with this orientation, helping to spread information about new ideas, best practices, possible pitfalls, and thought leaders that can be helpful in implementing programs to support innovative practices (Swindell & Thoreson, 2014). Some local governments, such as Durham, North Carolina, have set up an Idea Lab and have created staff positions to encourage and embed innovation in their organization.

Municipalities and counties can be run satisfactorily without being innovative, but they will not reach their full potential. Innovation and finding new ways of providing services or carrying out the functions of government, whether through an ASD option or some other method, will permit local governments to perform at their best. Both elected officials and citizens appreciate the recognition that comes with a local government that outperforms its peers.

NOTE

1. Services purchased to support governmental service production (such as legal services, tax assessing, title records, and vehicle maintenance) were excluded from Tables 9.2, 9.3, and 9.4.

REFERENCES

Carr, J. B. (2015). What have we learned about the performance of council–manager government? A review and synthesis of the research. *Public Administration Review, 75*(5), 673–689.

Damanpour, F. (1991). Organizational innovation: A meta-analysis of effects of determinants and moderators. *The Academy of Management Journal, 34*(3), 555–590.

Damanpour, F., & Schneider, M. (2009). Characteristics of innovation and innovation adoption in public organizations: Assessing the role of managers. *Journal of Public Administration Research and Theory, 19*(3), 495–522.

Delabbio, D. J., & Zeemering, E. S. (2013). Public entrepreneurship and interlocal cooperation in county government. *State and Local Government Review, 45*(4), 255–267.

DeSouza, K. C., Swindell, D., Smith, K. L., Sutherland, A., Fedorschak, K., & Coronel, C. (2015). Local government 2035: Strategic trends and implications of new technologies. *Brookings Issues in Technology Innovation, 27*. Retrieved March 22, 2017, from https://www.brookings.edu/wp-content/uploads/2016/06/desouza.pdf

Franzel, J. M. (2008). Urban government innovation: Identifying current innovations and factors that contribute to their adoption. *Review of Policy Research, 25*(3), 253–277.

Frost, P., Jr., & Egri, C. P. (1991). The political process of innovation. *Research in Organizational Behavior, 13*, 229–295.

Gabris, G. T. (2014). Public–private partnership. In K. Thurmaier (Ed.), *A handbook of alternative service delivery for local government* (pp. 117–138). Washington, DC: International City/County Management Association.

Gabris, G. T., Golembiewski, R. T., & Ihrke, D. (2001). Leadership credibility, board relations, and administrative innovation at the local government level. *Journal of Public Administration Research and Theory, 11*(1), 89–108.

Gaebler, T. A., Hilvert, C., & Holt, T. (2014). 100 years . . . and we are still reinventing government! In *The municipal year book 2014* (pp. 33–42). Washington, DC: International City/County Management Association.

Goldsmith, S., & Eggers, W. D. (2004). *Governing by network: The new shape of the public sector.* Washington, DC: Brookings Institution Press.

Gullet, B. M., & Bean, D. O. (1997, Winter). The Charlotte model for competition. *Popular Government*, 19–22.

Hilvert, C., & Swindell, D. (2013). Collaborative service delivery: What every local government manager should know. *State and Local Government Review, 45*(4), 240–254.

Jun, K.-N., & Weare, C. (2011). Institutional motivations in the adoption of innovations: The case of e-government. *Journal of Public Administration Research and Theory, 21*(3), 495–519.

Keltman, B., & Macy, J. (2016, May 17). DA: Former Beaumont officials siphoned $43 million. *The Desert Sun.* Retrieved March 22, 2017, from http://www.desertsun.com/story/news/crime_courts/2016/05/17/six-beaumont-officials-charged-embezzlement/84500932/

Lawrence, D. M. (2014). An overview of local government. In F. S. Bluestein (Ed.), *County and municipal government in North Carolina* (2nd ed., pp. 3–14). Chapel Hill: University of North Carolina School of Government.

Light, P. C. (1999). *The true size of government.* Washington, DC: Brookings Institution Press.

Miller, D. Y., & Cox, R. W., III. (2014). *Governing the metropolitan region: America's new frontier.* Armonk, NY: M.E. Sharpe.

Nelson, K. L. (2014). Managed competition. In Kurt Thurmaier (Ed.), *A handbook of alternative service delivery for local government* (pp. 43–68). Washington, DC: International City/County Management Association.

Nelson, K. L., Gabris, G. T., & Wood, C. H. (2011). Innovation management in local government: An empirical analysis of suburban municipalities. *International Journal of Organization Theory and Behavior, 14*(3), 301–328.

Nelson, K. L., & Svara, J. H. (2012). Form of government still matters: Fostering innovation in U.S. municipal governments. *The American Review of Public Administration, 42*(3), 257–281.

North Carolina General Assembly. (2016). *NC general statutes.* Retrieved March 21, 2017, from http://www.ncleg.net/gascripts/statutes/Statutes.asp

Osborne, D., & Gaebler, T. (1992). *Reinventing government: How the entrepreneurial spirit is transforming the public sector from schoolhouse to statehouse, city hall to the Pentagon.* Reading, MA: Addison-Wesley Publishing Company, Inc.

Perlman, B. J. (2013). The ins and outs of outsourcing. *State and Local Government Review, 45*(3), 180–182.

Perlman, B. J. (2015). Trust and timing: The importance of relationship and opportunity for interlocal collaboration and agreements. *State and Local Government Review, 47*(2), 116–126.

Rogers, E. M. (2003). *Diffusion of innovations* (5th ed.). New York, NY: Free Press.

Swindell, D., & Thoreson, K. (2014). Spreading innovation. In *The municipal year book 2014* (pp. 77–86). Washington, DC: International City/County Management Association.

Warm, D. (2011). Local government collaboration for a new decade: Risk, trust, and effectiveness. *State and Local Government Review, 43*(1), 60–65.

Warner, M. E., & Hefetz, A. (2009). Cooperative competition: Alternative service delivery, 2002–2007. In *The municipal year book 2009* (pp. 11–20). Washington, DC: International City/County Management Association.

Warner, M. E., & Hefetz, A. (2010). Service characteristics and contracting: The importance of citizen interest and competition. In *The municipal year book 2010* (pp. 19–27). Washington, DC: International City/County Management Association.

Whitaker, G. P. (2007). Service delivery alternatives. In C. W. Stenberg & S. L. Austin (Eds.), *Managing local government services: A practical guide.* Washington, DC: International City/County Management Association.

RESOURCE LIST/TO EXPLORE FURTHER

Books/Articles

Hecht, B. (2015). Breaking through barriers to innovation in local government. *Governing.* Available at http://www.governing.com/cityaccelerator/blog/Breaking-Through-Barriers-to-Innovation-in-Local-Government.html

Jacob, N. (2015). City accelerator guide for embedding innovation in local government. *Living Cities.* Available at https://www.livingcities.org/resources/286-city-accelerator-guide-for-embedding-innovation-in-local-government

Thurmaier, K. (Ed.). (2014). *Alternative service delivery: Readiness check.* Washington, DC: ICMA.

Web Resources

Alliance for Innovation. (2014). [Website]. Available at http://www.transformgov.org

THE MANAGER'S TOOLBOX

Public management is "a world of settled institutions designed to allow imperfect people to use flawed procedures to cope with insoluble problems."

—James Q. Wilson (1989, p. 375)

Managers are responsible for developing and sustaining a high-performing organization. There are many tools that managers have in their toolbox to help them achieve this goal. Some of these tools have been adopted from the private sector, others from local governments, and still others from state and federal agencies. This chapter focuses on the tools that are essential for managing contemporary local governments—strategic planning, performance measurement, program evaluation, budgeting for results, and succession planning—and provides examples of lessons learned from experience.

BUILDING ORGANIZATIONAL CAPACITY

As discussed in Chapter 7, managers work with elected officials as organizational capacity builders. This responsibility can be traced to the founding of council–manager government more than 100 years ago, when municipalities were growing rapidly and demanding infrastructure improvements to increase mobility and safety. Many managers at that time were trained engineers and brought to their jurisdiction public works experiences that were critical to constructing streets and sidewalks, lighting systems, water and sewer lines, and traffic controls as communities began their transformation from rural/agrarian to urban/industrial economic bases.

POSDCORB

The 1930s witnessed a second significant change in the manager's skills and abilities. As the field of public administration evolved, managers were expected to put basic systems in place for planning, managing, financing, and executing the work of local governments. Luther Gulick and Lyndall Urwick coined the acronym *POSDCORB* to capture seven basic principles that, in their judgment, were applicable to all organizations regardless of purpose, place, or clientele—planning, organizing, staffing, directing, coordinating, reporting, and budgeting. The manager's job was to apply these principles to enhance organizational performance in a quest for efficiency. At that time, administrative orthodoxy held that administration was a science, that politics and administration were separate, and that public administrators were neutrally competent and value free. These themes began to change with World War II, the explosion of the federal government's domestic role in the postwar period, and changes in the field of public administration in the behavioral era. But POSDCORB remained the dominant theme of managerial work and efficiency (Gulick & Urwick, 1937).

Federal Bureaucratic Reforms

Beginning in the 1960s, POSDCORB principles were joined in the manager's toolbox with reforms incorporating innovations and best practices from the private sector and other governments. These reforms were intended to not only improve government efficiency but to also connect expenditures to performance outcomes. Bureaucratic reform efforts since the 1960s have focused on budgeting, personnel, and performance management (see the summary in Table 10.1).

One such approach to maximizing efficiency was the planning–programming–budgeting system (PPBS), championed by Secretary of Defense Robert McNamara based on his experience as chief executive officer of the Ford Motor Company. PPBS was an example of rational decision making, in which "the goal of any activity, including governmental programs, is to get the biggest return for any investment. Simply put . . . to get the most bang for the buck" (Kettl, 2015, p. 265). PPBS had three phases: (1) senior managers developed five-year plans and strategies for defense; (2) strategies were translated into detailed weapons systems and other programs with delivery schedules; and (3) the plans and programs were presented as budget requests each year. In these ways, the annual budgeting process was linked to longer-range objectives, emphasis was placed on the program rather than organizational unit (i.e., program budgeting), and inputs were tied to outcomes.

TABLE 10.1 ■ Bureaucratic Reform Models		
Reform Effort	**Description**	**Year Instituted**
Planning–programming–budgeting system (PPBS)	Management tool designed to use data and analysis to support budgeting choices. Also called *output budgeting*	1961
Management by Objectives (MBO)	Personnel management method in which staff set measurable personal goals that align with organizational goals	1973
Zero-based budgeting (ZBB)	Budgeting method in which all expenditures in a given period must be justified; begins with a zero base instead of an incremental increase from the previous fiscal year	1977
National Performance Review (NPR)	Customer-focused management model in which citizens are customers and governments should find the ways that serve their customers best, whether that is in-house or through alternative service delivery methods	1992

President Lyndon Johnson thought the PPBS results in the defense area were impressive, so in 1965, he directed that program budgeting be expanded to include nearly all federal departments and agencies. Managers were directed to submit to the Bureau of the Budget five-year plans on future programming and related financial requirements, accompanied by cost-benefit analyses of alternatives. Not surprisingly, PPBS soon became characterized by wish lists, excessive paperwork, and disconnects between program desires and financial realities. There was no buy-in from Congress, who was not consulted, did not receive PPBS information and analysis, and continued to follow its traditional approach to budgeting. Strong bureaucratic resistance to innovation and change also could not be overcome:

Lower organizational units were upset that PPBS appeared to rob them of authority . . . that it shifted analytical work from agency staffs knowledgeable about an agency's policy area to PPBS technicians skilled in quantifying but unacquainted with the agency's policy area, and that it required an enormous amount of paperwork without discernible impact on decision making. (Kettl, 2015, p. 268)

PPBS was abandoned by the federal government in 1971. However, as will be seen, components of PPBS remained in place and were incorporated into subsequent administrative reforms.

Other federal reform efforts were instituted in subsequent administrations, but none gained enough traction with Congress and the federal bureaucracy to be sustained for the long term. The two most widely cited were management by objectives (MBO) and zero-based budgeting (ZBB). MBO is a personnel management tool that was instituted by the Nixon administration (1973–1974). Organizations using MBO encourage management and staff to work together to develop individual goals and align them with organizational goals. Progress on goal accomplishment is then tracked over time. While MBO was only used for a short time at the federal level, a recent study found that 17% of 893 municipalities responding to a survey were using MBO alone or in combination with other management models (Holliman & Bouchard, 2015).

ZBB was implemented by the Carter administration between 1977 and 1979. Using this method of budgeting, each unit of the organization was required to zero out the base and justify every expenditure each fiscal year. The rationale behind this method is that government budgeting tends to be incremental; each year, a percentage increase is added to the prior year's budget without reexamining base spending. In theory, ZBB would encourage staff to consider whether any given program was necessary to continue or whether the programs could be provided in a more cost-efficient way. ZBB requires an enormous amount of paperwork and time to do correctly. In practice today, ZBB is nearly nonexistent at the local level (Kavanagh, 2011).

Reinventing Government

Perhaps the most significant reform that has influenced the manager's toolbox was the Reinventing Government movement of the 1990s. Reinventing Government was different in scope, substance, and impact from earlier bureaucratic reform efforts. It also challenged many traditional assumptions about the roles of public agencies and public administrators. Launched by two books, *Reinventing Government* (1992) by consultant David Osborne and former city manager Ted Gaebler and *Banishing Bureaucracy* (1997) by David Osborne and former Michigan Department of Commerce official Peter Plastrik, the tone of the movement was captured in the subtitle of the former: "How the Entrepreneurial Spirit is Transforming the Public Sector from Schoolhouse to Statehouse, City Hall to the Pentagon." The broad appeal of Reinventing Government's theme was underscored by *Reinventing Government* achieving *New York Times* best-seller list status. Unlike earlier models,

Reinventing Government was originally developed at the local government level. It was embraced by the Clinton administration, principally through the National Performance Review (NPR) initiative, led by Vice President Al Gore between 1993 and 2001, that promised to make government work better and cost less.

The rationale for Reinventing Government was based on a number of trends, issues, and developments that are still relevant today. These include citizen desires for more for less from government amidst significant resource constraints; the chilling effect of the four *D*s—deficits, debt, defense, and demographics—on the federal government's ability to financially support domestic programs; the public's confidence in lower levels of government as service providers; the appeal and applicability of models from the private sector, such as rightsizing, delayering, and lean management; and the straitjacket effects of Progressive Era reforms, such as civil service requirements and line-item budgets that sought to insulate and isolate the public service from partisanship and corruption but also impeded the ability of government officials to respond nimbly and effectively.

According to Osborne and Gaebler (1992), traditional government program approaches, where monopolistic organizations spend appropriated public funds to deliver a service, have several flaws. First, they are subjected to the desires and demands of powerful constituency groups instead of customers. Second, they are driven by political pressure (which waters down and blurs goals) and not by rational plans and policies. Third, they devote too much attention to turf and custody battles over programs and clientele and not enough to effective management. Fourth, they fragment service delivery systems, each of which has its own procedures and none of which are user friendly. Fifth, they have no self-correcting mechanisms when results or outcomes are not being achieved; sometimes success is penalized (such as when all appropriated funds are not spent, raising questions about demand for services) and failure is rewarded (such as when public administrators ask for more money because they are unable to achieve goals). Sixth, they rarely achieve a fiscal magnitude that is necessary to attain their mission, such as ending poverty, achieving national K–12 education goals, and rebuilding neighborhoods. Finally, they function on a command–control, top-down system rather than an incentive basis, and often, the commands are not followed by subordinates or cannot be enforced by senior managers. In the view of Osborne and Gaebler (1992), the role of governments is to steer the ship of state, leaving the rowing to others, including private firms and nonprofit organizations (pp. 285–290).

Twenty-five years after the publication of *Reinventing Government*, many of the principles, practices, and protocols that formed the foundation of the movement have been adopted at all levels of government and have affected both the strategies and the tools managers have available to do their work. Some of these core principles that the reinventers contend should drive practice include the following:

- Governments should use alternatives to in-house delivery and focus on making policy and conducting oversight while other organizations, especially the private sector, handle implementation (e.g., charter schools, trash collection, corrections, parking meters).

- Public agencies should be driven by their mission rather than by the rule book.

- Public administrators should be outcome and results oriented instead of input and process oriented, and performance assessments and funding awards should be based on the former.

- Clients should be considered customers, and their needs as stakeholders should be taken into account in determining plans, priorities, and delivery systems.

- Public administrators should work to empower citizens to participate in the planning and coproduction of services through neighborhood councils and community groups (e.g., recreation services, senior citizen and veteran assistance, crime prevention).

- Competition should be encouraged within the public sector, such as competitive bidding for service delivery, as well as between government agencies and private sector organizations (e.g., school choice and voucher plans).

- Authority and responsibility should be decentralized.

- Public agencies should be authorized to earn money through fees, run surpluses and retain a portion of unspent appropriations for use in the next fiscal year, and leverage the marketplace through incentives for investment.

Adoption of these principles would make government at all levels more nimble, entrepreneurial, and customer focused. As noted earlier, the Clinton administration's NPR was established in 1993 to spearhead adoption of reinvention approaches by federal departments and agencies as well as by state and local governments that received federal funding. The promise of NPR, for a government that works better and costs less and moves from red tape to results, was partly achieved by reducing the federal civilian workforce by 272,900 positions (about a 12% cut), producing the smallest workforce since 1967 and about $108 billion in savings, some of which were offset by relying on private contractors to do the work formerly performed by civil servants (Kettl, 1998, pp. 2–3). Many of these positions were so-called checkers, who were viewed as being guilty of overcontrol and micromanagement, resulting in stifled creativity and reduced flexibility. These personnel included supervisors, personnel specialists, budget analysts, procurement specialists, auditors, accountants, and middle managers—the very people who help ensure accountability, neutrality, and efficiency. Clearly, the focus was more on *costs less* than *works better*. The NPR also adopted reengineering strategies by using computer systems and telecommunications to transform service delivery and replace obsolete structures. And the NPR included customer service, streamlined procurement, decentralized decision making, and employee empowerment among the components of a continuous improvement strategy (NPR, 1993).

In 1998, the Brookings Institution issued a five-year report card on the Clinton administration's efforts to embed Reinventing Government into the cultures and operations of federal agencies through the NPR. The principal investigator was Donald Kettl, who observed, "No administration in history has invested such sustained, high-level attention to management reform efforts" (1998, p. ix). NPR's overall grade was *B*, with the highest grades given to effort (*A+*) and procurement reform (*A*) and the lowest to relations with Congress (*D*) and identifying objectives of government (*D*). When George Bush became President, the NPR was terminated. Nevertheless, similar to PPBS, components of Reinventing Government remained in place in the executive branch, including strategic planning, outsourcing, performance measurement, purchasing cards, and customer service components.

Not surprisingly, some leaders in the public administration community criticized the reinvention movement. Many practitioners also were skeptical. Robert and Janet Denhardt, for instance, advocated a New Public Service model, arguing that public administrators should serve citizens not customers and not try to steer society in new directions. They should be attentive to more than marketplace forces and accountability mechanisms and especially be responsible to law, community values, political norms, professional standards, and the interests of citizens. In their view, citizenship should be valued above entrepreneurship (Denhardt & Denhardt, 2011).

THE MANAGER'S TOOLBOX

The preceding highlights of significant administrative reform efforts provide a context for discussing five of the most important tools that should be in the manager's toolbox. Four of the five tools covered—strategic planning, performance measurement, program evaluation, and budgeting for results—are survivors in the sense that they have been components of administrative reform efforts over the years under various names and led by different levels of government. The fifth— succession planning—is a relative newcomer, but it will be an essential tool given the anticipated changes in public sector workforce demographics. There are variations in each approach, and the following overview will highlight best practices and provide managers with potential challenges they should be aware of when applying them. Emphasis will be placed on strategic planning, performance measurement, and budgeting as the three most comprehensive and integrative tools for managers to utilize.

Strategic Planning

Strategic planning originated in the private sector and its use in government is relatively recent. Beginning in the 1980s, however, strategic planning spread widely across the intergovernmental system. Its growth was first spurred by the publication of a pathbreaking book by former Ohio Budget Director John Olsen and consultant Douglas Eadie in 1982 entitled *The Game Plan: Governance with Foresight* and then by the Reinventing Government movement and the Government Performance and Results Act (GPRA) of 1993. All federal agencies now produce and revise strategic plans, and most states and localities have engaged in this practice as well (Bryson, Berry, & Yang, 2010, pp. 499–500). A 1999 survey of state administrators by Jeffrey Brudney, Ted Hebert, and Deil Wright found that strategic planning was the most widely implemented of the Reinventing Government reforms.

John Bryson (2010) defines strategic planning as "a deliberate, disciplined effort to produce fundamental decisions and actions that shape and guide what an organization (or other entity) is, what it does, and why it does it" (p. S256). Strategic planning has two organizational benefits: (1) It helps promote strategic thought and action through systematic information gathering, negotiating performance measures, clarifying future directions, and establishing priorities for action and (2) it improves decision making and organizational effectiveness by focusing attention on current issues and emerging challenges, providing a framework for decisions, improving coordination and collaboration across levels and functions, and building administrative capacity over time. Through strategic planning, an organization can gain legitimacy with its stakeholders by engaging them in the process, soliciting their assessment of how well the organization is performing, and relating goals and objectives to their expectations. It can also improve employee morale and connect an individual's work to larger organizational mission and goals (Bryson, 2010, p. S255).

Despite these benefits, the strategic planning record is mixed and, as Theodore Poister (2010) observed, "the extent to which these efforts are worthwhile is not all that clear" (p. S247). It is difficult to assess the impact of strategic planning, as there are so many variables involved in implementation and some activities may not be measurable. However, Bryson's review of the record in the more than 25 years since publication of *The Game Plan: Governance with Foresight* concluded, "strategic planning does produce positive benefits on a modest scale, and in some instances, produces quite outstanding positive results" (2010, p. S258). The challenge to public managers is to get the most benefit from this tool.

Strategic planning is an excellent illustration of the rational approach to decision making. The process has eight fundamental components: (1) a situational analysis of strategic issues, sometimes called a SWOT analysis (strengths, weaknesses, opportunities, and threats) or, more positively, a SOAR analysis (strengths, opportunities, aspirations, and results); (2) a mission statement of why and for whom the organization exists, why it is distinctive or unique, what the core functions are, and how it adds value; (3) a values statement regarding what the organization stands for and how it treats its employees and customers; (4) a vision statement of what the organization will look like and the impact it will have when the plan is fully implemented; (5) goals statements, usually from three to five, describing the major activities to be undertaken through operationalizing the plan; (6) objectives statements for each goal, quantifying what progress is expected over time as implementation proceeds and embracing SMART (specific, measurable, aggressive but attainable, results-oriented, and time-bound) principles; (7) strategies and action plans, indicating strategies such as adaptive market entry or withdrawal and positioning, resources and time lines, and responsible parties (sometimes called *champions*); and (8) performance measures.

Figure 10.1 frames these components in the context of three questions: What should we do? How do we do it? How are we doing? The chart reveals the strategic planning process as a disciplined system. Ideally, over time, the process would move full circle. Unfortunately, in the experience of the University of North Carolina School of Government's Strategic Public Leadership Initiative, few counties and municipalities have completed the full model. Instead, various components have been adopted, such as visioning, goal setting, and performance measurement, but for several reasons, the dots have not been connected into a more systematic approach.

FIGURE 10.1 ■ Strategic Public Leadership: Setting Priorities and Getting Results

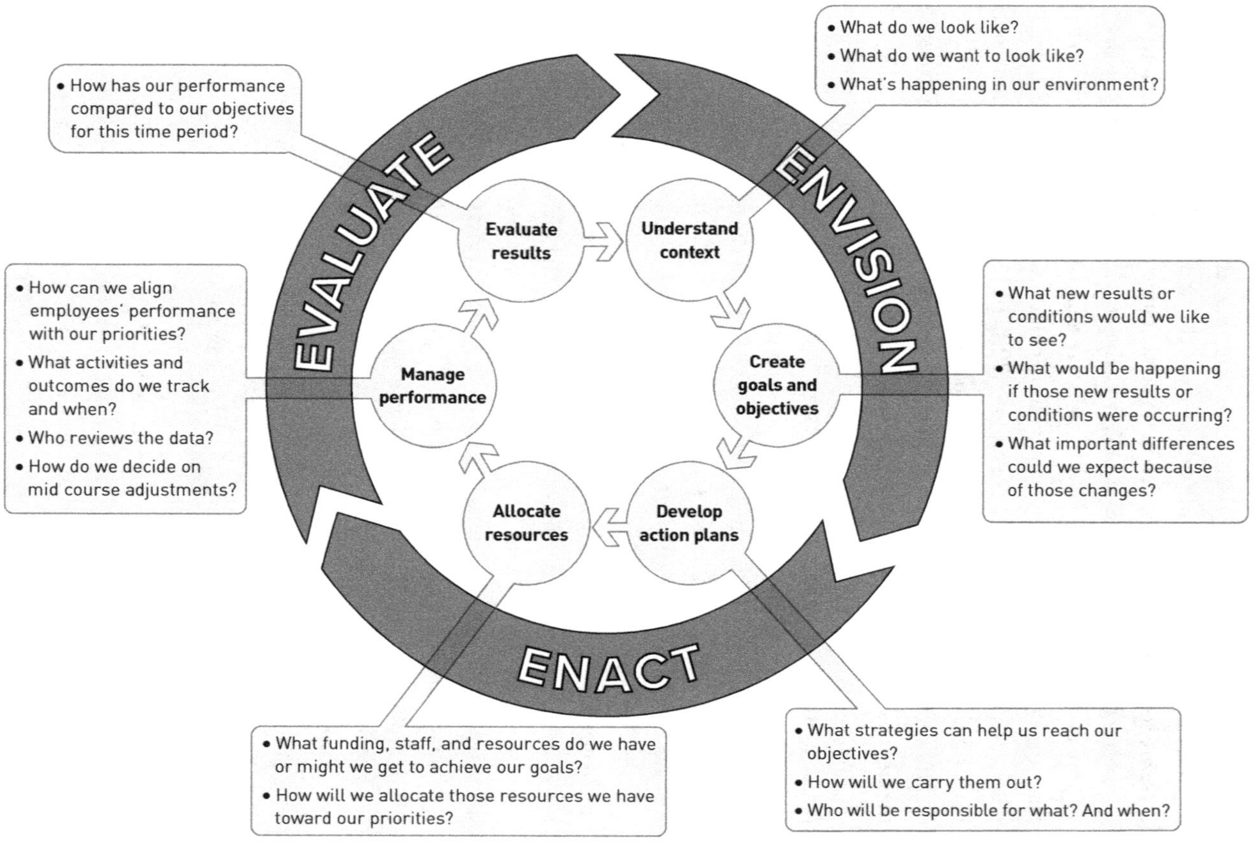

- What do we look like?
- What do we want to look like?
- What's happening in our environment?

- What new results or conditions would we like to see?
- What would be happening if those new results or conditions were occurring?
- What important differences could we expect because of those changes?

- What strategies can help us reach our objectives?
- How will we carry them out?
- Who will be responsible for what? And when?

- What funding, staff, and resources do we have or might we get to achieve our goals?
- How will we allocate those resources we have toward our priorities?

- How has our performance compared to our objectives for this time period?

- How can we align employees' performance with our priorities?
- What activities and outcomes do we track and when?
- Who reviews the data?
- How do we decide on mid course adjustments?

ENVISION

ENACT

EVALUATE

Understand context

Create goals and objectives

Develop action plans

Allocate resources

Manage performance

Evaluate results

Source: UNC School of Government. Reprinted with permission.

212

According to Bryson (2010), there are a number of reasons for the spread of strategic planning across the United States since the early 1980s. Particularly for smaller jurisdictions, strategic planning may only occur under coercion—for example, when small jurisdictions are required to prepare plans as a condition of receiving grants-in-aid. In larger jurisdictions, there may be normative pressures for strategic planning to be considered necessary for innovation or to be a top-performing organization because it is identified as a best practice by practitioners and academics. In other cases, strategic planning may be seen as a fad or "the flavor of the year" reform. In these situations, it is understandable why some managers and elected officials resist going beyond minimum compliance responses, have a "check the box" mentality, and let the plan sit on the shelf and not drive decision making. Even though Bryson concludes that strategic planning is "here to stay," Table 10.2 indicates some of the challenges identified by researchers that make it difficult to make strategic planning real.

These challenges are formidable, but managers can overcome them. Bryson and others argue that governments should make the journey from strategic planning to strategic management. This involves the ongoing integration of strategic planning across an organization—including performance measurement and management, evaluation, budgeting, and human capital management—in order to fulfill

---

TABLE 10.2 ■ Common Strategic Planning Challenges

Unwillingness to engage stakeholders and incorporate their feedback and expectations

Including too many goals or goals that are too vague

Failing to prioritize goals and identify crosscutting goals

Lowering the bar on SMART objectives due to fear of reprisals

Confusing outputs with outcomes

Failing to cross-walk budget requests to long-term goals and short-term objectives

Using inappropriate performance data

Underestimating financial, human, and other resources needed to achieve goals

Holding administrators responsible for objectives that depend on conditions beyond their agency's control

Unwillingness to seek feedback, assess implementation, and take corrective actions

---

Sources: Bryson, 2010, p. S263; Poister, 2010, p. S247.

its mission, meet mandates and expectations, and create public value. As will be considered next, it involves collecting and analyzing data on a regular basis and routinely conducting "Groundhog Day," where the management team and elected officials review plan execution, identify problems, and celebrate progress. Because strategic management is ongoing, continuous organizational learning takes place as the organization becomes more future ready by identifying possible scenarios, taking steps to adapt to its changing environment, and responding to feedback on its implementation strategies and actions.

Performance Measurement

Performance measurement has become an increasingly important component of strategic planning. Once an organization decides where it wants to go in terms of goals and the related strategies, measuring progress using the SMART objectives or performance targets tells administrators, elected officials, and stakeholders how much progress is being made, what corrective actions are required to stay on course, how much more work needs to be done, and what resources will be needed. It also enables an organization to compare itself to its peers and to benchmark itself against them or to the best in field, region, or country. Organizations can also benchmark against themselves from year to year. According to Steven Cohen and William Eimicke (1998):

> The benchmarking process has value even if the desired improvements are not achieved. By continuously seeking to identify the best-in-class and to duplicate or surpass their performance, an organization shapes its culture and behavior with a strong spirit of competitiveness, pride, confidence, energy, and a drive to always do better. (p. 75)

As such, performance measures are a tool to use to help an organization understand, manage, and improve what it does. In addition, accountability is strengthened, employees are empowered by having clear goals and targets to manage and measure, and teams and teamwork are encouraged.

At the national level, two reforms gave performance measurement a substantial boost. In the executive branch, the Program Assessment Rating Tool (PART) was adopted as a key component of President George W. Bush's management agenda as a successor to the NPR. Red, yellow, and green "Stoplight Scores" were assigned by the Office of Management and Budget (OMB) to agencies based on their success in advancing and achieving outcome-based performance targets. Although a latecomer to management reform, in 1993, Congress passed the GPRA, which required federal agencies and funding recipients to prepare strategic plans covering a three- to five-year time period and containing goals, objectives, and measures. In 2010, Congress passed the GPRA Modernization Act, which directed agencies to prepare a four-year plan and submit it to Congress one year after a President is elected or reelected, using common definitions of such terms as *goals* and *objectives*. Under the new law, the OMB is required to conduct annual strategic reviews of agency performance relative to their plans, develop cross-agency priority goals, and designate a lead federal official for each (Kamensky, 2013, p. 8).

Despite these breakthroughs, an assessment of experience by Beryl Radin concluded that these legislative and executive branch performance measurement systems have created conflict between the branches, fragmentation of responsibilities with congressional authorizing and appropriating committees, and variations of roles and responsibilities within federal departments and agencies. Radin concluded that there is very little evidence that performance information has been actually used in decision making by federal-level public managers and that they were "basically invisible" in congressional authorization and appropriations processes (2011, p. S130).

As with strategic planning, Radin's research underscores that there are formidable challenges associated with making performance measurement real to decision makers. First, just as "strategic planning is defined and implemented in vastly different ways across organizations," taking a one-size-fits-all approach to the collection of performance information ignores the diversity of agencies and programs (Poister, Pitts, & Edwards, 2010, p. 539).

As James Q. Wilson pointed out in his classic book *Bureaucracy* (1989), the work of "production organizations" such as state and local transportation, welfare, and public works departments is much easier to measure in terms of both outputs and outcomes than that of "coping organizations" such as schools and police departments, where neither outputs nor outcomes can be readily observed or connected and multiple factors influence performance. For instance, is there a linkage between the number of traffic tickets written (output) and the reduction of traffic accidents, injuries, and fatalities (outcome) (pp. 159–163, 168–171)? Grant programs such as the Community Development Block Grant, in which the federal government provides a sum of funds to accomplish a broadly defined purpose but allows local recipients to exercise considerable flexibility and discretion in setting priorities and determining uses of federal monies, also create performance-monitoring challenges compared to those having more national direction, specificity, and administrative oversight (Radin, 2006).

Second, with respect to the quantity and quality of data, when GPRA's reporting requirements were enacted, some critics said that they did not consider widely varying databases, information collection systems, and analytical capabilities at the state and local levels. Martin O'Malley's leadership and commitment to data and analytics while mayor of Baltimore (CitiStat) and governor of Maryland (StateStat) received national recognition. Both CitiStat and StateStat are versions of PerformanceStat. Originally called CompStat (a system created in the 1990s by the New York City police department to reduce crime), today's PerformanceStat programs are used more broadly in public agencies. These systems use a combination of data analytics, performance measurement, and accountability to improve government performance. However, across the country, the performance measurement spotlight did not shine widely or brightly on other elected leaders who must have buy-in if such efforts are to succeed. As Robert Behn's examination of 21 municipal PerformanceStat programs across the country discovered, the job of elected and administrative leaders involves much more than collecting statistics. Buy-in entails the following:

> A jurisdiction or agency is employing a PerformanceStat *leadership strategy* if, in an effort to achieve specific public *purposes*, its leadership team *persists* in holding an ongoing series of *regular, frequent, integrated meetings* during which the chief executive and/or the principal members of the chief executive's leadership team plus the director (and the top managers) of different subunits use *current data* to *analyze* specific, previously defined aspects of each unit's recent *performance*; to provide *feedback* on recent progress compared with *targets*; to *follow-up* on previous decisions and commitments to produce *results*; to examine and *learn* from each unit's efforts to improve *performance*; to identify and solve *performance-deficit* problems; and to set and achieve the next *performance targets*. (Behn, 2014, p. 1)

Personnel cutbacks that were made in the wake of the Great Recession thinned the ranks of statisticians and analysts who were charged with gathering and reporting performance information. Funds to train staff in performance measurement methods and best practices had dried up in many jurisdictions. While local economies are rebounding, filling vacancies in analyst and evaluator positions ranks far below police, firefighter, teacher, public works, and librarian positions.

Third, if not carefully managed, performance measurement systems can take on a "blame and shame" nature. An example here is the PART's "Stoplight Scores." Programs were rated *effective, moderately effective, adequate, ineffective*, and *results not demonstrated* in terms of four factors—their purpose and design, strategic planning, program management, and results (Radin, 2011, p. S129). These scores were used by the OMB to help determine budget recommendations. Agency personnel who disagreed with the rating could appeal to the OMB's political executives—not an attractive option. This approach raises the accountability stakes, but it also creates distrust and conflict between careerists and political appointees as well as between managers and elected officials. In fact, there may be understandable reasons why an agency or program has failed to meet its strategic objectives and performance targets—such as unrealistic goals, insufficient funding, short implementation time lines, and inadequate staff—that might not be brought to light.

Where this "gotcha" mentality persists, a typical bureaucratic response is to game the measures to satisfy departmental leadership. Donald Kettl believes that "all performance measures are gamed" (2014, p. 16) and asserts that measures create incentives that may be dysfunctional if punishment rather than progress is the focus. In the federal government, the effort of the Department of Veterans Affairs senior managers to disguise wait times for appointments in VA hospitals is illustrative. And in New York City's police department, which launched a crime statistics collection and analysis system (CompStat) to much fanfare, senior management's pressure to drive down crime rates led officers to cook the books:

> When a victim reported a theft, for example, officers would use eBay and other websites to find a lower value for the stolen item than the value the victim claimed. If they could drive the amount down to less than $1,000, it would become a misdemeanor instead of a felony, which are reported to the FBI [Federal Bureau of Investigation] as major crimes. Officers also claimed they were under pressure to convince victims not to report crimes at all or to adjust the facts to allow the police to downgrade the charge. (Kettl, 2014, pp. 16–17)

The PART experience shows that performance ratings are not objective or politically neutral. Studies have found that during the Bush administration, programs that were established under Republican presidents received more favorable scores than those created under Democratic presidents. Programs that reflected more liberal values such as equity, resource redistribution, and environmental protection also received low ratings. In this context, the wariness of careerists about PART and desire to game the system are understandable (Lavertu & Moynihan, 2012, pp. 527–529). PART was discontinued when the Obama administration took office.

So while more performance-related information is being collected at all governmental levels, there are concerns that it is not being used, or used as intended, by public administrators and elected officials. Research has found, for instance, that federal managers consider both PART and GPRA "primarily as a compliance exercise rather than an opportunity to generate purposeful performance information use" (Moynihan, 2013, p. 502). To be an effective tool, especially for local strategic plans and websites, managers will need to find ways to routinely include this data and analysis in program assessments, budget requests, personnel appraisals, and day-to-day administration. As with strategic planning, managers must work to embed performance management in their organizational culture.

Program Evaluation

A frequent comment on the current public administration scene is "what gets measured gets done." For many years, information collected through regular evaluations of programs and services in management studies, consultant reports, and employee surveys, among other instruments, has been used by managers to examine their effectiveness and to identify ways to improve performance. Having performance measurement systems in place that are more than just compliance exercises proves critical to evaluation success.

Program evaluation is one of the most commonly used tools. A mid-1990s survey of municipalities between 25,000 and one million population found that 70% of the respondents had used program evaluation citywide or in a specific area (Poister & Streib, 1994). Whether the research is quantitative or qualitative, contemporary information technology enables managers to evaluate how well their jurisdiction's programs and services are working on several fronts, including stakeholder assessments (e.g., citizen surveys), efficiency and effectiveness indicators (e.g., using geographic information systems to track neighborhood trash collections), and benchmark comparisons against peers using dashboards (e.g., water and sewer fees, police and fire response times, and K–12 graduation or dropout rates).

Growing interest in evidence-based decision making, open data, and analytics should bolster traditional program evaluation efforts and make local government operations more transparent and accountable. Of course, these tools entail investments in information technology, professional staff, and consultants that may be difficult for smaller and less affluent local governments to make. One promising development is the emphasis that most master of public administration and master of public policy programs now place on developing the data collection and analytical competencies of their graduates, who could fill entry-level positions in budget or evaluation units or the manager's office.

Budgeting for Results

Budget reforms also have been common instruments of administrative reform, although many of the initiatives have been short-lived and achieved fad or gimmick status. Proposed systems since PPBS have a variety of names: zero-based budgeting, program budgeting, budgeting for results, performance-based budgeting, responsibility-centered budgeting, and budgeting for outcomes. From a toolbox perspective, their common purpose is to move away from object-based line-item decisions focusing on incremental adjustments of the base. While these conventional approaches offer relative simplicity and are embraced by elected officials, they assume that the local government operates on autopilot in terms of its strategic direction, needs, and priorities. According to David Osborne and Peter Hutchinson (2004):

> The true outrage is that traditional budget cutting focuses entirely on what we cut (or hide), while ignoring what we keep. It does little to improve the effectiveness of the 85 or 90 percent of public dollars that continue to be spent. It never broaches the question of how to maximize the value of the tax dollars we collect. (p. 5)

At the core of budget reform, whatever terminology is used, is an effort to change the rules of the budget game by aligning resources with results. The process involves systematically connecting plans and programs with budget requests at the outset and then monitoring, evaluating, and providing feedback on results. Performance information is an integral part of budget development, execution, and evaluation (Barnett & Atteberry, 2007).

Such cross-walking can take time and consume staff resources and cause the eyes of elected officials to glaze over. But the payoffs in terms of showing elected officials the returns on the investment of taxpayer dollars and enabling them to ask good questions to staff regarding the impact of proposed expenditures are worthwhile. Focusing on these questions raises the conversation during budget season to the policy and program levels and helps keep policy makers from getting lost in the weeds and preoccupied with small line-item requests. Doing so will prove challenging to managers, as governing body members are often inclined to focus on budget details that they understand and are comfortable with and to micromanage staff proposals that are on the voter's radar screen instead of looking at the long-term big picture. An important lesson from past efforts is that it makes little sense to introduce a new budget system into the executive branch without consulting with legislators and encouraging them to use it.

One facilitating factor is the growing use of local websites to showcase how taxpayer dollars are spent through the budget, indicate current budget priorities and emerging needs, track spending trends, and compare budget allocations against peer jurisdictions. A wealth of data on local budgets and operations is available for managers to use to package information and communicate in ways that are understandable to elected officials, citizens, and other stakeholders.

Another benefit of budgeting for results systems is that the groundwork is in place for a more informed dialogue among elected officials and with citizens during the annual budget process. Performance information can be used to identify and justify both budget increases and cuts. Many local governments are required under state statute or local ordinance to conduct a public hearing on the proposed budget. Of course, budget work sessions are open to the public and media, but they rarely attract crowds. While hearings may not be an ideal way to convey information about the budget or to give useful feedback to decision makers, there are steps that managers can take to help promote an informed dialogue. These include making available a "citizen's budget" highlighting major or sensitive initiatives and related rationales and expected outcomes, cross-walking strategic goals and objectives to budget requests, and holding hearings in neighborhood facilities such as community centers as well as at the county courthouse or city hall.

Succession Planning

A fifth tool for managers that is gaining attention is succession planning. The focus here is on human capital (not plans, budgets, and evaluations), and it is driven by the so-called silver tsunami. Depending on the jurisdiction, a substantial number of the baby boomer generation are making retirement plans. For example, as indicated in Chapter 5, ICMA has reported that approximately 60% of the managers currently serving communities will be eligible for retirement within 10 years. The potential size of the retiree exodus and resulting amount of lost institutional knowledge and experience have raised serious concerns about who will fill the local management pipeline. This is especially the case in view of the growing popularity of the nonprofit management specialization in graduate programs.

Municipal and county managers have been encouraged by their professional associations to prepare succession plans for key departmental and management team personnel. Such plans identify the knowledge, skills, and abilities that will be necessary to fill a particular position as well as possible internal candidates who could be groomed to move into vacated positions. The latter sometimes involves a detailed management training and leadership development curriculum as well as job rotations in key positions in the organization. Where succession planning works, there is a smooth transition of personnel out of and into key positions.

Despite the anticipated critical need for talent and the organizational performance benefits, succession planning is not widely practiced. Some organizations simply do not have the resources to develop a succession planning system or have too few management-potential employees to make it realistic. There is also a concern that investing money in developing employees may be wasted if the new training makes them more marketable to other organizations. Some managers prefer to bring in fresh perspectives and new faces from outside the organization rather than to rely on internal candidates who might be wedded to the current culture and ways of doing business. Elected officials may not be supportive of a long-range succession plan, so they may be unwilling to agree in advance to groom individuals for senior management positions, especially where turnover occurs on the governing board and elected official–professional staff trust levels are not high. A legal hurdle also may exist. Civil service requirements, grant conditions, and human resource office practices may mandate that recruitment for all positions be wide open and that no favoritism should be shown toward particular candidates.

THE JOURNEY FROM PLANNING AND MEASUREMENT TO MANAGEMENT

Earlier in this chapter, Bryson (2010) was quoted with respect to the importance of moving from strategic planning to strategic management. Even though each of the five tools highlighted may be underutilized and its potential not fully realized, looking at each one's application in terms of a more integrated or comprehensive framework may pay dividends. As Bryson (2010) notes regarding the move toward strategic management, "the move includes integrating strategic planning, budgeting, human resource management, and performance measurement and management" (p. S262). In their review of the state of public strategic management research, John Bryson, Frances Berry, and Kaifeng Yang (2010) observe:

> Strategic management theory now emphasizes the development and alignment of an organization's mission, mandates, strategies, and operations, along with major strategic initiatives such as new policies, programs, or projects, while also paying careful attention to stakeholders seen as claimants on the organization's attention, resources, or outputs, or as affected by that output. (p. 496)

In these respects, all five of the instruments in the manager's toolbox are well aligned.

Turning to performance management, Theodore Poister (2010) distinguishes it from strategic management as follows: "Whereas strategic management focuses on taking actions now to position the organization to move into the future, performance management is largely concerned with managing ongoing programs and operations at present" (p. S251). Poister points out that large, complex organizations use a wide variety of performance measurements and systems at different management levels, different units, and different program areas. Performance measurement and performance management systems are more encompassing than strategic planning and management. Harry Hatry (2002), an Urban Institute program evaluation expert, has asserted that performance can improve in the absence of strategic planning, even though it would lead to an emphasis on the immediate situation and diminish attention to where the organization should be going in the future.

Performance management lags behind performance measurement in terms of adoption, and it should not be assumed that more performance measurement leads to better performance management. Poister cites a 2008 report by the Government Performance Project—a joint venture by the Pew Charitable Trusts, Syracuse University, and *Governing* and *Government Executive* magazines—that graded states on their attention to management issues such as human capital, financial management, and information technology. The results indicated that 24 states received a *C* or *D* grade on their effort to generate performance information and use it to support decision making. Only six states received an *A* (Poister, 2010, p. S250). The Government Performance Project also examined 75 large counties and municipalities and found that only eight merited an *A* or *A-* in the "managing for results" category (Ammons, Liston, & Jones, 2013, pp. 172–173). The grades could have been worse except for the efforts of public managers in some states to hasten work on their management reforms in anticipation of the public reporting of grades.

A survey of 72 county and municipal governments having a reputation for good performance management found that most (49%) focused on systems for collecting, compiling, and improving performance data, with another 24% indicating that their emphasis was limited to upgrading performance measures. Only 28% connected it with a managerial philosophy. The latter localities collected more information and used it to improve operations and services (Ammons et al., 2013, p. 175). The authors concluded:

> City and county governments that embrace performance management as their management philosophy may enjoy advantages in the pursuit of particular types of benefits over those regarding performance management as a system or tool, and both of these sets of governments are likely to anticipate and receive more benefits from performance management than municipalities and counties that are focused simply on upgrading their performance measures. (p. 178)

Among the reasons for this spotty record are the low priority elected officials give to administrative oversight, except when there is a crisis. Governing bodies often lack political will to make decisions and incur costs necessary to achieve substantial performance gains. And, recalling the straightjacket effects of rules identified by Reinventing Government advocates, public administrators sometimes lack flexibility and discretion to manage programs to improve performance.

An example of how strategic planning and performance budgeting linkages can atrophy if not adequately supported is Alabama's SMART initiative that was launched in 2004. The acronym stood for "specific results, measurable key goals, accountable to stakeholders, responsive to customers and, finally, transparent to everyone" (Barrett & Greene, 2012, p. 68). Partly due to worsening fiscal conditions, by late 2011, state agencies were no longer required to submit their budget requests connected with SMART, although they continued to plan and set goals. Lack of legislator buy-in, uneven support from departmental and agency leadership, outmoded technology, and disconnects between annual goals and statewide strategies were among the reasons for the demise of performance budgeting.

The state of Washington provides another interesting example. In 2007, the Council of State Governments gave its first Governance Transformation Award to the state's Government Management Accountability and Performance (GMAP) system that had been put in place two years earlier. Among the many illustrations of how processes were streamlined and response times were improved was Child Protective Services, which acted on 69% of referrals within 24 hours in 2005 and rose to 90% by 2007. GMAP was a proud accomplishment of Governor Christine Gregoire's administration, but when she convened a meeting to assess the impact of the six years of program experience, the feedback was eye-opening. According to Wendy Korthuis-Smith, GMAP's director:

> Some of the directors felt like the measures weren't relevant anymore but that they couldn't or shouldn't change them. . . . Some saw the GMAP meetings with the governor as "dog and pony shows." . . . The system we'd built didn't feel flexible and nimble. . . . There was too much focus on polishing presentations, when what we really wanted were cycles of experimentation, improvement, and results. (Buntin, 2016, p. 28)

GMAP was becoming "just another stale compliance regime" (Buntin, 2016, p. 28).

This is not to say that managers should stay on the sidelines in the struggle to move to the next level of organizational planning and performance. Table 10.3 indicates a number of managerial levers that could be pulled to steer organizations in this direction.

TABLE 10.3 ■ Levers to Encourage Strategic Performance Management
Tracking Implementation Progress by Monitoring Performance Measures
Assessing and adjusting performance data in strategy review sessions to ensure that appropriate performance metrics are being used
Cross-walking programmatic and budgetary proposals, requests, and initiatives to strategic plans and communicating this information to elected officials
Aligning budget requests and manager's work plans with strategic priorities
Incorporating progress on goal and objective accomplishment into administrator appraisals and compensation decisions
Communicating progress to stakeholders and engaging them in SOAR (strengths, opportunities, aspirations, results) assessments and program performance reviews
Promoting vision, mission, and goal recognition with employees throughout the organization by using signage, newsletters, websites, and award ceremonies

An important, and unanswered, question is, "So what?" Have local governments that use these tools performed more effectively than those that have not done so? Have the tools bolstered relationships between managers, elected officials, and citizen stakeholders? Empirical evidence is lacking or, at best, mixed. Benedict Jimenez conducted research to determine whether municipalities that had comprehensive strategic plans in place were better able to adjust to the economic crisis during the Great Recession and minimize their budget deficits. He found that "managers from cities with comprehensive strategic planning are more confident of the fiscal outlooks of their governments amidst a generally worsening local fiscal climate" (2012, p. 597). This confidence, while subjective, can inspire a sense of control and capacity to act at a time of declining morale, confused direction, and decision paralysis. While it might be hypothesized that local governments operating under reformed forms of government—such as the council–manager system featuring professionally trained managers, nonpartisan and at-large election systems, and unified decision making—were more efficient, there was no confirming evidence that structure affected fiscal policy and that such reforms impacted taxing and spending levels (Morgan & Pelissero, 1980). Clearly, more evidence-based research is needed here.

USING THE TOOLS AS MANAGER

The journey to better local government performance could prove difficult, lengthy, and frustrating in many organizations. Immediate problems and pressing needs often trump long-range thinking, planning, and acting. The attention span of local elected officials is relatively short as they seek to satisfy constituents' current concerns and bolster their reelection prospects; indeed, their definition of *the future* might well be the next election, not the time frame of a strategic plan. Competing values such as efficiency, effectiveness, and equity sometimes produce political decisions that do not reflect managerial recommendations and are satisfactory but not optimal. The wide diversity of public organizations and need for collaborative approaches to problem solving complicates planning, execution, and accountability. And of course, while looking to the future strategically and acting on the basis of forecasts and trends are important, as the Great Recession reminds us, there are always unforeseen events and unintended consequences.

Yet, according to David Ammons (2002), despite their limitations, using these tools in the decision-making process has benefits:

> Thoughtful analysis normally elevates the quality of debate on an issue. Important aspects of a decision and its likely ramifications become more apparent. Sometimes the analysis is so compelling that its recommendations are adopted in full; sometimes recommendations are modified to be more politically acceptable, but are nevertheless adopted with most characteristics intact. Even when its recommendations are rejected, careful analysis permits decision makers to proceed with eyes wide open, fully aware of the likely consequences of a particular decision. (p. 222)

For local governments, there has been progress on the strategic planning, performance, and budgeting fronts in a relatively short time period. While challenges remain, these tools are here to stay. More and better information is now available to policy makers and managers that can help them adapt to changing environments, improve decisions and outcomes, and create greater public value for their work. The key challenge is to embed these tools into the organizational cultures and management systems of public agencies and into the mindsets of elected officials.

Local governments need both strategic management and performance management. They must be nimble in terms of both identifying and dealing with compelling current issues and needs while remaining focused on long-term goals and adapting to a rapidly changing environment. Using the tools highlighted in this chapter will enable managers to successfully embark on and complete this journey.

REFERENCES

Ammons, D. N. (2002). *Tools for decision making: A practical guide for local government.* Washington, DC: CQ Press.

Ammons, D. N., Liston, E. G., & Jones, J. A. (2013). Performance management purpose, executive engagement, and reported benefits among leading local governments. *State and Local Government Review, 45*(3), 172–179.

Barnett, C. C., & Atteberry, D. (2007). Your budget: From axe to aim. *Public Management, 89*(5), 6–12.

Barrett, K., & Greene, R. (2012). SMART is stumped. *Governing, 26*(1), 68–70.

Behn, R. (2014). *Bob Behn's performance leadership report.* Washington, DC: Brookings Institution Press.

Brudney, J. L., Hebert, F. T., & Wright, D. S. (1999). Reinventing government in the American states: Measuring and explaining administrative reform. *Public Administration Review, 59*(1), 19–30.

Bryson, J. M. (2010). The future of public and nonprofit strategic planning in the United States. *Public Administration Review, 70*(Supplement 1), S255–S264.

Bryson, J. M., Berry, F. S., & Yang, K. (2010). The state of public strategic management research: A selective literature review and set of future directions. *The American Review of Public Administration, 40*(5), 495–521.

Buntin, J. (2016). The reinventors: 25 years after first "reinventing government" states are still tinkering with how to get it right. *Governing, 29*(12), 26–33.

Cohen, S., & Eimicke, W. (1998). *Tools for innovators: Creative strategies for managing public sector organizations.* San Francisco, CA: Jossey-Bass Publishers.

Denhardt, J. V., & Denhardt, R. B. (2011). *The new public service: Serving, not steering* (3rd ed.). Armonk, NY: M.E. Sharpe.

Gulick, L., & Urwick, L. (Eds.). (1937). *Papers on the science of administration.* New York, NY: Institute of Public Administration.

Hatry, H. (2002). Performance measurement: Fashions and fallacies. *Public Performance and Management Review, 25*(4), 352–358.

Holliman, A. E., & Bouchard, M. (2015). The use of management by objectives in municipalities: Still alive? *Review of Public Administration and Management, 3*, 1. Retrieved March 24, 2017, from https://www.omicsonline.com/open-access/the-use-of-management-by-objectives-in-municipalities-still-alive-2315-7844-1000150.pdf

Jimenez, B. S. (2012). Strategic planning and the fiscal performance of city governments during the Great Recession. *The American Review of Public Administration, 43*(S), 581–601.

Kamensky, J. M. (2013). The strategic plans are coming! *PA Times, 36*(5), 8, 11.

Kavanagh, S. (2011). *Zero-base budgeting: Modern experiences and current perspectives.* Chicago, IL: Government Finance Officers Association.

Kettl, D. F. (1998). *Reinventing government: A fifth-year report card.* Washington, DC: The Brookings Institution.

Kettl, D. F. (2014). Gaming the system. *Governing, 27*(11), 16–17.

Kettl, D. F. (2015). *Politics of the administrative process* (6th ed.). Washington, DC: SAGE/CQ Press.

Lavertu, S., & Moynihan, D. P. (2012). Agency political ideology and reform implementation: Performance management in the Bush administration. *Journal of Public Administration Research and Theory, 23*(3), 521–549.

Morgan, D. R., & Pelissero, J. P. (1980). Urban policy: Does political structure matter? *American Political Science Review, 74*(4), 999–1006.

Moynihan, D. P. (2013). Advancing the empirical study of performance management: What we learned from the program assessment rating tool. *The American Review of Public Administration, 43*(5), 502.

National Performance Review. (1993). *From red tape to results: Creating a government that works better & costs less.* Washington, DC: U.S. Government Printing Office.

Olsen, J. B., & Eadie, D. C. (1982). *The game plan: Governance with foresight.* Washington, DC: The Council of State Planning Agencies.

Osborne, D., & Gaebler, T. (1992). *Reinventing government: How the entrepreneurial spirit is transforming the public sector from schoolhouse to statehouse, city hall to the Pentagon.* Reading, MA: Addison-Wesley Publishing Company, Inc.

Osborne, D., & Hutchinson, P. (2004). *The price of government: Getting the results we need in an age of permanent fiscal crisis.* New York, NY: Basic Books.

Osborne, D., & Plastrik, P. (1997). *Banishing bureaucracy: The five strategies for reinventing government.* Reading, MA: Addison-Wesley Publishing Company, Inc.

Poister, T. H. (2010). The future of strategic planning in the public sector: Linking strategic management and performance. *Public Administration Review, 70*(Supplement 1), S246–S254.

Poister, T. H., Pitts, D. W., & Edwards, L. H. (2010). Strategic management research in the public sector: A review, synthesis, and future directions. *The American Review of Public Administration, 40*(5), 522–545.

Poister, T. H., & Streib, G. D. (1994). Municipal management tools from 1976 to 1993: An overview and update. *Public Productivity & Management Review, 18*(2), 115–125.

Radin, B. A. (2006). *Challenging the performance movement: Accountability, complexity, and democratic values.* Washington, DC: Georgetown University Press.

Radin, B. A. (2011). Federalist no 71: Can the federal government be held accountable for performance? *Public Administration Review, 71*(Supplement 1), S128–S133.

Wilson, J. Q. (1989). *Bureaucracy: What government agencies do and why they do it.* New York, NY: Basic Books.

RESOURCE LIST/TO EXPLORE FURTHER

Books/Articles

Altman, L., Henderson, M., & Mamlin, V. (2017). *Strategic planning for elected officials: Setting priorities.* Chapel Hill: University of North Carolina School of Government.

EMERGING ISSUES AND MANAGEMENT CHALLENGES FACING LOCAL GOVERNMENTS

Growth is inevitable and desirable, but destruction of community character is not. The question is not whether your part of the world is going to change. The question is how.

—Edward T. McMahon (2012)

As this text demonstrates, the challenges of managing local governments are numerous.[1] Many of the issues local governments face today exceed jurisdictional boundaries but these governments are not accustomed to working together to develop solutions to problems. The housing crisis and resulting financial market collapse that began in 2008 created a new normal for local governments (Martin, Levey, & Cawley, 2012), causing them to lose significant revenues and make cutbacks in both personnel and services. Some local governments may never return to prerecession resource or service levels.

Collaborative efforts between jurisdictions and with private organizations have become a necessity and will take on increasing importance in the future as the population growth trends continue to move from rural to urban/suburban. Previous chapters have highlighted both the opportunities and challenges that come with collaboration. Unfortunately, the rise in local partisanship, single-issue candidates, and declining citizen trust in government make collaboration more difficult.

This final chapter discusses trends that are affecting local governments today and those that will continue to influence local governments in the future. Municipal and county managers will be on the forefront in the efforts to overcome these challenges and build communities that can thrive in an environment that is full of complex problems and tough issues.

WICKED PROBLEMS FACING LOCAL GOVERNMENTS

As discussed in Chapter 4, most of the important problems or issues that affect local governments cross geographic boundaries. Therefore, it is unlikely that a single government can solve these problems alone. Given the existing governmental fragmentation in U.S. metropolitan areas, addressing these problems may call for collaboration by more than a handful of jurisdictions. These types of problems are often called *wicked* not to indicate that they are evil but that they are highly resistant to a solution.

The term *wicked problem* was coined in 1973 by planners at the University of California, Berkeley. They contrasted wicked problems with what they called *tame problems*, which may be complex but can be defined and a solution can be identified in a linear, rational way (Rittel & Webber, 1973). Wicked problems are socially based, so a single, short-term solution is not sufficient. In most cases, the solution would involve modifying the behavior of individuals, so a large-scale policy may not be appropriate.

The interjurisdictional, interdependent, and intercausal nature of the wicked problems require some type of long-term solution. However, shifts in culture, ideology, and the understanding of the problem itself make attempting to find a solution similar to shooting a moving target. Adding to the difficulty is the fact that the problem being addressed may actually be a symptom of another problem, so the solution may lie in first mitigating the original problem. Developing a solution without understanding the cause may lead to unintended consequences.

When asked to define a wicked problem and/or the solution to a wicked problem, different people or groups will define it in different ways. In some cases, all may not even agree that there is a problem, therefore, it would not be possible to get consensus about solving it. There is no single, agreed-upon cause, so there can be no single, agreed-upon solution. In contrast, some problems are called *valence issues*, for which there is widespread agreement about the issue being problematic and an optimal solution can be developed. Instead, policies are developed that manage the problem rather than solve it.

An example of a wicked problem is the illegal narcotic trade and use in the United States. Table 11.1 explains why the problem is a wicked one. All levels of government—federal, state, and local—have been working for more than 40 years to reduce or eliminate the illegal drug trade, with little to show for it except for new problems created by increased enforcement attempts.

Complex problems such as these require a systematic approach to solving them. Most of these issues are, at least in part, caused by choices of individuals. To truly solve them requires finding a way to modify human behavior. This is not something that can be accomplished simply through legislative or executive means. It requires that the government work with the private sector and nonprofit organizations to develop comprehensive strategies for resolution or mitigation.

TABLE 11.1 ■ Illegal Narcotics as a Wicked Problem

Sale and Use of Illegal Narcotics in the U.S.—A Wicked Problem

What is the underlying cause?

No agreement—drug addiction, organized crime, other

What secondary problems does it cause?

Overdose deaths, greater criminal activity, higher health care cost burden

What is the solution?

If you believe drug addiction is the cause, then the solutions include methadone clinics, addiction support, or other treatments for addiction.

If you believe organized crime is the cause, then the solutions include zero-tolerance policies and increased police activity.

Which government is affected by illegal narcotic use?

Federal, state, counties, municipalities

What has the government done and has it worked?

Nixon and Reagan administrations implemented a War on Drugs—both administrations greatly expanded drug enforcement operations.

Illegal drug trade continues with no evidence of permanent change.

What are the unintended consequences of the War on Drugs?

Increased prison populations—racially disproportionate

Increased production of homemade drugs, such as methamphetamine

Wasted taxpayer money

CURRENT AND EMERGING ISSUES FOR LOCAL GOVERNMENTS

What are the issues facing local governments in the future that could be considered wicked? Some of the most commonly referenced current local government problems are those that will likely continue into the future. County and municipal managers will need to understand these issues and how they affect their community in order to meet the challenges these problems present.

Unchecked Growth

Prior to the Great Recession, a widespread housing boom led to rampant sprawl throughout the country. The massive levels of development resulted in the enlargement of metropolitan areas, in some cases leading to creation of a megalopolis. Lang and Dhavale (2005) argue that there are ten megapolitan areas as defined by ten characteristics. The primary features of a megalopolis are that it combines at least two existing metropolitan areas, has a population that will reach 10 million by 2040, and is linked through a transportation network. The image in Figure 11.1 graphically shows the merging of major population centers in the United States. Called the "nighttime map" by the U.S. Census Bureau (2010), the map uses dots to indicate population density. The map shows that by 2010, a highly dense population ran continuously between New York and Boston.

According to the U.S. Census Bureau, in 2010, more than 83% of the U.S. population lived in one of the country's 366 metropolitan areas. Some metropolitan areas experienced record-setting growth between 2000 and 2010. The Palm Coast, Florida, region grew the most (92%). Those with population growth rates over 40% include St. George, Utah; Las Vegas, Nevada; Cape Coral, Florida; and Raleigh, North Carolina (U.S. Census Bureau, 2010).

Although growth has slowed somewhat since the recession, some metropolitan areas are again expanding rapidly. Even areas that have slowed or stalled but grew quickly prerecession bear the legacy of unchecked growth. As mentioned in Chapters 2 and 4, sprawl has significant environmental and economic implications. The reliance on the automobile as the primary transportation method in even high-growth regions leads to air and water pollution, high noise levels, and traffic congestion. Rapid growth consumes a great deal of green space, increasing the risk to air and water cleanliness. In addition, the out-migration of residents from central cities to suburban areas can result in central city decline.

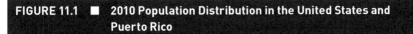

FIGURE 11.1 ■ **2010 Population Distribution in the United States and Puerto Rico**

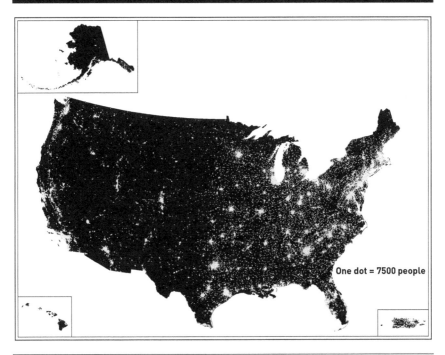

One dot = 7500 people

Source: U.S. Census Bureau, 2010.

To address some of the problems of sprawl, the use of light rail has been introduced or proposed for many of these high-growth regions. However, this option is not a panacea. While proponents cite its ability to reduce traffic congestion and pollution while providing affordable transportation to low-income residents, research has shown that the costs of light rail may be more substantial than the benefits. One study of 24 rail transit systems in the U.S. found that none of the systems provided net social welfare gains without accounting for externalities (Guerra, 2010). Externalities are the benefits for nonriders, such as pollution and traffic reduction. Five of the systems in the study showed no net benefits even when accounting for these externalities.

The Urban–Suburban–Rural Divide

Closely related to the rapid growth and sprawl around metropolitan areas in the U.S. are regional economic problems that occur when parts of a state are growing while other parts are shrinking. In a number of states, primarily in the south and southwest, there are significant economic disparities between urban, suburban, and rural areas. Much of the growth in urban and suburban areas has come at the expense of population in rural areas. In 2015, 14% of U.S. residents lived in nonmetropolitan counties (United States Department of Agriculture, 2016). Between 2010 and 2012, U.S. rural counties experienced an overall population loss (Cromartie, 2013). The graph in Figure 11.2 shows that population growth rates in nonmetropolitan areas have been considerably lower than those of metropolitan areas since the 1990s.

Although in-migration of people leaving rural areas to seek jobs in urban centers drives some of the differences in population change, there has also been natural shrinking of rural population (Maciag, 2013). The average age in rural areas is higher than that of urban areas, leading to lower fertility rates. In 2012, more than 1,000 counties had death rates that exceeded birth rates, meaning a natural population loss (Maciag, 2013).

Hundreds of small municipal governments are at risk of disincorporation because these communities rely on a limited property tax base, given their small populations and lack of commercial development. In some states, urban/suburban cities are

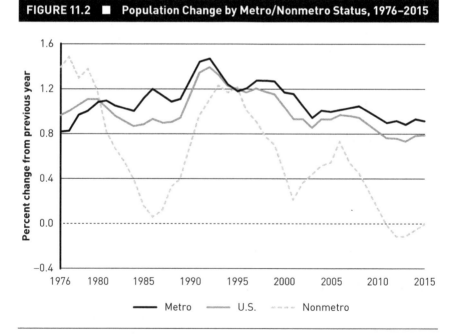

FIGURE 11.2 ■ Population Change by Metro/Nonmetro Status, 1976–2015

Source: U.S. Department of Agriculture Economic Research Service, 2016.

flourishing while rural towns are barely making ends meet. When a municipality fails to collect sufficient revenue to cover basic services, dissolution may be offered as a solution. Should this occur, service responsibility is typically transferred to the county. Between 1900 and 2000, there were close to 250 municipal dissolutions (Anderson, 2012).

Further complicating the economic issues that occur due to urban–suburban–rural disparities are the ideological differences that often exist between these areas in the same state. People who live in rural areas tend to be more conservative than those who live in urban areas, so they elect representatives for the state legislature who are unlikely to agree on major policy choices. However, small, rural communities will likely need to partner with counties and larger municipalities in the future if they are to survive.

Erosion of Public Infrastructure

Another challenging issue for local governments currently and into the future is the significant erosion of infrastructure that was allowed to continue virtually unchecked during the Great Recession. Municipalities and counties deferred maintenance on infrastructure so funds could be directed to maintaining essential services. Compounding the problem are declining revenues from the state and federal governments for infrastructure spending.

In 2013, the American Society of Civil Engineers updated its Infrastructure Report Card. Although the overall grade for the U.S. went up from a D to a D+, the U.S. continues to trend mostly downward when it comes to the condition of our public infrastructure (see Table 11.2). The amount of funding needed to get public infrastructure into good shape is estimated to be over $2 trillion (Kemp, 2012).

While funding for public infrastructure construction, repair, and maintenance comes from all levels of government, only the federal government is positioned to complete an overhaul of the public infrastructure system. Unfortunately, since the 1980s, the federal government has left much of the infrastructure work to the state and local governments. The climate at the national level seems to be changing, however. In December 2015, Congress passed a $305 billion infrastructure bill to fund work on bridges, roads, and rail lines. While significantly less than what is needed for a complete overhaul, as a five-year reauthorization, it is the longest-term measure in more than ten years (Berman, 2015). Although it is too early to determine whether additional legislation for public infrastructure improvements will pass in Congress, the Trump administration has repeatedly called for additional spending on infrastructure.

TABLE 11.2 ■ American Society of Civil Engineers Infrastructure Report Card

	1988	2009	2013
Overall Grade for the U.S.	C–	D	D+
Aviation	B–	D	D
Bridges	C+	C	C+
Drinking water	B–	D–	D
Hazardous waste	D	D	D
Public parks and recreation		C–	C–
Roads	C+	D–	D
Solid waste	C–	C+	B–
Transit	C–	D	D
Wastewater	C	D–	D

Sources: American Society of Civil Engineers, 1988, 2009, 2013.

Some local governments have turned to private companies to fill the gap. While this may seem like a quick way to infuse cash into local government coffers, there may be unintended negative outcomes from the decision to privatize. For example, the city of Chicago agreed to a 75-year lease of its parking meters for $1 billion. While the deal seemed good to the Daley administration at the time, later analysis revealed that the contract amount was half of the value. Rules in the contract that required the city pay the company for lost revenue during parades and other events added further costs to the city. Other examples of public infrastructure that may be privatized are airports, water systems, sewer systems, and toll roads.

Other Issues Affecting Local Governments

In 2011, Elizabeth Kellar identified five "mega issues" that would affect local governments for many years to come: a long-term economic outlook, strained relationships with state governments, demographic challenges, resource challenges, and new media and technology. (See Chapter 8 for a discussion of how technology is being used to engage citizens.) Some of these issues have been discussed in other chapters but not in the context of the future of local governments.

As stated earlier, the Great Recession hit local governments very hard, and many still have not recovered. This means that for the long-term economic outlook, some counties and municipalities will be struggling to simply return to prerecession service levels. Some cuts, such as those to health care and retirement benefits for employees, may be permanent.

In many parts of the country, local governments have entered a period of strained relationships with their state governments. Actions by states that limit the power of local governments and examples of "carrot and stick" state strategies for leveraging local change were explored in Chapters 3 and 4. More broadly, state governments turned to local governments as a source of revenue to meet their own budget shortfalls during the recession. The choice by states to shift responsibilities to local governments with unfunded mandates, limit local government authority through tax and expenditure limitations and legal restrictions, and reduce funding has created an adversarial rather than collaborative relationship between state and local officials in several states. At a time when complex problems require collaborative efforts to resolve, the state–local relationship is critically important. The jury is still out with respect to the question about whether states will be partners or adversaries of local governments in the future.

As baby boomers reach retirement age, communities throughout the country are experiencing a rising proportion of senior residents. This population can pose challenges for local service delivery. However, it also can present opportunities in the form of a large volunteer labor pool and an economic boon to communities that attract retirement-age populations. Perhaps the most significant shift due to the greying of America will be in the implications for the workforce. Recall the discussion in Chapter 5 about the impending wave of municipal and county manager retirements. The retirement wave will affect both the public and private sectors, having implications for succession planning in many industries but particularly for senior management positions in local government.

SKILLS NEEDED IN FUTURE MANAGERS

For the 100th anniversary of the local government management profession, the managers' professional organization, the International City/County Management Association (ICMA), asked members, "Where do you see the future of local government?" Those responding spoke about the future environment of local government and the skills managers would need to succeed amidst the challenges. In addition to the necessary manager skills and competencies listed in Chapter 1, future managers will need to excel at bringing people together in multiple contexts.

One theme from those responses is that managers will need to be good communicators and facilitators. Managers interact with local and state elected and appointed officials, community stakeholders, and the public. The ability to relate to people of different backgrounds and communicate with them is an essential skill. As discussed earlier in the book, managers are the ones who are tasked with bringing people together—whether it is their elected board members or members from neighboring communities. One manager observed, "[A required skill is] finding a way to communicate with more than five generations living, working, and playing in our communities. We have to connect and engage with all of them" (ICMA, 2014, p. 1).

A related skill that was repeated by the managers was the ability to engage citizens in a meaningful way, as covered in Chapter 8. Future managers should be prepared to incorporate citizens into the governing process to a greater degree than is in widespread use today. As one manager said, it is critical to "[work] with citizens to identify needs, values, and wants" (ICMA, 2014, p. 2).

A final point that responding managers made was that there needed to be greater diversity in the profession—more women and minorities—to more closely relate to the community members they serve. Despite ICMA's efforts to promote the profession to diverse groups, as noted in Chapter 5, there has been little change in the percentage of minorities and women in the profession. Declining public trust in government makes the manager's work harder. Research has shown that bureaucratic representativeness leads to several positive benefits for government, including greater trust, an increased willingness to coproduce public services, and greater perceived legitimacy of police (Riccucci, Van Ryzin, & Li, 2016). These potential benefits mean that increased diversity in the local government is not only good for the managing profession itself but for the community overall.

TACKLING WICKED PROBLEMS

The realization of the magnitude of some of the policy issues affecting local governments has led to increasing efforts to engage collaboratively with other governments and the private sector. As discussed in Chapter 3, the growth of suburban communities has created a mass of interconnected and overlapping sets of governments in many U.S. metropolitan areas. The importance of collaboration was discussed in Chapter 4 from the perspective of working across boundaries to address regional problems and in Chapter 5 from the perspective of the local government manager as leader and catalyst of collaborative efforts.

The question left to unravel is this: How can local government managers address these complex problems? The short answer is that no one is sure yet how to solve wicked problems, but clearly the solution must be both collaborative and innovative. As observed in the previous chapter, public managers play an important role in ensuring that their organizations are prepared to work with others and in using modern management tools to achieve efficient, effective, and equitable service delivery. Local government managers should consider ways to bolster innovation capacity in their organizations, as pointed out during the Reinventing Government movement. Government organizations tend to be rigid, hierarchical, and risk averse—characteristics that hinder innovation—so managers must develop ways to manage risk and accept that risk is necessary to foster innovation.

Consideration of the underlying and interrelated causal factors to wicked problems requires a long-term process of analysis and policy development. Elected officials tend to have a shorter time horizon (such as the next election) and are therefore not able to take on the responsibility of developing these long-term solutions. That responsibility will fall to the public manager.

There is limited research into coping with wicked problems that offers some insights. Nancy Roberts (2000) argues that it is critical to first determine how power is dispersed among the problems' stakeholders. She offers three possible strategies:

- Authoritative—assign responsibility to a single group or individual and have the others agree to abide by the decision made by that entity.

- Competitive—assume a win–lose outcome in which various entities compete for resources to address the problem.

- Collaborative—seek a win–win outcome in which stakeholders partner across boundaries to develop a solution.

Roberts maintains that the collaborative approach has the most promise, given the boundary-spanning nature of the most complex problems. Other researchers agree that collaborative approaches are the answer to wicked problems (Head & Alford, 2015; Weber & Khademian, 2008).

Clarke and Stewart (1997) also offer advice on dealing with wicked problems. They stress that it is essential that the definition of the problem not be narrowed and that people be open to the definition evolving over time. Addressing wicked problems requires holistic/broad thinking. Returning to the example of the narcotics problem in the U.S., putting people in jail for longer terms is unlikely to address the problem itself and leads to a different problem—prisons exceeding capacity.

Other research suggests that some of the basic functions of managing government must be rethought to deal with wicked problems. Table 11.3 summarizes the suggestions by Head and Alford (2015) for more effectively analyzing,

TABLE 11.3 ■ How to More Effectively Deal with Wicked Problems
Improve analysis of the problem:
Construct a metaframe of conflicting perspectives on the problem.
Use systems theory to think about the problem holistically.
Use complexity theory to analyze complex trends and challenges.
Use collaborative networks to enhance understanding of the problem:
Help to better understand the nature of the problem.
Increase the likelihood of finding provisional solutions.
Facilitate the implementation of solutions.
Examine the role of leadership in addressing wicked problems:
Adaptive leadership will work better than transformational leadership. Use the process of shared leadership to help people work collectively.
Use inclusive leadership (dialogue-based work across stakeholders).
Use collaborative leadership (occurs without formal authority).
Change structures and processes to facilitate solutions:
Implement flexible organizational structure, such as project teams.
Use flexible budgeting and financial systems; allow for pooled budgeting of collaborating organizations.
Make changes in performance measurement and program evaluation to focus on results.
Make changes in human resources management to focus on finding and hiring people well-suited to collaborative and adaptive situations.

understanding, and addressing wicked problems. They also argue for a rethinking of typical organizational structures and processes to better equip the organization to deal with these complex problems.

Local government managers seeking to tackle wicked problems should also find ways to effectively engage citizens and other stakeholders. To deal with wicked problems, managers must authentically engage citizens as part of the solution. As covered in Chapter 8, engaging citizens as stakeholders can improve the success of policy implementation and often can enlighten policy makers of decision consequences they may be unaware of.

This is particularly important when it is necessary to influence sustained changes in the behavior of individuals to allay the problem. For example, if a county wants to improve environmental sustainability countywide, residents must choose to recycle and use less water and electricity. To reduce the sale of illegal narcotics, the demand for drugs must decline among individuals. To address childhood obesity, children need to eat healthier. Affecting sustained change in individual behavior is perhaps the most difficult challenge of solving wicked problems.

An example of how one community engaged its citizens to solve some of their most intractable problems is found in Eau Claire, Wisconsin's Clear Vision Civic Engagement Initiative (Huggins, 2016). Through the Initiative, citizens were trained in relational problem solving, a process that encourages participants to see themselves as partners in developing public policy and making decisions. The citizens who received the training then led efforts in areas such as "performing arts facilities, community gardens, jobs for the underemployed, community parks, homeless shelters, bicycle routes, environmental education, and elementary school partnerships" (Huggins, 2016).

As noted in several chapters, local governments have a number of advantages over other governments that may make them the best advocates for solving the most intractable public-sector problems. Local governments are smaller organizations than the state and federal governments, therefore, they can act more quickly. Also, citizens hold the highest levels of trust for their local governments versus the state and federal governments. Although trust has declined for all levels of government in the past 20 years, the lowest drops have been for local government. Local governments may be best at taking a long-term view of public policy, given the high percentage of municipal and county governments that are professionally managed. Finally, local governments are closest to the people they serve. Citizens are more likely to know one of their elected officials personally, they have greater immediate access to their local government, and it is much easier for citizens to become engaged with local governments.

CONCLUSION

A recurring message in this text is that demographic shifts, suburban expansion, the growth of special-purpose governments, and the increase in multijurisdictional problems have created a complex local governance system. Today, most residents of the United States live in metropolitan America, not rural America. Unlike in the past, when a local government manager only had to consider the quality of life and issues faced in the community he or she managed, the counties and municipalities that make up metropolitan America today cannot exist in a bubble.

During the Great Recession, local governments suffered considerable losses in revenue—and in some cases, population—and many have still not recovered. Adding capacity through the increase of property or sales taxes is not an option for many local governments. The most obvious way to add capacity and to attempt to solve the complex problems of these local governments is to engage in regional and/or cross-sectoral collaboration.

However, despite many discussions and research supporting metropolitan or regional collaboration as the best way to add capacity, the days when we truly think and act regionally are still far away. It remains difficult for elected officials to think beyond their own borders to consider the ways in which working with other governments will lead to greater benefits to their own communities. Finding ways to work across local boundaries to address wicked problems while at the same time preserving community character and contributions to quality of life will be among the manager's highest priorities.

Fortunately, most local governments in the U.S. are professionally managed. The training and experience that municipal and county managers bring to their jobs allows their communities to build resiliency to withstand the challenges of the future. Although the pace of regional reform has been glacial, some experts have made positive predictions about what lies ahead for local governments and metropolitan areas in an era where the federal and state "cavalries" are no longer able or willing to provide significant financial support. To these observers, metropolitan areas will become more powerful economic engines while local governments will become more active innovators, experimenters, and entrepreneurs.

Former ICMA Executive Director Robert O'Neill, for example, considers the second decade of the twenty-first century the "decade of local government" in which an important facilitating factor in addressing critical issues such as jobs, education, safety, health care, the environment, and infrastructure is the trust citizens have in local government. In this context, O'Neill (2013) finds that:

> leadership will have to span the normal boundaries of the local government organization and the political boundaries of the jurisdiction: (1) to match the geography and scale of significant issues, and (2) to reach all of the sectors and disciplines necessary to make meaningful change. At the same time, local governments will need to preserve their own sense of "place" and what distinguishes their community and makes it special.

Bruce Katz and Jennifer Bradley (2013) of the Brookings Institute point out that even as ideological divides, bureaucratic inertia, and dysfunctionality paralyze the federal government and many of the states, a metropolitan revolution is underway across the country.

County and municipal managers will play critical roles in this revolution. While wicked problems and other challenges and trends discussed throughout this book are formidable, they present exciting and rewarding opportunities to serve on the front lines in transforming communities and organizations. Managers are well-poised to make significant contributions to improved governance and citizen service. We hope that the information, ideas, and insights presented in the preceding chapters will inspire students to embark on a career in local management and will help those who are new to the profession to navigate the dynamic world of local government.

NOTE

1. See Chapter 4 for an in-depth discussion of metropolitan America and its associated problems and issues.

REFERENCES

American Society of Civil Engineers. (1988). *1998 report card for America's infrastructure*. Reston, VA: Author.

American Society of Civil Engineers. (2009). *2009 report card for America's infrastructure*. Reston, VA: Author.

American Society of Civil Engineers. (2013). *2013 report card for America's infrastructure*. Reston, VA: Author.

Anderson, M. W. (2012). Dissolving cities. *Yale Law Journal, 121*(6), 1286–1583.

Berman, R. (2015, December 4). A major infrastructure bill clears Congress. *The Atlantic*. Retrieved March 27, 2017, from http://www.theatlantic.com/politics/archive/2015/12/a-major-infrastructure-bill-clears-congress/418827/

Clarke, M., & Stewart, J. (1997). *Handling wicked issues—A challenge for government*. Birmingham, AL: University of Birmingham.

Cromartie, J. (2013). *How is rural America changing?* Washington, DC: United States Department of Agriculture. Retrieved March 27, 2017, from https://www.census.gov/newsroom/cspan/rural_america/20130524_rural_america_slides.pdf

Guerra, E. (2010). *Valuing rail transit: Comparing capital and operating costs to consumer benefits*. Retrieved March 26, 2017, from https://iurd.berkeley.edu/wp/2010-04.pdf

Head, B. W., & Alford, J. (2015). Wicked problems: Implications for public policy and management. *Administration and Society, 47*(6), 711–739.

Huggins, M. (2016, March 8). *Leadership skills for managing wicked problems in local government.* ICMA Knowledge Network blog. Retrieved March 27, 2017, from http://icma.org/en/icma/knowledge_network/blogs/blogpost/4493/Leadership_Skills_for_Managing_Wicked_Problems_in_Local_Government.

International City/County Management Association. (2014). *The future of local government.* Retrieved March 27, 2017, from https://www.google.com/url?sa=t&rct=j&q=&esrc=s&source=web&cd=&ved=0ahUKEwizpaHk6-LRAhVLQCYKHRtwB1MQFggjMAE&url=http%3A%2F%2Ficma.org%2F-Documents%2FDocument%2FDocument%2F305645&usg=AFQjCNGkvkb9QQgW0hXofVXyTqEJzNE8cw

Katz, B., & Bradley, J. (2013). *The metropolitan revolution: How cities and metros are fixing our broken politics and fragile economy.* Washington, DC: Brookings Institution Press.

Kellar, E. (2011). Five mega issues drive local changes: Managers tackle future challenges with resolve. *Public Management, 93*(1), 6–11.

Kemp, R. L. (2012). The condition of America's infrastructure. In R. Kemp (Ed.), *The municipal budget crunch, a handbook for professionals* (pp. 225–228). Jefferson, NC: McFarland and Company.

Lang, R. E., & Dhavale, D. (2005). America's megapolitan areas. *Land Lines, 17*(3), 1–4.

Maciag, M. (2013). America's rural–urban divide is growing. *Governing.* Retrieved March 27, 2017, from http://www.governing.com/blogs/by-the-numbers/gov-americas-rural-urban-divide-is-growing.html

Martin, L. L., Levey, R., & Cawley, J. (2012). The "new normal" for local government. *State and Local Government Review, 44*(Supplement 1), S17–S28.

McMahon, E. T. (2012, April 4). The distinctive city. *Urbanland.* Retrieved April 6, 2017, from http://urbanland.uli.org/development-business/the-distinctive-city/

O'Neill, B. (2013). Leadership and the profession: Where to from here? Be reformers or be reformed? *Public Management, 95*(2), 20–23. Retrieved March 27, 2017, from http://webapps.icma.org/pm/9502/public/feature2.cfm?title=SPECIAL%20REPORT%3A%20Leadership%20and%20the%20Profession%3A%20Where%20to%20From%20Here%3F%20&subtitle=Be%20reformers%20or%20be%20reformed%3F&author=Bob%20O%E2%80%99Neill

Riccucci, N. M., Van Ryzin, G. G., & Li, H. (2016). Representative bureaucracy and the willingness to coproduce: An experimental study. *Public Administration Review, 76*(1), 121–130.

Rittel, H. W. J., & Webber, M. M. (1973). Dilemmas in a general theory of planning. *Policy Science, 4*, 155–169.

Roberts, N. (2000). Wicked problems and network approaches to resolution. *International Public Management Review, 1*(1), 1–19.

U.S. Census Bureau. (2010). *2010 population distribution in the United States and Puerto Rico.* Retrieved March 27, 2017, from https://www.census.gov/geo/maps-data/maps/2010popdistribution.html

U.S. Department of Agriculture. (2016). *Population and migration.* Retrieved March 27, 2017, from https://www.ers.usda.gov/topics/rural-economy-population/population-migration/

U.S. Department of Agriculture Economic Research Service. (2016). *Population change by metro/nonmentro status, 1976–2015*. Retrieved March 27, 2015, from https://www.ers.usda.gov/topics/rural-economy-population/population-migration/

Weber, E. P., & Khademian, A. (2008). Wicked problems, knowledge challenges, and collaborative capacity builders in network settings. *Public Administration Review, 68*(2), 334–349.

RESOURCE LIST/TO EXPLORE FURTHER

Books/Articles

Reese, E., & Berner, M. (2014). *Wicked problems: What can local governments do?* Chapel Hill: University of North Carolina School of Government.

Web Resources

ICMA. (2016, March 8). *Leadership skills for managing wicked problems in local government*. Available at http://icma.org/en/icma/knowledge_network/blogs/blogpost/4493/Leadership_Skills_for_Managing_Wicked_Problems_in_Local_Government

National Association of Counties. (2015). *National city–county task force on the opioid epidemic*. Available at http://www.naco.org/national-city-county-task-force-opioid-epidemic

National League of Cities. (2016). *Emerging issues*. Available at http://www.nlc.org/emerging-issues

Video

Pahlka, J. (2012, February). *Jennifer Pahlka: Coding a better government* [Video file]. Retrieved from https://www.ted.com/talks/jennifer_pahlka_coding_a_better_government?language=en

ICMA

INTERNATIONAL CITY/ COUNTY MANAGEMENT ASSOCIATION (ICMA) CODE OF ETHICS WITH GUIDELINES

The ICMA Code of Ethics was adopted by the ICMA membership in 1924, and most recently amended by the membership in April 2015. The Guidelines for the Code were adopted by the ICMA Executive Board in 1972, and most recently revised in June 2015.

The mission of ICMA is to create excellence in local governance by developing and fostering professional local government management worldwide. To further this mission, certain principles, as enforced by the Rules of Procedure, shall govern the conduct of every member of ICMA, who shall:

Tenet 1. Be dedicated to the concepts of effective and democratic local government by responsible elected officials and believe that professional general management is essential to the achievement of this objective.

Tenet 2. Affirm the dignity and worth of the services rendered by government and maintain a constructive, creative, and practical attitude toward local government affairs and a deep sense of social responsibility as a trusted public servant.

GUIDELINE

Advice to Officials of Other Local Governments. When members advise and respond to inquiries from elected or appointed officials of other local governments, they should inform the administrators of those communities.

Tenet 3. Be dedicated to the highest ideals of honor and integrity in all public and personal relationships in order that the member may merit the respect and confidence of the elected officials, of other officials and employees, and of the public.

GUIDELINES

Public Confidence. Members should conduct themselves so as to maintain public confidence in their profession, their local government, and in their performance of the public trust.

Impression of Influence. Members should conduct their official and personal affairs in such a manner as to give the clear impression that they cannot be improperly influenced in the performance of their official duties.

Appointment Commitment. Members who accept an appointment to a position should not fail to report for that position. This does not preclude the possibility of a member considering several offers or seeking several positions at the same time, but once a bona fide offer of a position has been accepted, that commitment should be honored. Oral acceptance of an employment offer is considered binding unless the employer makes fundamental changes in terms of employment.

Credentials. An application for employment or for ICMA's Voluntary Credentialing Program should be complete and accurate as to all pertinent details of education, experience, and personal history. Members should recognize that both omissions and inaccuracies must be avoided.

Professional Respect. Members seeking a management position should show professional respect for persons formerly holding the position or for others who might be applying for the same position. Professional respect does not preclude honest differences of opinion; it does preclude attacking a person's motives or integrity in order to be appointed to a position.

Reporting Ethics Violations. When becoming aware of a possible violation of the ICMA Code of Ethics, members are encouraged to report the matter to ICMA. In reporting the matter, members may choose to go on record as the complainant or report the matter on a confidential basis.

Confidentiality. Members should not discuss or divulge information with anyone about pending or completed ethics cases, except as specifically authorized by the Rules of Procedure for Enforcement of the Code of Ethics.

Seeking Employment. Members should not seek employment for a position having an incumbent administrator who has not resigned or been officially informed that his or her services are to be terminated.

Tenet 4. Recognize that the chief function of local government at all times is to serve the best interests of all of the people.

GUIDELINE

Length of Service. A minimum of two years generally is considered necessary in order to render a professional service to the local government. A short tenure should be the exception rather than a recurring experience. However, under special circumstances, it may be in the best interests of the local government and the member to separate in a shorter time. Examples of such circumstances would include refusal of the appointing authority to honor commitments concerning conditions of employment, a vote of no confidence in the member, or severe personal problems. It is the responsibility of an applicant for a position to ascertain conditions of employment. Inadequately determining terms of employment prior to arrival does not justify premature termination.

Tenet 5. Submit policy proposals to elected officials; provide them with facts and advice on matters of policy as a basis for making decisions and setting community goals; and uphold and implement local government policies adopted by elected officials.

GUIDELINE

Conflicting Roles. Members who serve multiple roles—working as both city attorney and city manager for the same community, for example—should avoid participating in matters that create the appearance of a conflict of interest. They should disclose the potential conflict to the governing body so that other opinions may be solicited.

Tenet 6. Recognize that elected representatives of the people are entitled to the credit for the establishment of local government policies; responsibility for policy execution rests with the members.

Tenet 7. Refrain from all political activities which undermine public confidence in professional administrators. Refrain from participation in the election of the members of the employing legislative body.

GUIDELINES

Elections of the Governing Body. Members should maintain a reputation for serving equally and impartially all members of the governing body of the local government they serve, regardless of party. To this end, they should not participate in an election campaign on behalf of or in opposition to candidates for the governing body.

Elections of Elected Executives. Members shall not participate in the election campaign of any candidate for mayor or elected county executive.

Running for Office. Members shall not run for elected office or become involved in political activities related to running for elected office, or accept appointment to an elected office. They shall not seek political endorsements, financial contributions or engage in other campaign activities.

Elections. Members share with their fellow citizens the right and responsibility to vote. However, in order not to impair their effectiveness on behalf of the local governments they serve, they shall not participate in political activities to support the candidacy of individuals running for any city, county, special district, school, state or federal offices. Specifically, they shall not endorse candidates, make financial contributions, sign or circulate petitions, or participate in fundraising activities for individuals seeking or holding elected office.

Elections Relating to the Form of Government. Members may assist in preparing and presenting materials that explain the form of government to the public prior to a form of government election. If assistance is required by another community, members may respond.

Presentation of Issues. Members may assist their governing body in the presentation of issues involved in referenda such as bond issues, annexations, and other matters that affect the government entity's operations and/or fiscal capacity.

<u>Personal Advocacy of Issues.</u> Members share with their fellow citizens the right and responsibility to voice their opinion on public issues. Members may advocate for issues of personal interest only when doing so does not conflict with the performance of their official duties.

Tenet 8. Make it a duty continually to improve the member's professional ability and to develop the competence of associates in the use of management techniques.

GUIDELINES

<u>Self-Assessment.</u> Each member should assess his or her professional skills and abilities on a periodic basis.

<u>Professional Development.</u> Each member should commit at least 40 hours per year to professional development activities that are based on the practices identified by the members of ICMA.

Tenet 9. Keep the community informed on local government affairs; encourage communication between the citizens and all local government officers; emphasize friendly and courteous service to the public; and seek to improve the quality and image of public service.

Tenet 10. Resist any encroachment on professional responsibilities, believing the member should be free to carry out official policies without interference, and handle each problem without discrimination on the basis of principle and justice.

GUIDELINE

<u>Information Sharing.</u> The member should openly share information with the governing body while diligently carrying out the member's responsibilities as set forth in the charter or enabling legislation.

Tenet 11. Handle all matters of personnel on the basis of merit so that fairness and impartiality govern a member's decisions, pertaining to appointments, pay adjustments, promotions, and discipline.

GUIDELINE

Equal Opportunity. All decisions pertaining to appointments, pay adjustments, promotions, and discipline should prohibit discrimination because of race, color, religion, sex, national origin, sexual orientation, political affiliation, disability, age, or marital status. It should be the members' personal and professional responsibility to actively recruit and hire a diverse staff throughout their organizations.

Tenet 12. Public office is a public trust. A member shall not leverage his or her position for personal gain or benefit.

GUIDELINES

Gifts. Members shall not directly or indirectly solicit, accept or receive any gift if it could reasonably be perceived or inferred that the gift was intended to influence them in the performance of their official duties or if the gift was intended to serve as a reward for any official action on their part.

The term "Gift" includes but is not limited to services, travel, meals, gift cards, tickets, or other entertainment or hospitality. Gifts of money or loans from persons other than the local government jurisdiction pursuant to normal employment practices are not acceptable.

Members should not accept any gift that could undermine public confidence. De minimus gifts may be accepted in circumstances that support the execution of the member's official duties or serve a legitimate public purpose. In those cases, the member should determine a modest maximum dollar value based on guidance from the governing body or any applicable state or local law.

The guideline is not intended to apply to normal social practices, not associated with the member's official duties, where gifts are exchanged among friends, associates and relatives.

Investments in Conflict with Official Duties. Members should refrain from any investment activity which would compromise the impartial and objective performance of their duties. Members should not invest or hold any investment, directly or indirectly, in any financial business, commercial, or other private transaction that creates a conflict of interest, in fact or appearance, with their official duties.

In the case of real estate, the use of confidential information and knowledge to further a member's personal interest is not permitted. Purchases and sales which might be interpreted as speculation for quick profit should be avoided (see the guideline on "Confidential Information"). Because personal investments may appear to influence official actions and decisions, or create the appearance of impropriety, members should disclose or dispose of such investments prior to accepting a position in a local government. Should the conflict of interest arise during employment, the member should make full disclosure and/or recuse themselves prior to any official action by the governing body that may affect such investments.

This guideline is not intended to prohibit a member from having or acquiring an interest in, or deriving a benefit from any investment when the interest or benefit is due to ownership by the member or the member's family of a de minimus percentage of a corporation traded on a recognized stock exchange even though the corporation or its subsidiaries may do business with the local government.

Personal Relationships. Members should disclose any personal relationship to the governing body in any instance where there could be the appearance of a conflict of interest. For example, if the manager's spouse works for a developer doing business with the local government, that fact should be disclosed.

Confidential Information. Members shall not disclose to others, or use to advance their personal interest, intellectual property, confidential information, or information that is not yet public knowledge, that has been acquired by them in the course of their official duties.

Information that may be in the public domain or accessible by means of an open records request is not confidential.

Private Employment. Members should not engage in, solicit, negotiate for, or promise to accept private employment, nor should they render services for private interests or conduct a private business when such employment, service, or business creates a conflict with or impairs the proper discharge of their official duties.

Teaching, lecturing, writing, or consulting are typical activities that may not involve conflict of interest or impair the proper discharge of their official duties. Prior notification of the appointing authority is appropriate in all cases of outside employment.

Representation. Members should not represent any outside interest before any agency, whether public or private, except with the authorization of or at the direction of the appointing authority they serve.

<u>Endorsements.</u> Members should not endorse commercial products or services by agreeing to use their photograph, endorsement, or quotation in paid or other commercial advertisements, marketing materials, social media, or other documents, whether the member is compensated or not for the member's support. Members may, however, provide verbal professional references as part of the due diligence phase of competitive process or in response to a direct inquiry.

Members may agree to endorse the following, provided they do not receive any compensation: (1) books or other publications; (2) professional development or educational services provided by nonprofit membership organizations or recognized educational institutions; (3) products and/or services in which the local government has a direct economic interest.

Members' observations, opinions, and analyses of commercial products used or tested by their local governments are appropriate and useful to the profession when included as part of professional articles and reports.

APPENDIX 2

ICMA UNIVERSITY

INTERNATIONAL CITY/COUNTY MANAGEMENT ASSOCIATION (ICMA) PRACTICES FOR EFFECTIVE LOCAL GOVERNMENT MANAGEMENT

International City/County Management Association (ICMA) members have agreed that certain defined practices are essential for effective local government management. For convenience, these practices were originally organized into eight groupings. With the development of the Management Practices Assessment, it became clear that for professional development purposes, the practices more clearly fall into 18 core content areas, as shown below. These are the same practices that members developed and approved; they are simply organized differently.

1. **Staff Effectiveness:** Promoting the development and performance of staff and employees throughout the organization (requires knowledge of interpersonal relations, skill in motivation techniques, and the ability to identify others' strengths and weaknesses). Practices that contribute to this core content area are

   - **coaching/mentoring:** providing direction, support, and feedback to enable others to meet their full potential (requires knowledge of feedback techniques and the ability to assess performance and identify others' developmental needs);
   - **team leadership:** facilitating teamwork (requires knowledge of team relations, the ability to direct and coordinate group efforts, and skill in leadership techniques);

- **empowerment:** creating a work environment that encourages responsibility and decision making at all organizational levels (requires skill in sharing authority and removing barriers to creativity); and
- **delegating:** assigning responsibility to others (requires skill in defining expectations, providing direction and support, and evaluating results).

2. **Policy Facilitation:** Helping elected officials and other community actors identify, work toward, and achieve common goals and objectives (requires knowledge of group dynamics and political behavior; skill in communication, facilitation, and consensus-building techniques; and the ability to engage others in identifying issues and outcomes). Practices that contribute to this core content area are

   - **facilitative leadership:** building cooperation and consensus among and within diverse groups, helping them identify common goals and act effectively to achieve them, recognizing interdependent relationships and multiple causes of community issues, and anticipating the consequences of policy decisions (requires knowledge of community actors and their interrelationships);
   - **facilitating council effectiveness:** helping elected officials develop a policy agenda that can be implemented effectively and that serves the best interests of the community (requires knowledge of role/authority relationships between elected and appointed officials, skill in responsibly following the lead of others when appropriate, and the ability to communicate sound information and recommendations); and
   - **mediation/negotiation:** acting as a neutral party in the resolution of policy disputes (requires knowledge of mediation/negotiation principles and skill in mediation/negotiation techniques).

3. **Functional and Operational Expertise and Planning (a component of service delivery management):** Practices that contribute to this core content area are

   - **functional/operational expertise:** understanding the basic principles of service delivery in functional areas (e.g., public safety, economic development, human and social services, administrative services, public works; requires knowledge of service areas and delivery options) and
   - **operational planning:** anticipating future needs, organizing work operations, and establishing timetables for work units or projects (requires knowledge of technological advances and changing standards,

skill in identifying and understanding trends, and skill in predicting the impact of service delivery decisions).

4. **Citizen Service (a component of service delivery management):** Determining citizen needs and providing responsive, equitable services to the community (requires skill in assessing community needs and allocating resources and knowledge of information-gathering techniques).

5. **Quality Assurance (a component of service delivery management):** Maintaining a consistently high level of quality in staff work, operational procedures, and service delivery (requires knowledge of organizational processes, the ability to facilitate organizational improvements, and the ability to set performance/productivity standards and objectives and to measure results).

6. **Initiative, Risk Taking, Vision, Creativity, and Innovation (components of strategic leadership):** Setting an example that urges the organization and the community toward experimentation, change, creative problem solving, and prompt action (requires knowledge of personal leadership style; skill in visioning, shifting perspectives, and identifying options; and the ability to create an environment that encourages initiative and innovation). Practices that contribute to this core content area are

    -   **initiative and risk taking:** demonstrating a personal orientation toward action and accepting responsibility for the results as well as resisting the status quo and removing stumbling blocks that delay progress toward goals and objectives,
    -   **vision:** conceptualizing an ideal future state and communicating it to the organization and the community, and
    -   **creativity and innovation:** developing new ideas or practices as well as applying existing ideas and practices to new situations.

7. **Technological Literacy (a component of strategic leadership):** Demonstrating an understanding of information technology and ensuring that it is incorporated appropriately in plans to improve service delivery, information sharing, organizational communication, and citizen access (requires knowledge of technological options and their application).

8. **Democratic Advocacy and Citizen Participation:** Demonstrating a commitment to democratic principles by respecting elected officials,

community interest groups, and the decision-making process; educating citizens about local government; and acquiring knowledge of the social, economic, and political history of the community (requires knowledge of democratic principles, political processes, and local government law; skill in group dynamics, communication, and facilitation; and the ability to appreciate and work with diverse individuals and groups and to follow the community's lead in the democratic process). Practices that contribute to this core content area are

- **democratic advocacy:** fostering the values and integrity of representative government and local democracy through action and example as well as ensuring the effective participation of local government in the intergovernmental system (requires knowledge and skill in intergovernmental relations) and
- **citizen participation:** recognizing the right of citizens to influence local decisions and promoting active citizen involvement in local governance.

9. **Diversity:** Understanding and valuing the differences among individuals and fostering these values throughout the organization and the community.

10. **Budgeting:** Preparing and administering the budget (requires knowledge of budgeting principles and practices, revenue sources, projection techniques, and financial control systems as well as skill in communicating financial information).

11. **Financial Analysis:** Interpreting financial information to assess the short-term and long-term fiscal condition of the community, determine the cost effectiveness of programs, and compare alternative strategies (requires knowledge of analytical techniques and skill in applying them).

12. **Human Resources Management:** Ensuring that the policies and procedures for employee hiring, promotion, performance appraisal, and discipline are equitable, legal, and current as well as ensuring that human resources are adequate to accomplish programmatic objectives (requires knowledge of personnel practices and employee relations law as well as the ability to project workforce needs).

13. **Strategic Planning:** Positioning the organization and the community for events and circumstances that are anticipated in the future (requires knowledge of long-range and strategic planning techniques, skill in

identifying trends that will affect the community, and the ability to analyze and facilitate policy choices that will benefit the community in the long run).

14. **Advocacy and Interpersonal Communication:** Facilitating the flow of ideas, information, and understanding between and among individuals as well as advocating effectively in the community's interest (requires knowledge of interpersonal and group communication principles; skill in listening, speaking, and writing; and the ability to persuade without diminishing the views of others). Practices that contribute to this core content area are

    - **advocacy:** communicating personal support for policies, programs, or ideals that serve the best interests of the community and
    - **interpersonal communication:** exchanging verbal and nonverbal messages with others in a way that demonstrates respect for the individual and furthers organizational and community objectives (requires the ability to receive verbal and nonverbal cues and skill in selecting the most effective communication method for each interchange).

15. **Presentation Skills:** Conveying ideas or information effectively to others (requires knowledge of presentation techniques and options and the ability to match the presentation to the audience).

16. **Media Relations:** Communicating information to the media in a way that increases public understanding of local government issues and activities and builds a positive relationship with the press (requires knowledge of media operations and objectives).

17. **Integrity:** Demonstrating fairness, honesty, and ethical and legal awareness in personal and professional relationships and activities (requires knowledge of business and personal ethics as well as the ability to understand issues of ethics and integrity in specific situations). Practices that contribute to this core content are

    - **personal integrity:** demonstrating accountability for personal actions and conducting personal relationships and activities fairly and honestly;
    - **professional integrity:** conducting professional relationships and activities fairly, honestly, legally, and in conformance with the ICMA Code of Ethics (requires knowledge of administrative ethics, specifically the ICMA Code of Ethics); and

- **organizational integrity:** fostering ethical behavior throughout the organization through personal example, management practices, and training (requires knowledge of administrative ethics as well as the ability to communicate ethical standards and guidelines to others).

18. **Personal Development:** Demonstrating a commitment to a balanced life through ongoing self-renewal and development in order to increase personal capacity (includes maintaining personal health, living by core values, continuous learning and improvement, and creating interdependent relationships and respect for differences).

Source: © ICMA. Used with permission.

INDEX

Great Depression, 36
Greatest good, 108, 108 (figure)
Great Recession
  housing developments, 232
  infrastructure erosion, 235
  long-term economic outlook, 236–237
  personnel cutbacks, 216
  state restructuring incentives, 76
  strategic planning practices, 224, 225
  tax revenue losses, 42, 242
Greenblatt, A., 41, 42
Greene, R., 223
Gregoire, Christine, 223
Grubert, W. A., 26
Guerra, E., 233
Gulick, L. H., 101, 204
Gullet, B. M., 195

Haines, M. R., 19
Hamilton, D. K., 84
Hanbury, G. L., 104
Hanchett, T. W., 27
Hannah-Spurlock, S., 81
Harding, C., 175
Harlow, L., 113
Harrigan, J. J., 64
Harrison, S., 105
Hart, V., 21
Hassett, W. L., 92, 95
Hatry, H., 222
Hawaii, 45, 47, 48 (table)
Hayden, D., 18–19, 27
Hays, S. P., 25
Head, B. W., 239
Hebert, F. T., 210
Hecht, B., 202
Hefetz, A., 185, 186, 186 (table), 188, 190,
    190 (table), 191 (table), 193
Henderson, M., 227
Hendrick, R., 61
Hickory, North Carolina, 118
High-performing habits, 134–135
High-quality local government
    leadership, 104
High-speed Internet access, 172, 173
Highway systems, 28
Hill, M. B., Jr., 39, 73
  see also Krane, D.

Hilvert, C., 67, 189, 192
  see also Gaebler, T. A.
Hiring/firing practices, 89–91, 103,
    118–120, 138, 199, 221
Hirschhorn, B., 26
Hobbs, F., 29 (figure)
Hofstadter, R., 33
Holliman, A. E., 206
Holt, T., 189
  see also Gaebler, T. A.
Home rule, 11, 40–41, 51, 64, 74, 182, 187
Hopkins, G. B., 25
Horne, Bill, 102
Horses, 22, 22 (photo)
Housing Act (1949), 29
Housing Act (1954), 29, 68
Housing conditions, 23
Housing demand, 27 (figure), 27–28
How the Other Half Lives (Riis), 23
Huggins, M., 241
Human resources policies, 138, 141–143,
    199, 221
Hurricane Sandy, 173
Hutchinson, P., 219

Idaho, 48 (table)
Ihrke, D. M., 104, 199
Illinois
  forms of government, 48 (table), 52, 53
  independent school districts (ISDs), 45
  infrastructure erosion, 236
  local government consolidation, 47
  percentage of paved streets, 21 (table)
  political reforms, 25
  population growth, 18
  regional cooperative approaches, 69
Illinois Compiled Statutes, 138
Illinois General Assembly, 138
Immigrant populations, 19 (table), 19–20,
    23–24
Implementation grants, 79
Incentive opportunities, 199
Inclusive leadership, 240 (table)
Independent school districts (ISDs),
    4, 43–44, 44 (table), 45, 47,
    48–50 (table)
Indiana, 45, 47, 49 (table), 51, 195–196
Indianapolis, Indiana, 195–196

suburbanization impacts, 28–30
three-tier reforms, 73–76
Miami, Florida, 73
Michigan, 47, 49 (table)
Micromanagement, 123, 134, 141, 209
Mid-America Regional Council, 181
Miller, D. Y., 62, 65, 66, 69, 71, 73, 74, 75–76, 182
Minneapolis, Minnesota, 73–74
Minnesota, 45, 49 (table), 63, 73–74
Minority populations, 28–29, 89, 238
Mission statements, 211
Mississippi, 50 (table)
Missouri, 21 (table), 42, 49 (table)
Model Cities Act (1966), 156, 167
Monkkonen, E. H., 18
Montana, 49 (table)
Moreira, J., 40
Morgan, D. R., 224
Morganton, North Carolina, 118
Morris, R., 105
Morrisville, North Carolina, 71
Morse, R. S., 76, 175, 178
Mortality rates, 19
Mortgage policies, 28, 29
Moynihan, D. P., 104, 217
Muckrakers, 24
Mullins, D. R., 41, 42
Municipal governments
  alternatives to service delivery (ASD), 187–197, 190 (table), 191 (table)
  authority and control policies, 118–119
  authorized services and functions, 181–183, 184–185 (table), 187
  emerging issues and trends, 8–9, 229–237
  forms of government, 51 (table), 51–55
  home rule policies, 182, 187
  infrastructure erosion, 235–236, 236 (table)
  job requirements and qualifications, 90–91
  management challenges, 64–66
  management philosophy, 222–223
  new technology use, 197–200
  retirement-age populations, 237
  types and distribution, 44 (table), 45, 47, 48–50 (table)

  see also Chief administrative officers (CAOs); Citizen engagement; Managers
Municipal managers
  critical skills and abilities, 12–15
  jurisdictional challenges, 3–5, 7, 9, 187, 242
  new technology use, 197–200
  politics–administration dichotomy, 106–107
  regional cooperative approaches, 66–73, 67 (table), 80–81, 242–243
  roles and responsibilities, 118–119
  tools and techniques, 209–225, 212 (figure), 213 (table), 224 (table)
Murphy, K., 54 (table)
Mutual assistance agreements, 180–181
Mutual expectations, 137–149

Nabatchi, T., 177
Nalbandian, C., 133
Nalbandian, J., 65, 94, 100, 124, 128, 128 (table), 129, 131, 133, 135, 141, 174, 175
Nash, G. B., 18
Nashville–Davidson County, Tennessee, 63
National Association of Counties (NACo), 14, 54, 245
National Association of Regional Councils (NARC), 69
National Civic League, 118, 142
National Council for Public–Private Partnerships, 192
National Fire Protection Association, 157
National government
  see Federal government
National League of Cities, 14, 42, 63, 245
National Municipal League, 26, 96
National Performance Review (NPR), 209
National Performance Review (NPR) initiative, 207, 208–209
Nebraska, 49 (table)
Necessary and Proper Clause (U.S. Constitution), 12
Neighborhood priority/advisory boards, 169–170

CPSIA information can be obtained
at www.ICGtesting.com
Printed in the USA
JSHW021508110621
15750JS00006B/136